COURAGE, CONVICTION AND CONSCIOUSNESS

365 Days of Inspiration
From the Women of New Thought

May the Lord repay you for what you have done.
May you be richly rewarded by the Lord, the God of Israel,
under whose wings you have come to take refuge.
Ruth 2:12 NIV

REV. DR. C. WILLIAM MERCER
2016
FIRST EDITION

COURAGE, CONVICTION AND CONSCIOUSNESS
365 Days of Inspiration From the Women of New Thought

Copyright © 2016, C. William Mercer

All rights reserved. No portion of this book may be reproduced in any form -- mechanically, photographically, electronically or by any other means, including photo-copying, phonographic recording; nor may it be stored or by any information storage and retrieval system now known or later developed, transmitted or otherwise be copied for public or private use, other than for -- fair use as brief quotations embodied in articles and reviews -- without the prior written permission of the author.

ISBN: 978-0-578-17302-3

Cover Photo: Florence Scripps Kellogg, author of "My Hand in God's," is a classic example of all the intelligent and intriguing women included in this book. Floy's bearing and forward-looking profile convey the very courage, conviction and consciousness that speak for the Women of New Thought.

DEDICATION

Sédare, I love you more today than yesterday…
and less than tomorrow!

SPIRITUAL DEDICATION

Bertha June Cobb
1902-1942

In 1920, a young African-American woman named Bertha June Cobb traveled from her home in Glastonbury, Connecticut to resettle in Los Angeles, California. The cross-country trip cannot have been an easy one for a young black woman during the era of Jim Crow. The motivation for her relocation remains unclear to us, as does the source of her spiritual upbringing and education. Nonetheless we know that within a short time after arriving in Los Angeles she was teaching metaphysics and New Thought principles in the living room of her own home. Her popularity grew through the ensuing years to a point in 1938 when she and her congregation completed the June Cobb Teaching Institute at 1195 E. 55th Street. The Institute thrived under June's dynamic leadership through the time of her untimely passing caused by the onset of an organic ailment in 1942.

Following June's transition her Institute and ministry continued to grow and thrive in the same location under a succession of strong leaders. In 1963 Dr. Daniel Morgan assumed the pulpit and achieved the agreement of the congregation to reconstitute the Institute as the June Cobb Church of Religious Science. By January 1967 Dr. Morgan moved on to establish Guidance Church of Religious Science, now Guidance Church CSL at 7225 Crenshaw Boulevard. "Dr. Dan's" Guidance Church ministry grew rapidly through the

1970s and 1980s, bringing forth many of today's New Thought leaders -- among them Rev. Nirvana Gayle and Dr. Michael Bernard Beckwith.

The June Cobb Heart Space Spiritual Center continued to operate as a Church of Religious Science and later as a Center for Spiritual Living, most recently under the leadership of Rev. Clara Ma Mosley. In 2013 the June Cobb ministry was folded into Guidance Church.

The legacy of Rev. June Cobb's work is clear. Although her written works have found their way into the ethers for the present, we know that nothing is lost in Spirit. For now we remember and honor her for the visionary courage, conviction and consciousness with which she pursued the advancement of New Thought in her own California community against all odds in the 1920s and 1930s. We bless her and thank her.

ACKNOWLEDGEMENTS

I thank God for the inspiration to develop this volume and the divine guidance that was present throughout the process. That guidance frequently led to unimagined discoveries and epiphanies. As a result, this book became a source of great spiritual fulfillment for me as I was writing it. There were healings accomplished for many people on many levels as the work progressed. Some were my own. I am especially grateful for the opportunity to witness and participate in some of these compelling demonstrations as the efforts to discern and locate the unpublished work of certain women moved forward.

A work of this kind enlists the support and assistance of many. Archival centers always are of critical value. God bless them all. Dr. Blaine Mays provided special assistance in locating several photographs for the book from INTA's Addington Archives. Rev. Eric Page of the Unity Archives and Library at Unity Village helped uncover some long-hidden information on key women from the Unity movement. Together we also added to the existing record for some of the women found in this book. Kathy Mastroianni, Executive Director of the Science of Mind Archives and Library Foundation kindly allowed me to perform onsite research at the Archives in Golden, Colorado. This visit was very fruitful in sourcing documentary details and photos regarding significant women from the Religious Science/Science of Mind movement. Barbara Stewart at the DSFI Headquarters in Rutland, Vermont was invaluable in researching several items related to Divine Science history. Finally, Rev. Dr. Jonathan Ellerby graciously provided me one last opportunity to rummage for Divine Science treasure in the basement of the Althea Center, formerly the First Divine Science Church of Denver. Even this brief foray actually netted two photos (Claudine Whitaker and Carrie Munz) included in the book.

Dr. Sheila McKeithen, President of the Universal Foundation for Better Living (UFBL) as well as Rev. Whilmetta Harrell, Rev. Joyce Anderson and Tawnicia F. Rowan were key in sourcing information about women from the Universal Foundation for Better Living (UFBL) and Christ Universal Temple in Chicago, Illinois.

Rev. Candice Gee of Agape International Spiritual Center provided priceless information regarding the ministries of several pioneering African-American women in California. In too many cases ministries such as these have gone largely unheralded outside their immediate communities. I was determined to change this pattern, to bring these marvelously spiritual women forward and to recognize them for the heroic figures that they are in the shared heritage of New Thought.

Individual church leaders and officials across the spectrum of New Thought were intrigued with the project and when contacted were uniformly and unselfishly helpful in locating sermon material and photos long since filed away. Thanks to Rev. Terry Keenan of The Santa Anita Church for sending materials written by Ethel Barnhart, founder of the church he now pastors. Thanks to Dr. Deirdre Y. Sermons of Guidance Church for her able assistance with the materials of Dr. Juanita Bryant-Dunn. Thanks also to Dr. Gregory Pitts for his loving help in locating materials for his grandmother and Triangular Church founder Mother Pearl C. Wood.

As with Dr. Gregory Pitts, the direct involvement of these people in my research generated heartwarming acts of love and remembrance on behalf of their loved ones. Sons, grandsons, brothers, husbands, sisters, sisters-in-law, daughters, granddaughters, great-granddaughters, friends, former students as well as fellow ministers, teachers and practitioners became invaluable in accessing the written legacy of women who may be well-known, but whose written or recorded works are somewhat more obscure at the present time.

Similar help came in locating rare photographs of some of these women. Individual snapshots and other photos were sometimes scanned after being removed from framed collections hung on church walls. Sometimes they were scanned from grainy photocopies of copies of other documents, sometimes from old newspapers and fliers. Amazingly, the only known photo of Cora B. Mayo was accidentally located in the Archives of the Denver Museum of Nature and Science! This truly was God-directed work with God-directed people. I loved every minute of it! Each person who helped in this process receives special thanks and a blessing.

I am especially grateful to Rev. Cynthia James and Dr. Michael Bernard Beckwith for graciously offering the Special Forewords for this book. Their participation touches my heart. I first met both of them in 2008 while I attended Mile Hi Church in Lakewood, Colorado. Cynthia was powerful in the pulpit the first Sunday I visited Mile Hi in February of that year and I have been a continuing admirer. I first had occasion to witness Michael's spiritual energy and high consciousness that same spring at Naropa Institute in Boulder, Colorado and again at Mile Hi a few months later. Each of them brings me to a place of awe every time I hear them speak. Each of them also brings unique perspective to the varied historic roles of women in New Thought as well as their involvement in today's movement. I am truly honored by their words.

Spiritual encouragement came from virtually everyone who became aware of the project. The positive energy they conveyed for me and this book represented a real Presence in bringing it to fruition. I also confess that as I prepared the book I felt the energy of many of the special souls that are the subject of it – urging me forward. Meeting each one of them unvarnished through their words and their thoughts was a singular experience on my own spiritual journey.

My beloved wife, Sédare Coradin-Mercer, to whom this book is fondly dedicated, gave me enormous love as always, maybe even a little extra dose of love as she might put it, and provided ongoing prayer treatment to bring forth this work in the most loving and meaningful way possible.

Special thanks to Cris Wanzer of "Manuscripts To Go" who once again provided great advice and assistance in completing this book for publication.

For the love of these people and others too numerous to mention, I am forever grateful.

SPECIAL FOREWORD

In 1979 I was handed a book, *The Game of Life and How To Play It,* by a woman named Florence Scovel Shinn. I devoured the information. It was the first time that I had seen, in writing, what I had believed all of my life. It was the first time that someone was saying that I had a direct connect to Spirit and could create the life of my dreams.

Shortly after that, I entered my first Religious Science community and was amazed that there were women ministers and teachers and that the classes referenced the teachings of great metaphysical women. I never had heard of Emma Curtis Hopkins, Mary Baker Eddy or Malinda Cramer. I was astounded to read their books and writings. It gave me such a wonderful feeling of being empowered. It was also insightful to learn that Ernest Holmes, whose wisdom I loved, was taught by a woman called the "Teacher of Teachers."

The religion of my childhood did not lift up women as teachers. In fact, women were not exalted as thought leaders, healers, and gifted philosophers. My grandmother took me to see a woman named Kathryn Kuhlman, a faith healer, when I was quite young. I loved her presence but it didn't mean much because many people in my church considered her a fake. It was many years later, when I was on a committed spiritual path that I realized what she was preaching from the stage was new thought wisdom.

As I grew I learned how many women have played incredible roles as prominent figures in religion. The mainstream audience is aware that there has been great intrigue about Esther, Ruth, Mary Magdalene, St. Claire of Assisi, Hildegard Von Bingen, Joan of Arc, St. Theresa of Avila and Mother Theresa. Each of these women was gifted at bringing the message of divinity in their own unique way. However, many New Thought women were as profound and prolific as those mentioned above.

C. Will Mercer has assembled a powerful book of writings and quotes from an extraordinary list of historical and contemporary New Thought women. *Courage, Conviction and Consciousness* is a perfect title. The women in this book are authors, teachers and healers. Each woman's writing invites the reader to explore different avenues of divine inspiration. Each teacher took a stand for her beliefs when it was not easy or accepted. They were often misunderstood and pushed away for honoring their convictions. Even so, they stood and encouraged us all to look within and discover the divinity that lives at the core of our being.

I invite you to read this book from cover to cover. Use it as a daily guide to support your shifts, challenges and growth opportunities. The wisdom in these pages will lift your spirits, invite you to contemplate more deeply and give you opportunities to dive deeper into the minds of amazing women. Enjoy!

Rev. Cynthia James,
Author, Speaker, Teacher
Mile Hi Church, Special Ministries
Denver, Colorado
Photo Credit: Carl Studna

SPECIAL FOREWORD

Some months ago, my editor presented me with a manuscript accompanied by a letter from its author inquiring if I would consider contributing a foreword to his soon-to-be published book. The title piqued my immediate interest, but it was upon turning to the first page that I blurted out, "It's about time!" And indeed it is, because as the history of New Thought proves, it was its women teachers and students who, beginning in the 1800s, pioneered and grounded a movement that to this day impacts our post-modern spiritual and cultural landscape.

Most notable among them is Emma Curtis Hopkins, who was known to have been a feminist in her generation, as well having said that she and the women she ordained were messengers of "the new era of the Holy Mother Spirit." She also taught many suffragettes, including Ella Wheeler Wilcox who, in 1915, sold 50,000 copies of her booklet, *What I Know About New Thought*, which was published by Elizabeth Towne, president of the International New Thought Alliance in 1924. From Myrtle Fillmore and Nona Brooks to more contemporary teachers such as Johnnie Colemon and Mary Tumpkin, these visionary ministers and practitioners filled positions of leadership under the umbrella of New Thought including Mental Science, Divine Science, Unity, and Religious Science.

The women whose works are included and celebrated in this book were contributors not only to New Thought, but also to a new formation of selfhood for women, one that to this day affects political, social, spiritual, and economic reform. Nowhere will you find such a comprehensive collection of Spirit-inspired writings by such extraordinary women as Dr. Will Mercer has brought together within these pages.

May you draw great inspiration, encouragement, and heartfelt enthusiasm to cultivate your own spiritual practice that this book offers as a teaching in how to live a life centered in Spirit, unconditional love, compassion, peace, creativity, wholeness and abundance in harmony with the laws governing the universe.

Michael Bernard Beckwith
Founder, Agape International Spiritual Center
Author of *Spiritual Liberation* and *Life Visioning*
www.agapelive.com
Photo Credit: C. William Mercer

TABLE OF CONTENTS

DEDICATION iii
SPIRITUAL DEDICATION iv
ACKNOWLEDGEMENTS vi
SPECIAL FOREWORD ix
SPECIAL FOREWORD xi
INTRODUCTION xiv
TABLE OF DATES xix

☙

- JANUARY 1
- FEBRUARY 35
- MARCH 67
- APRIL 101
- MAY 133
- JUNE 167
- JULY 199
- AUGUST 233
- SEPTEMBER 267
- OCTOBER 299
- NOVEMBER 333
- DECEMBER 365

☙

TRIBUTE 399
HISTORIAN'S DILEMMA 401
CONTRIBUTOR INDEX 403
REMEMBERED 457
OTHER BOOKS BY REV. DR. C. WILLIAM MERCER 458
ABOUT THE AUTHOR 459

INTRODUCTION

The flowering of the female voice in American literature began early in the nineteenth century. Women like Hannah Adams, Harriet Beecher Stowe, Louisa May Alcott and Emily Dickenson opened wide the doors of expression for women in this country. Their presence evidenced a shift in the social landscape of the mid 1800s and played an instrumental role in the significant increase in the number of women seeking to verbalize their own views and values outside the home.

Literary exploration and expression by women extended to the very nature of their relationship with God as well as matters of worship and religious instruction, self-healing and spirituality beginning in the era of Mary Baker Eddy in the 1860s. The women of *Courage, Conviction and Consciousness* all share in that marvelous lineage as both participants in and products of the flame of New Thought teachings.

With the onset of the American Civil War in 1861 the role of women in white society, both North and South, changed dramatically. As men went off to war – an unexpectedly lengthy one -- women increasingly headed households, ran businesses and in many ways replaced the missing thread of men in the social fabric. If these women had not already found their faith and their voice, many passionately sought after them now.

One cannot overlook the impact of both slavery and emancipation on the stirring souls of African-American women during this same time. The war began with slavery at its ugly and awful zenith. Even with slavery "abolished" in 1863, both black women and men continued to suffer tremendous abuse and loss of life. In the aftermath of the war Reconstruction, Redemption and the era of Jim Crow marginalized them for at least another one hundred years. Strides made by particular women in education and social enfranchisement often began within the church setting where they found community, solace, spiritual knowledge, strength and the determination to be victorious in their expression – to be heard.

Following the war, the women's movement burgeoned with the demand for increased access to education and greater rights overall. The aspiration for women's voting rights took flight in America, joining similar suffrage movements across the globe. Although a woman's right to vote was fully established in Australia by 1902, American, British, and Canadian women did not win the right to vote until the end of World War I. (It is well to remember that the Women's Suffrage movement here began in Seneca Falls, New York in 1848.) Women who sought higher education found their own outlets for expression. Although not an activist, Nona L. Brooks is known to have written on the subject of women's suffrage at least once during the year she spent at Wellesley College in 1891, some fifteen years before she became a force in New Thought.

The rise of women socially and politically fairly mirrored their rise in New Thought. The increasing visibility of women in the developing New Thought movement also reflected the changing social structure throughout the western world. In some cases the faces and voices of women were primarily seen and heard in the wake of men like Charles Fillmore, Horatio Dresser, and even Ernest Holmes and company. At the same time others were differently courageous and equally victorious in striking out entirely on their own, as with Emma Curtis Hopkins, Malinda Elliott Cramer, Harriett Hale Rix together with her sister Annie Rix Militz, June Cobb, Helen Wilmans, Pearl C. Wood, Ethel Barnhart and Johnnie Colemon. Individually and collectively their work shone brightly within the movement. These women came from a place of pure illumination, their conviction was strong and they were fearless in meeting the challenges of their place and time. In many respects both invisibly and visibly women led the way in energizing and developing the expansive theology and body of spiritual literature that characterizes New Thought.

Mary Baker Eddy's *Truth and Health,* which was formally published in 1875 (an earlier version having appeared in 1870), awakened Ursula Gestefeld and Emma Curtis Hopkins as Christian Science students before becoming independent forces in New Thought theology and literature. Without Emma Curtis Hopkins, Helen Wilmans, Jane Yarnall and Myrtle Fillmore might not have come forth as they did. It is appropriate to remember that Myrtle came to the healing faith that underlined the early Unity movement before Charles did, despite the fact that he gets most of the recognition as the driving force in the founding of Unity. It also should be remembered that the Fillmores recruited a female homeopathic physician, H. Emilie Cady, to write *Lessons in Truth*, a book that quickly became the primary text of the Unity School of Christianity. Even today her book is arguably the most widely read in all of New Thought literature.

Divine Science sprang from the heart and soul of Malinda Elliott Cramer and fanned the flame for two of the Brooks sisters who became recognized New Thought writers in their own right: Fannie Brooks James and Nona L. Brooks. The early Divine Science movement in Denver was the product of a powerful cadre of women that surrounded Nona and Fannie including Ada B. Fay, Agnes Lawson, Alice R. Ritchie, Agnes Galer, Anna L. Palmer, Ida B. Elliott, Caroline Munz, Daisy Baum, Ruth B. Smith and Kathleen M. H. Besly. Other voices followed such as Elizabeth Carrick-Cook, Hazel Deane, Elizabeth Searle Lamb, Grace L. Faus, Elizabeth R. McLellan, Margaret M. Stevens, F. Bernadette Turner, Helen Zagat and Lucile Frederick. Elizabeth A. Nordman and Barbara L. Wolfe are key female voices from the St. Louis branch of Divine Science which grew in tandem with Denver led by Rev. Herman H. Schroeder from the days of Malinda Elliott Cramer.

Unity had its own wellspring of female ministers and writers including Myrtle Fillmore, Hannah More Kohaus, Jennie Croft, Frances W. Foulks, Martha Smock, Vera Dawson Tait, Evelyn Whitell, Dana Gatlin, Cora Dedrick Fillmore, May Rowland and Clara Beranger. Other important voices also came from Unity like those of Clara A. Palmer, Imelda Octavia Shanklin, Mary L. Kupferle, Ella Pomeroy, Georgiana Tree West, Elizabeth Sand Turner, Sue Sikking, Carol Ruth Knox, Marguerite Lewis, and more recently Rosemary Fillmore Rhea, Dorothy M. Pierson, Sallye Taylor, Nancy Purcell and Jennifer Holder.

The Religious Science movement gained critical mass a full generation after the early expansion of New Thought across the country. It quickly attracted and developed its own impressive corps of female practitioners, ministers and writers including Helen Van Slyke, Hazel Foster Holmes, Augusta E. Rundel, Josephine Holmes Curtis, Alberta Smith, Lola Pauline Mays, Cornelia Addington, Elena Goforth Whitehead, Vetura Papke, Claudine Whitaker, Pearl C. Wood and in more recent years Peggy Bassett, Norah Boyd, Doris Jones, Jane Claypool, Betty Jean House, Marian G. Moon and Juanita Bryant-Dunn.

The Universal Foundation for Better Living, founded in 1974 and following the Fillmore tradition, produced gifted writers in both Johnnie Colemon and Mary A. Tumpkin. The writings and pioneering UFBL ministries of Olga Una Barker and Judith G. Weekes came to the fore in UFBL's *Daily Inspiration for Better Living* and other UFBL publications, as did that of Christina Knox-Walthall of Christ Universal Temple in Chicago.

Other more independent voices, while not necessarily identified exclusively with one of the major denominations, were a vital part of New Thought from the beginning and are to be heard as well: Clara H. Fiske Scott, Ella Wheeler Wilcox, Annie Rix Militz and Harriet Hale Rix of the Home of Truth, Mildred Mann, Nora Smith Holm, Julia Seton Sears, Elizabeth Towne, Florence Scripps Kellogg, Vida Reed Stone, Annie S. Greenwood, Florence Scovel Shinn, Ruth E. Chew, Agnes Sanford, Evelyn Underhill, Edna M. Lister, Ethel Barnhart, Helen Brungardt, Eva Bell Werber, Helen Schucman, and even Peace Pilgrim.

The writing of these ministers, poets, authors and activists routinely appeared in publications across the spectrum of New Thought without regard to denomination. This natural tendency to cross-pollinate in matters of Thought continues to this day and follows a tradition adopted early in the movement. Perhaps in response to the rigid and proprietary actions of Mary Baker Eddy and her organization, Malinda Elliott Cramer, Myrtle Fillmore and Emma Curtis Hopkins chose the unfettered spread and growth of New Thought philosophy and theology over any proprietary concerns related to the expression of Truth and Principle.

Through the twentieth century a magnificent panoply of women's voices continued to pave the way for much of the fresh growth that occurred in the movement. Some of the women included here had training and often ordinations with more than one denomination. Claudine Whitaker, Helen Brungardt and Cornelia Addington are clear examples of this pattern of personal spiritual development which only added to the broadening and deepening of New Thought teachings over time.

Women of courage also led the way in preserving access to the written record of Truth and Principle that stands at the core of our shared teachings. We know that ministers Marge Flotron and Ruth F. Townsend were guided to bring forward the nearly forgotten work of Emma Curtis Hopkins and Malinda Elliott Cramer in the latter part of the twentieth century. Along with the Revelation Research group that supported Ruth's efforts, we thank them for their contributions to the recognition and revitalization of these two iconic pioneers of New Thought.

The powerful women of our own time found within these pages represent the vibrant leadership role that women continue to play in today's New Thought ministries – whether in the pulpit, the office, the boardroom, the classroom, the lab, the home, as practitioners, as writers or likely serving in a combination of such roles.

Other individuals may be revealed who might have been a part of this book. Great effort was made to be as inclusive as possible of all the magnificent women who have been sources of shared spiritual inspiration within the New Thought movement since its beginnings. My apologies to readers who perhaps will search in vain for their own favorite minister, teacher or writer. The book is intended to highlight the courage, strength, power, conviction, determination and high consciousness of more than one hundred women featured here as representatives of the larger population of spiritually stellar women in and around New Thought from 1870 forward.

A few significant voices from the past, like June Cobb, left too soon in a circumstance or at a time when preservation of their unpublished work was not deemed important or perhaps even feasible. One day their written works may yet be revealed, because in each case their Truth outlived them here on earth as expressed in the lives illumined by their love and ministry. Nothing is lost in Spirit. Alma Morse and probably a few others have known written legacies that are as yet to be explored outside their own environments of safekeeping. It's all good. We pray that their voices and others will continue to emerge.

It is very much hoped that this small collection of the inspired words of these women will lead the reader to inquire further, to explore their pamphlets, books, audio and video recordings and to plumb the depths of the meditations, notes, letters, poems, hymns, lessons, spiritual mind treatments, affirmations and prayers that they left for us. *Courage, Conviction and Consciousness* is their Timeless Truth expressed again for today's world.

As we know in metaphysics, there is no such thing as coincidence. Therefore, God bless you in your journey through the heartfelt messages of inspiration and high consciousness from the hearts of these strong and loving women. Apparently their messages were intended to be seen and enjoyed by you at this particular and perfect time in your life.

Rev. Dr. C. William Mercer
January 2016

TABLE OF DATES

January 1:   THERE IS GOOD FOR ME AND I OUGHT TO HAVE IT
                  Emma Curtis Hopkins

January 2:   FOR THE MORNING
                  Ursula Gestefeld

January 3:   NEW BEGINNINGS
                  Marian G. Moon

January 4:   THE IMPORTANCE OF THE BIBLE
                  Agnes M. Lawson

January 5:   THERE IS ALWAYS PLENTY
                  Florence Scovel Shinn

January 6:   HEAVEN HERE AND NOW
                  Juanita Bryant-Dunn

January 7:   WHAT I AM
                  Fannie Brooks James

January 8:   THE LORD'S PRAYER
                  Mary Baker Eddy

January 9:   THE HIGHEST IDEA OF GOD
                  Malinda Elliott Cramer

January 10:   GOD'S CONSTANCY
                  Imelda Octavia Shanklin

January 11:   DIVINE ENTHUSIASM
                  Cora Dedrick Fillmore

January 12:   GROWING OUT OR GROWING UP?
                  Doris Dickelman

January 13:	WORDS OF WISDOM Sallye Taylor
January 14:	THE HIDDEN GOOD Alice R. Ritchie
January 15:	WHEN YE PRAY Elizabeth Towne
January 16:	WHO'S IN CHARGE? Peggy Bassett
January 17:	BE NOT AFRAID Barbara L. Wolfe
January 18:	THE WILL OF GOD H. Emilie Cady
January 19:	OVERCOMING OUR COMMON FAULTS Clara Beranger
January 20:	PRAYER Myrtle Fillmore
January 21:	ONE'S HIGHER SELF Elizabeth Sand Turner
January 22:	THE LIGHT OF LIFE Jennie Croft
January 23:	THE OPEN DOOR Norah Boyd
January 24:	A CLEAN SLATE Jennifer Holder
January 25:	THE OAK AND THE LEAVES Helen Van Slyke

January 26: THOUGHTS OF PEACE
             Peace Pilgrim

January 27: BAPTISM OF SPIRIT
             Malinda Elliott Cramer

January 28: THE THRONE ROOM
             Eva Bell Werber

January 29: REJOICE! GOD REIGNS
             Edna M. Lister

January 30: MAKE YOUR LIFE SUCCESSFUL
             Clara M. Wright

January 31: LIFE IN PARADOX
             Nancy Purcell

February 1: STRENGTH
             Ella Pomeroy

February 2: KNOW THE TRUTH
             Annie S. Greenwood

February 3: BLESSED WITH TRUE PROSPERITY
             Christiana Knox-Walthall

February 4: LIFE'S RIVER
             Dorothy M. Pierson

February 5: THE SCIENCE OF SPIRIT
             Malinda Elliott Cramer

February 6: THE OBJECT OF THE GAME OF LIFE
             Florence Scovel Shinn

February 7: ATONEMENT
             Mary Baker Eddy

February 8:   NO LIMIT TO WHAT GOD CAN DO IN YOU
Elizabeth Towne

February 9:   NINETEEN WORDS
F. Bernadette Turner

February 10: I AM SPIRITUAL ENERGY
Judith G. Weekes

February 11: GIVING THANKS VS. COMPLAINING
Jane Yarnall

February 12: CONTEMPLATION
Helen Brungardt

February 13: SILENCE SELF, AND LISTEN
Fannie Brooks James

February 14: DIVINE LOVE
May Rowland

February 15: PRACTICE PRAISING GOD
Margaret M. Stevens

February 16: SPIRITUAL PRINCIPLE
Elizabeth Sand Turner

February 17: HAPPINESS
Alberta Smith

February 18: IT WORKS IF YOU WORK IT
Johnnie Colemon

February 19: DIVINE LOVE
Agnes J. Galer

February 20: SERENITY
Vida Reed Stone

February 21:	FINDING THE CHRIST IN OURSELVES H. Emilie Cady	
February 22:	LEARNING TO KNOW GOD Barbara L. Wolfe	
February 23:	THE MAGIC OF BELIEVING Cora B. Mayo	
February 24:	AFFIRMATIONS Florence Scovel Shinn	
February 25:	A BELOVED MINISTER'S WISDOM Marguerite Lewis	
February 26:	IMMORTALITY – THE CELEBRATION OF LIFE Betty Jean House	
February 27:	OLD UNWANTED HABITS CANNOT BIND ME Olga Una Barker	
February 28:	MY MEDITATION Elizabeth R. McClellan	
February 29:	LIFE'S REVERIE Rosemary Fillmore Rhea	
March 1:	DEVELOPING OUR FACULTIES Myrtle Fillmore	
March 2:	GOD'S HAND H. Emilie Cady	
March 3:	EXPERIMENT IN PRAYER Agnes Sanford	
March 4:	DEEDS NOT RESULTS Eva Bell Werber	

March 5:   PEACE
           Helen Van Slyke

March 6:   LOVE: THE KEYNOTE OF JESUS' TEACHING
           Grace L. Faus

March 7:   GODLINESS AND THE SUBSTANCE OF RICHES
           Annie Rix Militz

March 8:   WISDOM
           Ella Pomeroy

March 9:   THE INFERIORITY COMPLEX
           Augusta Rundel

March 10: MEDITATION ON GOD'S LOVE
           Jane Paulson

March 11: FATHER, I'M TRUSTING
           Mary L. Kupferle

March 12: THE ETERNAL RHYTHM
           Vida Reed Stone

March 13: ONENESS WITH GOD
           H. Emilie Cady

March 14: WORLD CREATED BY THE WORD OF GOD
           Elizabeth Sand Turner

March 15: HEAVEN'S FIRST LAW
           Clara A. Palmer

March 16: JESUS CHRIST: RICH OR POOR?
           Harriet Hale Rix

March 17: WHAT KIND OF GOD DO YOU HAVE?
           Mildred Mann

March 18:	WINTER-SPRING DROPS OF GOLD	Emma Curtis Hopkins
March 19:	REMEMBER	Lillian DeWaters
March 20:	REALIZE CHRIST WITHIN	May Rowland
March 21:	I AM A CHILD OF THE LIVING GOD	Josephine Holmes Curtis
March 22:	APPLIED TRUTH	Nona L. Brooks
March 23:	HOW TO REALIZE ILLUMINATION OR UNDERSTANDING	Fannie Brooks James
March 24:	JOY	Daisy Baum
March 25:	POWER	Ella Pomeroy
March 26:	THE POWER OF INVOCATION	Ethel Barnhart
March 27:	IN HIS NAME	H. Emilie Cady
March 28:	BEATITUDES (1)	Elizabeth Sand Turner
March 29:	BEATITUDES (2)	Elizabeth Sand Turner
March 30:	KEYS TO PROSPERITY	Elizabeth Carrick-Cook

March 31:	THE SUBCONSCIOUS Myrtle Fillmore
April 1:	GIVE AND RECEIVE Ella Wheeler Wilcox
April 2:	GOD IS ALL IN ALL Betty Jean House
April 3:	WHAT IS MAN? Grace L. Faus
April 4:	DIVINE LOVE HEALS ME Claudine Whitaker
April 5:	CONQUERING FAITH Caroline Munz
April 6:	IN ALL THE WORKS OF THY HANDS Mary L. Kupferle
April 7:	THE ESSENTIAL DORIS JONES Doris Jones
April 8:	LETTING GO Marian G. Moon
April 9:	TWENTY-THIRD PSALM Ruth B. Smith
April 10:	MIND VS. MENTAL Malinda Elliott Cramer
April 11:	FATHER, THE HOUR IS COME Adela Rogers St. Johns
April 12:	I AM WHERE I AM BY LAW, NOT BY CHANCE Alice R. Ritchie

April 13:	THE SAVIOR'S MISSION Mary Baker Eddy
April 14:	I RESOLVE TO GROW Elena Goforth Whitehead
April 15:	THE DRAMA OF LIFE Nona Brooks
April 16:	LIFE A MINISTRY H. Emilie Cady
April 17:	I SHALL SUCCEED Evelyn Whitell
April 18:	ONENESS Vida Reed Stone
April 19:	IMAGINATION Ella Pomeroy
April 20:	OMNIPRESENCE OF SPIRIT Kathleen M. H. Besly
April 21:	THE ETERNAL NOW F. Bernadette Turner
April 22:	THE HIGHROAD OF PROSPERITY Annie Rix Militz
April 23:	ILLUMINATION – UNDERSTANDING Emma Curtis Hopkins
April 24:	COURAGE IN SEEKING GOD Carol Ruth Knox
April 25:	DEMONSTRATION Myrtle Fillmore

April 26:	WHAT IS GOD, METAPHYSICALLY CONSIDERED? Georgiana Tree West
April 27:	TODAY, I AM SHOWN Christina Knox-Walthall
April 28:	SUPPLICATION VS. ACKNOWLEDGEMENT Harriet Hale Rix
April 29:	OUR FATHER NEVER FAILETH Hannah More Kohaus
April 30:	GOD AND LOVE Ella Wheeler Wilcox
May 1:	PRAYER Fannie Brooks James
May 2:	COURAGE Helen Wilmans
May 3:	RICHES THE GIFT OF GOD Annie Rix Militz
May 4:	THE WAY OF LOVE Helen Brungardt
May 5:	UNITING WITH GOD Carol Ruth Knox
May 6:	CHOICES Peggy Bassett
May 7:	TEN OF JESUS' COMMANDMENTS Ada B. Fay
May 8:	RESOLUTIONS TO RESULTS Jennifer Holder

May 9:	WHO ARE GOD'S TEACHERS? Helen Schucman
May 10:	INFINITE SPIRIT OF SUBSTANCE Alberta Smith
May 11:	I AM DIVINELY PROTECTED Judith G. Weekes
May 12:	THE LAW OF PROSPERITY Harriet Hale Rix
May 13:	HOW WE FIND GOD Barbara L. Wolfe
May 14:	I RESPOND WITH JOY TODAY Elizabeth Searle Lamb
May 15:	LIFE TURNS TO US AS WE TURN TO IT Pearl C. Wood
May 16:	PRAYER Sallye Taylor
May 17:	INTELLIGENCE Caroline Munz
May 18:	GROWING IN SPIRITUAL UNDERSTANDING Daisy Baum
May 19:	OMNIPRESENT LIFE Helen Wilmans
May 20:	THE BODY TEMPLE Clara A. Palmer
May 21:	OLD UNWANTED HABITS CANNOT BIND ME Olga Una Barker

May 22:   THE PAST IS PRESENT
           Sue Sikking

May 23:   THE PEARL OF GREAT PRICE
           Caroline Munz

May 24:   THE DIVINE PLAN FOR YOUR LIFE
           May Rowland

May 25:   LET US LEARN
           Anna L. Palmer

May 26:   GOD
           Agnes Sanford

May 27:   WISDOM
           Cora Dedrick Fillmore

May 28:   MYSTICISM
           Evelyn Underhill

May 29:   SPRING-SUMMER DROPS OF GOLD
           Emma Curtis Hopkins

May 30:   SKEPTICISM
           Clara Beranger

May 31:   PURE POTENTIALITY
           Marian G. Moon

June 1:   THAT SECRET PLACE
           Annie S. Greenwood

June 2:   SEEK AND YE SHALL FIND
           Caroline Munz

June 3:   HER FINAL LESSON
           Marguerite Lewis

June 4:	IN THE NAME OF JESUS CHRIST Imelda Octavia Shanklin
June 5:	MEDITATION OF A PROSPERED CONSCIOUSNESS Frances W. Foulks
June 6:	OMNIPRESENCE Clara H. Scott
June 7:	MEDITATION Mary A. Tumpkin
June 8:	SUCCESS Julia Seton Sears
June 9:	BIBLE STUDY Agnes M. Lawson
June 10:	WE ARE LIFE Malinda Elliott Cramer
June 11:	TRUST Florence Scripps Kellogg
June 12:	SOMETHING IS WORKING FOR YOU F. Bernadette Turner
June 13:	TOLERANCE Helen Schucman
June 14:	GOD MAKES MY DAY GLORIOUS Claudine Whitaker
June 15:	ALPHABET OF PRINCIPLES Hazel Foster Holmes
June 16:	FORGIVE AND YE SHALL BE FORGIVEN Nora Smith Holm

June 17:	OCEAN OF SPIRIT Ruth B. Smith
June 18:	MEDITATIONS FOR WEDNESDAY NIGHT CLASSES Doris Jones
June 19:	MAKING HEAVEN HAPPEN Juanita Bryant-Dunn
June 20:	I AM AN IRRESISTIBLE MAGNET Vetura Papke
June 21:	BLESSING THE HOME Annie Rix Militz
June 22:	TRANSLATION Elizabeth Searle Lamb
June 23:	WHATEVER THE PROBLEM Dana Gatlin
June 24:	NO GOOD THING SHALL BE WITHHELD Agnes J. Galer
June 25:	JESUS' REVERENCE Ada B. Fay
June 26:	AFFIRMATIONS Grace L. Faus
June 27:	WHAT IS TREATMENT? Josephine Holmes Curtis
June 28:	HEALING AS RELEASE FROM FEAR Helen Schucman
June 29:	LISTEN AND SPEAK THE WORD OF GOD Daisy Baum

June 30:	EVERYDAY AFFIRMATIONS Jane Claypool	
July 1:	FOR HIGH NOON Ursula Gestefeld	
July 2:	WHERE IS GOD? Nona L. Brooks	
July 3:	TRAVELER'S PRAYER Imelda Octavia Shanklin	
July 4:	FREEDOM OF CHRIST Mary L. Kupferle	
July 5:	WILL Ella Pomeroy	
July 6:	GOD IS LIFE Helen Zagat	
July 7:	YOU ARE LIFE Helen Van Slyke	
July 8:	GOD'S HELP Mary L. Kupferle	
July 9:	COURAGE THAT DEFIES FAILURE Evelyn Whitell	
July 10:	THE REALM OF UNTOLD RICHES WITHIN Elizabeth Nordman	
July 11:	UNIFICATION WITH GOD Carol Ruth Knox	
July 12:	PEACE OF GOD Vida Reed Stone	

July 13:	I WILL HELP THEE Nora Smith Holm
July 14:	A HEALING TREATMENT Mary A. Tumpkin
July 15:	MY LIFE IS IN ORDER Lola Pauline Mays
July 16:	WORSHIP Hazel Deane
July 17:	NEW THOUGHT IN THE TWENTY-FIRST CENTURY Rosemary Fillmore Rhea
July 18:	SOWING AND REAPING Judith G. Weekes
July 19:	KNOWING I AM ALIVE Ruth E. Chew
July 20:	BITTERSWEET FAREWELLS Norah Boyd
July 21:	WHEN THERE IS A NEED FOR PATIENCE Ursula Gestefeld
July 22:	THE WONDER-WORKING POWER OF GOD Olga Una Barker
July 23:	DEMONSTRATION IS FOREVER Elena Goforth Whitehead
July 24:	SPIRITUAL MIND TREATMENT Vetura Papke
July 25:	SOUL FOOD Jane Yarnall

July 26:	GOD FILLS ALL SPACE Christina Knox-Walthall	
July 27:	WHEN THERE IS DIFFICULTY LETTING GO OF THE PAST (1) Ursula Gestefeld	
July 28:	WHEN THERE IS DIFFICULTY LETTING GO OF THE PAST (2) Ursula Gestefeld	
July 29:	DIVINE WISDOM Helen Zagat	
July 30:	GOD'S WILL MUST BE GODLIKE Nona L. Brooks	
July 31:	MEDITATION ON PEACE OF MIND Jane Paulson	
August 1:	THE PRAYER OF FAITH Hannah Moore Kohaus	
August 2:	UNDERSTANDING Ella Pomeroy	
August 3:	HIM THAT FILLETH ALL IN ALL Nora Smith Holm	
August 4:	THE FUNCTION OF A MIRACLE WORKER Helen Schucman	
August 5:	WHO AM I? Mildred Mann	
August 6:	THE FINAL WORD: AMEN Betty Jean House	
August 7:	IMPERSONALITY Lillian DeWaters	

August 8:	DIVINE IMAGINATION Cora Dedrick Fillmore
August 9:	THE RISE OF MAN Elizabeth Towne
August 10:	IN THE SHADOW OF HIS WINGS Agnes Sanford
August 11:	DESTINY AT MY COMMAND Vera Dawson Tait
August 12:	THE CHRIST WITHIN ME IS MY FULFILLMENT Cornelia Addington
August 13:	PURSUING WISDOM Jane Claypool
August 14:	TODAY IS A DAY OF PEACE Lola Pauline Mays
August 15:	DOMINION Georgia Carmichael Maxwell
August 16:	REAL LOVE Florence Scovel Shinn
August 17:	GOD NOT CHANGED BY PRAYER Harriet Hale Rix
August 18:	OPEN MY EYES Clara H. Scott
August 19:	THE SCIENCE OF BEING Ida B. Elliott
August 20:	I NOW FREE MY SELF Ruth E. Chew

August 21:   REMEMBER THAT YOU ARE HIS COMPLETION AND
              HIS LOVE
              Helen Schucman

August 22:   PROSPERITY'S TEN COMMANDMENTS
              Georgiana Tree West

August 23:   GOD MY MIND
              Fannie Brooks James

August 24:   NON-RESISTANCE
              Daisy Baum

August 25:   I WILL LIFT UP MINE EYES
              Agnes J. Galer

August 26:   NO REGRET
              Lucile Frederick

August 27:   MAN'S ASCENDING CONSCIOUSNESS
              Anna L. Palmer

August 28:   SPIRITUAL DISCRIMINATION
              Lillian DeWaters

August 29:   CUT THE TIES
              Johnnie Colemon

August 30:   I HAVE NO FEAR
              Dana Gatlin

August 31:   CONTACTING MYSELF
              Eva Bell Werber

September 1: THE PERFECT LOVE RELATIONSHIP WITH MYSELF
              Doris Jones

September 2: FEAR
              Augusta E. Rundel

September 3:   LAUGHTER AS A SPIRITUAL GIFT
                Jane Claypool

September 4:   SERVICE
                Elizabeth Searle Lamb

September 5:   THE WILDERNESS EXPERIENCE
                Grace L. Faus

September 6:   KINGDOM OF GOD WITHIN
                Ida B. Elliott

September 7:   SILENT UNITY LETTER
                Myrtle Fillmore

September 8:   GOD'S LIGHT WITHIN US
                Ruth Hammink Carr

September 9:   SPIRITUAL FORGIVENESS
                Alberta Smith

September 10: FAITH IN THE PROMISES OF GOD
                Ethel Barnhart

September 11: I AM IN GOD'S HANDS
                Lola Pauline Mays

September 12: TRUTH IS GOD
                Jane Yarnall

September 13: IMMUTABLE LAWS
                Josephine Holmes Curtis

September 14: IN THE SILENCE
                Elizabeth R. McClellan

September 15: COMMUNION
                Imelda Octavia Shanklin

September 16: POWER
    Helen Zagat

September 17: REALIZATION FOLLOWING MEDITATION
    Jennie Croft

September 18: THE CREATIVE FORCE
    Kathleen M. H. Besly

September 19: YOU ARE AN OVERCOMER
    Johnnie Colemon

September 20: LOOK NO LONGER
    Agnes J. Galer

September 21: FAVORITE AFFIRMATIONS
    Grace L. Faus

September 22: LOOKING AHEAD
    Peggy Bassett

September 23: DIVINE LOVE
    Cora Dedrick Fillmore

September 24: GOD IS LOVE
    Adela Rogers St. Johns

September 25: THE POWER TO CHOOSE
    Margaret M. Stevens

September 26: I ARISE
    Evelyn Whitell

September 27: TURNING ON THE LIGHT
    Agnes Sanford

September 28: WHAT IS IT THAT WE HAVE?
    Ruth E. Chew

September 29: GOD AS SPIRIT
Georgiana Tree West

September 30: PATIENCE
Helen Schucman

October 1: SONG IN MY HEART
Frances W. Foulks

October 2: LIVE IN THE NOW
Nancy Purcell

October 3: WHO IS GOD?
Elizabeth Towne

October 4: LABOR WITH LOVE
Doris Dickelman

October 5: FAITH
Alice R. Ritchie

October 6: TRINITY OF MIND
Elizabeth Carrick-Cook

October 7: THOU SHALT WALK IN THY WAY SAFELY
Nora Smith Holm

October 8: THE CHRIST IN ME IS THE CHRIST IN YOU
Cornelia Addington

October 9: THE FINISHER
Lillian DeWaters

October 10: THE CHRIST WITHIN
Helen Van Slyke

October 11: SPIRITUAL SUSTENANCE
Helen Zagat

October 12:	OMNIPRESENT LIFE Helen Wilmans	
October 13:	DO YOU WORK FOR A LIVING? Harriet Hale Rix	
October 14:	RECORD OF MYSELF Malinda Elliott Cramer	
October 15:	LORD'S PRAYER INTERPRETATION Judith G. Weekes	
October 16:	WHO'S DRIVING? Vera Dawson Tate	
October 17:	LIFE HEALING (1) Dana Gatlin	
October 18:	LIFE HEALING (2) Dana Gatlin	
October 19:	SEVEN STEPS IN DEMONSTRATION Mildred Mann	
October 20:	MY DEMONSTRATION IS SURE Claudine Whitaker	
October 21:	THOU SHALT LET GO AND LET GOD DO IT Georgiana Tree West	
October 22:	GIVE WITHOUT FEAR F. Bernadette Turner	
October 23:	REST AND RELAXATION Clara M. Wright	
October 24:	ONE SUBSTANCE Nona L. Brooks	

October 25:   PROGRESS
              Ella Wheeler Wilcox

October 26:   TWENTY-THIRD PSALM INTERPRETED
              Agnes J. Galer

October 27:   THE POTENTIAL OF YOUR WORD POWER
              Vetura Papke

October 28:   FEAR AND DOUBT
              Helen Zagat

October 29:   WHAT IS FAITH?
              Johnnie Colemon

October 30:   TRUTH
              Pearl C. Wood

October 31:   FAITH
              Georgia Carmichael Maxwell

November 1: THE SEEKERS OF THE LIGHT ARE ONE
             May Rowland

November 2: RESOLVE: I WILL THINK ONLY CONSTRUCTIVE
             THOUGHTS TODAY
             Nona L. Brooks

November 3: LET GO
             Martha Smock

November 4: DECLARATION OF LIFE PRINCIPLES
             Edna M. Lister

November 5: ALL THAT *IS* GOD CREATED
             Mary Baker Eddy

November 6: I AM STRONGER THAN MY FEARS
             Hannah More Kohaus

November 7: NO OTHER WAY
Martha Smock

November 8: CHRIST CONSCIOUSNESS
Julia Seton Sears

November 9: FINDING THE CHRIST IN OURSELVES
H. Emilie Cady

November 10: FORGIVENESS
Frances W. Foulks

November 11: WHAT IS SUPPLY?
Josephine Holmes Curtis

November 12: TODAY I FORGIVE MYSELF
Mary A. Tumpkin

November 13: MY HAND IN GOD'S
Florence Scripps Kellogg

November 14: COMPLETE IN THEE
May Rowland

November 15: WHY WE BELIEVE
Hazel Foster Holmes

November 16: THE PREMISE OF DIVINE SCIENCE
Ida B. Elliott

November 17: I REJOICE IN THE TRUTH
Cornelia Addington

November 18: ONE NATURE, NOT TWO
Malinda Elliott Cramer

November 19: I LIVE IN AWARENESS
Claudine Whitaker

November 20: OUR DIVINITY
Grace L. Faus

November 21: BE YE THANKFUL
Sue Sikking

November 22: HELL
Kathleen M. H. Besly

November 23: DEMONSTRATION
Jane Yarnall

November 24: MY JOY MAKES ME POROUS TO MY GOOD
Ruth E. Chew

November 25: AUTUMN-WINTER DROPS OF GOLD
Emma Curtis Hopkins

November 26: BLESS, PRAISE, GIVE THANKS
Annie Rix Militz

November 27: NEW THOUGHT – A WAY OF LIFE
Betty Jean House

November 28: SOUL
Mary Baker Eddy

November 29: FOR THE EVENING
Ursula Gestefeld

November 30: GUIDELINES TO PERSONAL PROSPERITY
Elizabeth Carrick-Cook

December 1: THIS PRESENT MOMENT
Dorothy M. Pierson

December 2: THE FULLNESS OF JOY
Grace L. Faus

December 3: THE STORY OF MAN'S SPIRIT
Evelyn Underhill

December 4: THOU SHALT NOT SEEK SOMETHING FOR NOTHING
Georgiana Tree West

December 5: I WILL HELP THEE
Nora Smith Holm

December 6: A CHANGE IN ATTITUDE
Johnnie Colemon

December 7: LET YOUR HEART LISTEN
Martha Smock

December 8: HOW I FOUND HEALTH
Myrtle Fillmore

December 9: TRUST THE SPIRIT WITHIN
Mary L. Kupferle

December 10: DIVINE GUIDANCE
Annie S. Greenwood

December 11: WHOLENESS FOR YOU
Clara A. Palmer

December 12: I HEAR THE SONG OF CHRISTMAS
Martha Smock

December 13: THE MEANING OF FREE WILL
Norah Boyd

December 14: BE STILL
Eva Bell Werber

December 15: THE MYSTIC EXPERIENCE
Mildred Mann

December 16: THE EVER-PRESENT NOW
Helen Van Slyke

December 17: PEACE PILGRIM'S BEATITUDES
Peace Pilgrim

December 18: MY DESIRE IS TO ACCOMPLISH THE WILL OF GOD
Olga Una Barker

December 19: ALMIGHTY GOD IS WITH ME
Elizabeth Nordman

December 20: I WILL COME AND HEAL
Christina Knox-Walthall

December 21: LOVE IS THE ESSENCE
Nona L. Brooks

December 22: FOR UNTO US A CHILD IS BORN
Emma Curtis Hopkins

December 23: WHERE I AM KING
Dana Gatlin

December 24: Christmas Thoughts
Ella Wheeler Wilcox

December 25: O WONDROUS NIGHT
Florence Scripps Kellogg

December 26: MIND RADIATES
Harriet Hale Rix

December 27: SONG IN MY HEART
Frances W. Foulks

December 28: GOD OMNIPOTENT
Alice R. Ritchie

December 29: MY CUP RUNNETH OVER
            Annie Rix Militz

December 30: WE CAN CHANGE
            Lucile Frederick

December 31: NEW-YEAR EVE MEDITATION
            Frances W. Foulks

JANUARY

January 1

THERE IS GOOD FOR ME AND I OUGHT TO HAVE IT

There is good for me and I ought to have it. You are sure of this. It is the foundation statement of your being. One may not admit that there is any God, or Great Being, to whom he owes allegiance, but he is always sure that there is good for him, which he ought to have. The good that we feel that we ought to have is our God. Every move we make we are making to get our God, to satisfy our idea of the good. This is one service of our God. Hence in all languages, God is called Good. Good is God. We seek the good. We long for the good. We expect the good. Good is God. There is no other God but Good. If everything and everybody is filled with the Good, then there is no place or space that this God is not. We can speak of the Good as omnipresent, and that which is not Good as nowhere present. God is omnipresent Good. Good has no other power to oppose it. It is omnipotent. God is omnipotent Good. Omnipotent Good has no other intelligence but itself. God is omniscient Good. This is striking the mind straight on to a foundation stone within itself.

Emma Curtis Hopkins, *How To Attain Your Good*, 1898, p. 6. No known copyright in effect.

January 2

FOR THE MORNING

The night of sense-consciousness is past, and I wake to the spiritual day -- the eternal Now. In the light of God I see my self anew. The shadows of the night are gone, and I am free from suffering, disease, and death. I am filled now with health, strength, and joy unspeakable. There is no room in me for any unlikeness to the Infinite One, for that One vibrates in every part of my being from least to greatest, and fills me with pulsating, invigorating, deathless life.

I rise from the passivity of the night to the activity of the day, in which I work the works of Him that sent me. I wash away the last remnants of clinging mortality from before my Vision, and I see only the Son of God. I cleanse my body from the impurity of false thought, and open every pore to the inflowing Divine Energy and Infinite Love, whose offspring I am. I feel within me their uplifting power.

I clothe myself with garments of light, woven on the loom of life by the ministering angels who show me His will. They are with me now, they never leave me, and I will not forsake them. I put from me all desire which could make me unworthy to wear the robe of righteousness, and their hands shall bear me above all temptation. I descend the stairs which lead from the upper chamber of recognition of my God-Likeness to the lower room of experience, where I must manifest that relation to the world. I eat the food which is the bread from on high, that certain and sure supply which is mine as a child of God. I draw from the great storehouse that which I need in my work of the day. I feed upon the Word, the true Thought. I assimilate it, I embody it, it works in me and through me, and naught can oppose or conquer it....

I am that I am. With me is the everlasting Peace.

Ursula Gestefeld, *The Breath of Life*, 1897, pp. 7-9. No known copyright in effect.

January 3

NEW BEGINNINGS

Every day is a new beginning. We can rethink our past and look forward to something new. A new year reminds us that we have a chance to start anew.

We may look back and assess our lives and look forward to something different. We can change our circumstances or not. It's up to us. It is a matter of choice in how we view our lives and the circumstances in which we find ourselves.

The important thing to know is that now is the only time we have. This moment can make us conscious of what is, at this very moment. To live in the moment clears any confusion we may have about the past or future.

This moment contains all we require for a full life. It is what we are aware of that counts. To be aware we see beyond limitations and lack. We see what has always existed. And what is that? That there is perfection in every experience. There is order and beauty and right action at work in the universe and in our lives right now.

To be aware is to be open to new insights for living freely each and every day. Be aware. Think about the newness of the moment and that all things are made new in consciousness. May your New Year be filled with clarity and peace.

Marian G. Moon, *Lessons of Truth*, 2012, p. 1. Reprinted with permission of her family.

January 4

THE IMPORTANCE OF THE BIBLE

Man is always striving up to God and the Bible is the Book of the Meeting. This book grows in value to us as we grow in the knowledge of spiritual things; it interprets our own spiritual experiences, and enables us to see the goal of mankind, the Resurrection of the human race, above material limitation and darkness. It is the inspiration alike for individual needs, national needs and international aspirations. It inspires the artist, the litterateur, the musician, the merchant and the housewife. It comforts the sorrowing, and heals the sick in mind and body. It reveals our relation to God, and inspires our association with our fellow man to reach a closer affiliation. It is therefore not only the book of the meeting of God and man; it is the book of the meeting of man and man, for we never meet our fellow man until we meet him in Spirit.

Agnes M. Lawson, *Hints to Bible Study*, 1920, p. 11. Copyrighted material reprinted with permission of Divine Science Federation International.

January 5

THERE IS ALWAYS PLENTY

There is always plenty on man's pathway. It can only be brought into manifestation through desire, faith or the spoken word. Jesus Christ brought out clearly that man must make the first move.

Getting into the spiritual swing of things is no easy matter for the average person. The adverse thoughts of doubt and fear surge from the subconscious. They are the "army of aliens" which must be put to flight. This explains why it is so often, "darkest before the dawn."

A big demonstration is usually preceded by tormenting thoughts. Having made a statement of high spiritual truth one challenges the old beliefs in the subconscious, and "error is exposed" to be put out. This is the time when one must make his affirmations of truth repeatedly, and rejoice and give thanks that he has already received, "Before ye call I shall answer." This means that "every good and perfect gift" is already man's awaiting his recognition.

Florence Scovel Shinn, *The Game of Life and How to Play It*, 1925, page 7. No known copyright in effect.

January 6

HEAVEN HERE AND NOW

We miss out on so much of the good life by not enjoying heaven here and now. In Matthew 3:2 it reads, "the kingdom of heaven is at hand." And then at Mark 1:15 we find "the kingdom of heaven is at hand." Right where we are, heaven is. Heaven is now.

At page 598 in *The Science of Mind* textbook our dean and founder, Dr. Ernest Holmes, wrote that heaven is a state of happiness. He said heaven is within us and that it is resident all about us; that it is the result of that atmosphere of conviction that our thought awakens within us. He also said that heaven is not a locality, it is not a place. It is a real state of reality… He also said that those of us who are looking for a heaven whose streets are paved with gold and gates are made of pearl will not find it. So you won't find heaven in a locality. Heaven is within us. Happiness is within us. Peace is within us. Once we can find that peace, that happiness, that heaven, we will experience heaven right here and right now.

Many people spend their time seeking the pearl of great price. What they are looking for, you already are, you already have…

I can't remember how many times I have visited hell in order to find heaven. Dr. Holmes said "We are all hell-bound for heaven." Then there are some people who are too lazy to get up from the couch to make it happen. With heaven comes responsibility. You don't get something for no-thing.

Do not postpone living your dreams. Live in the moment. Let us not put off until tomorrow what we can do today. I do believe in saving; but a lot of people are saving for a rainy day. Then they stop to look out the window not knowing that it's raining cats and dogs out there already.

Juanita Bryant-Dunn, from *The Voices of Guidance 43rd Anniversary Tribute*, 2010. Transcribed and printed with permission of Guidance Center for Spiritual Living, Los Angeles, California.

January 7

WHAT I AM

God worketh through me to will and to do of His good pleasure.
In Him I live, move, and have my Being.
I am Life within Eternal Life.
I am Substance within the Eternal Substance.
I am Strength within the Infinite Strength.
I am Mind within the Divine Mind.
I am Idea within the Divine Idea.
I am Consciousness within Divine Consciousness.
I am Truth. I am Freedom. I am Fullness. I am that I am.
My Life is complete now. I am eternally perfect.
My Health is a finished fact.
My Freedom is a changeless reality,
My Strength is Omnipotence.
My Understanding is Omniscience.

I now accept my always Perfect Health, my Changeless Freedom, my Unlimited Strength, my Divine Understanding and my Spiritual Substance from Thee, my Source.

All souls shall be in God, and shall be God, and nothing but God be.
— Festus

Fannie Brooks James, *Divine Science: New Light Upon Old Truths*, 1896, p. 121. No known copyright in effect.

January 8

THE LORD'S PRAYER

Our Father, which art in heaven,

Our Father-Mother God, all harmonious,

Hallowed be Thy name.

Adorable one.

Thy kingdom come.

Thy kingdom is come. Thou art ever-present.

Thy will be done in earth, as it is in heaven.

Enable us to know – as in heaven, so on earth – God is omnipotent, supreme.

Give us this day our daily bread,

Give us grace for today, feed the famished affections,

And forgive us our debts,
as we forgive our debtors.

And Love is reflected in love;

And lead us not into temptation,
but deliver us from evil;

And God leadeth us not into temptation, but deliver us from sin, disease and death.

For Thine is the kingdom,
and the power, and the glory, forever.

For God is infinite, all power, all Life, Truth, Love, over all, and All.

Mary Baker Eddy, *Science and Health*, 1875, pp. 16-17. No known copyright in effect.

January 9

THE HIGHEST IDEA OF GOD

Jesus was the highest idea of God visible to the senses, and the Christ is the Divine Principle (manifested by Jesus) which actuates and controls all things. Jesus the Christ as revealed in Christian science is the sense of dominion (the will and the power of God in everyone) lifting mankind above the thralldom of the senses, and re-establishing him in his normal condition – having absolute dominion over all things. "Thou hast put all things under his feet." Man is the idea of God, the conception of Eternal Mind, co-existent and co-eternal with It. We believe that the only absolute healing power is that demonstrated by our Elder Brother, Jesus, and that to follow in His footsteps -- casting out evil and healing the sick is the -- coming to Him, the straight and narrow way which leads to eternal life. This healing power is Mind. There is no Life, Substance or Intelligence, but that which is Spiritual, and that the salvation of man (as taught by Jesus) is in the consciousness of the supremacy and omnipotence of God, and the impotency of evil (any opposite to God).

Malinda Elliott Cramer, (1890), published in *Present At The Beginning*, (Mercer), 2014, p. 18.

January 10

GOD'S CONSTANCY

God does not change. He cannot change. If change were possible to God, our efforts to approach Him in character would be illogical and superfluous. The emotional man is a creature of changes, and to think of God as also being variable, would make existence take on the nature of a fantastic dance, a world of shadows, leaping and wavering in imitation of a master shadow. Prayers would be of no avail; faith would be of no avail; works would be of no avail. For if God were of one mind yesterday and of another mind today, by what adroitness of mental legerdemain could we hope to catch up with his mood of tomorrow?

In whatever study we make of God, it is imperative that we remember His constancy of nature. With that truth immovably fixed in us we can meet all the changes in phenomena and be unchanged by them. We can face all the fluctuations of the emotions and remain serene in the consciousness that the emotions may vary but that the mind of God in us never does.

Imelda Octavia Shanklin, *Selected Studies*, 1926, pp. 35-36. Copyrighted material reprinted with permission of Unity, Unity.org.

January 11

DIVINE ENTHUSIASM

The law of divine enthusiasm, spiritual zeal, is one of the most powerful laws operative in the kingdom of the heavens. To speak always fearlessly, truthfully, and courageously makes for enthusiasm and establishes a confidence, a sureness that even the angels of heaven must notice and honor.

The world has been zealous in advocating reforms. The trouble with all reforms has been that those who were behind them have tried to compel others to change their ways without changing their hearts. When the principles of practical Christianity get a deep hold on one's consciousness, one is not only willing to change but to work continuously to lay hold of the spiritual powers that will transform him.

Application of the fundamental principles of Christianity, that is, of love toward God and humanity, makes new creatures of men and women. This is true today, as it has been true all down the ages. But no great inspiration is going to emanate from a lukewarm religion; one must be zealous in one's work. Courageous, zealous religion is the power that transforms one, that makes one want to be on the right side of every proposition.

Cora Dedrick Fillmore, *Christ Enthroned in Man*, 1937, pp. 79-80. Copyrighted material reprinted with permission of Unity, Unity.org.

January 12

GROWING OUT OR GROWING UP?

There are times when all of us doubt that we matter very much, because life…tends to obliterate the importance of the individual. Except for our families and a few friends, it seems like we're becoming more and more depersonalized. But to grow afraid under pressure, manipulations, devaluations, is unworthy of our divine heritage. In God's sight there are no anonymous or unimportant people.

Each one of us is important because each one of us has been created in the "image" of God – "So God created man in his own image, in the image of God created He him…" not in terms of physical form, but in terms of creative *thinking* entities. The New Testament affirms: "Beloved, now are we the sons of God, and it doth not yet appear what we shall be…" namely, to what heights we may grow. We are important, you and I, because God needs us to express Himself. Whatever our education, social or financial status, or color, God needs us to express abundance in living; to express freedom in terms of constructive activity – to be our true self, to exercise our Divine potential, but not in terms of license or action at the expense of others.

The person who is able to appreciate himself as a Divine incarnation, who knows that a mistake doesn't lessen but only delays his good – but will help him grow if he will but benefit from it – has solved one of the riddles of life. The world belongs, the very wise have said, to him who accepts this truth humbly, acts upon it courageously, and fulfills it grandly.

Doris Dickelman, published in *Science of Mind,* August 1969, p.10. Copyrighted material reprinted with permission of SOM Publishing.

January 13

WORDS OF WISDOM

Sometimes we think we can improve our self-identity, our consciousness of who we are, by making a change in the outer. We think that we can improve our self-concept by getting a new suit of clothes; but all you're going to get is a new suit of clothes. That's only dealing with the outer. Whatever you do in the outer represents only ten percent of the work to be done. Ninety percent of the work has to be done on the inner, changing our consciousness and changing our heart.

The change in our life from our place of limitation to a place of unlimited freedom and our greater good is an inside job. The work that must be done must be done from the inside. This inside job was described by Jesus as "the narrow way."

Enter through the narrow gate. For wide is the gate and broad is the road that leads to destruction, and many enter through it. But small is the gate and narrow the road that leads to life, and only a few find it.
— Matthew 7:13-14

Sallye Taylor, transcribed from her recorded lesson delivered at the Unity Church of Austin, January 24, 2010. No known copyright in effect.

January 14

THE HIDDEN GOOD

Whether we believe it or not, there is an invisible, inexhaustible Supply that is ever seeking to express Its Life, Its Substance, Intelligence, Power and Love. These blessings can be expressed through each one of us. They will be manifested by means of us when we mentally see their Omnipresence and Omnipotence. No demand can be made upon you that you cannot supply through the Power of Almighty God in you. Suppose lack is apparent in your world; you need money and the things that money can buy so that you may be suitably fed and housed. You have the wisdom and the power to manifest this supply....

Begin now to affirm that you are one with the Source of all abundance. You are an inseparable, individualized center in the Presence of Love. Affirm and feel that your supply comes from God through your consciousness of your oneness with God.

Alice R. Ritchie, published in *Bulletin,* Federation of Divine Scientists, March 1930, p. 15. Copyrighted material reprinted with permission of Divine Science Federation International.

January 15

WHEN YE PRAY

Whether kneeling down to God is necessary or not, depends upon the kneeler. As you think in your heart, so it is.

The attitude of kneeling means submission, and it comes from the time when kings struck down their enemies in front of them, and the enemy crouched and begged for his life.

I see no reason for crouching before God, nor do I see a reason for begging from God that which God already knows is within me. Therefore when I pray I choose any position which affords me a sense of freedom from consciousness of the body.

Elizabeth Towne, published in *Washington News Letter*, (ed. Sabin), March 1917, p. 381. No known copyright in effect.

January 16

WHO'S IN CHARGE?

In Genesis God tells us that man has dominion over everything on earth. This includes the fact that we're in charge of everything in our lives. We are expressions of the divine life of God and we have the freedom to take charge of our lives. We tend to engage in a victim mentality that blames external forces for the outcomes in our lives. We have generally not understood that we have the power to declare full freedom to take charge of our lives.

Our freedom is God-given. Despite this fact, we are all born into the human condition where there is an external power that dictates to us what role we will play and what expectations others will have for us. We have allowed ourselves to be bound by society's rules, by this external power.

Author Gary Zukav acknowledges external power; but also speaks to us of our "authentic power," that is the internal power we have to live life as we choose. This power does not judge things that it sees; it has the ability to see meaning and purpose trying to break through in the chaotic condition of the world today.

In back of all the confusion and chaos there is a purpose to life. This power is resident in each of us. As we awaken to who we are as children of God, we are able to claim our power and to exercise it. We learn that we are God in expression. With this freedom and dominion comes the responsibility to take charge of our lives and truly become channels for God.

This authentic power activates us and moves us in the direction of our dreams. We must be committed to being free, standing up and following our own hearts. It is a process, and in recognizing that life is a process we understand that our unfoldment occurs over time, step-by-step. Activating our freedom and dominion is such a process.

Peggy Bassett, from her lesson at Huntington Beach Church of Religious Science, July 15, 1990. Transcribed and printed with permission of Huntington Beach Center for Spiritual Living, Huntington Beach, California.

January 17

BE NOT AFRAID

*God hath not given us the spirit of fear; but of power,
and of love, and of a sound mind.*
2 Timothy 1:7

God has not given us the "spirit of fear." If fear is not a gift of God, whence does it come? And why do we accept it as a reality?

In the Old Testament, and also in the New, there are hundreds of verses which tell us in many ways: "Fear not, be not afraid, take courage. God is here!"

Let us give some time each day to quiet thought, to deep meditation upon some of these comforting and strengthening words from the Bible. We claim the power, the love and the sound mind which we are promised, as gifts of God – ours now.

Barbara L. Wolfe, *Be Not Afraid*, 1998, p. 3. Copyrighted material reprinted with permission of Divine Science Federation International.

January 18

THE WILL OF GOD

Or what man is there of you, who, if his son shall ask him for a loaf, will give him a stone; or if he shall ask for a fish, will give him a serpent? If ye then, being evil, know how to give good gifts unto your children, how much more shall your Father who is in heaven give good things to them that ask him.
– Jesus

God's will for us is not sorrow, poverty, loneliness, death, and all the other forms of suffering that we usually associate with the expression "Thy will be done."

"That creature in which the Eternal Good most manifesteth itself, shineth forth, worketh, is most known and loved, is the best."

Paul expresses the same idea when he says, "It was the good pleasure *of the Father* that in him [Christ] should all the fullness dwell." This means fullness of love, fullness of life, fullness of power, fullness of joy, fullness of all good; and Christ abideth in you, "Of his fullness we all received." "And in him ye are made full."

H. Emilie Cady, *The Will of God,* pamphlet, 1959, p. 1. Copyrighted material reprinted with permission of Unity, Unity.org.

January 19

OVERCOMING OUR COMMON FAULTS

Just what do we mean by sin? It is defined as a transgression of the divine law and an offense against God, as a violation of some religious or moral principle or of some standard of taste or propriety. Being a transgression, a violation of some law or principle is not a thing in itself, not a quality, but a lack of will or ability to develop positive qualities. It is not a principle but a departure from a principle, which by immutable law of sowing and reaping carries within itself its own punishment.

When we know a principle to be right and fail to live up to it, we are committing a sin against ourselves. It may be a comparatively minor infraction, such as yielding to the temptation to overeat, which probably harms no one but ourselves. Yet because overeating is a disregard of the principle of temperance, it brings the punishment of physical discomfort, perhaps even physical disease. The greater the transgression, the greater the penalty.

We cannot hope to grow spiritually until we rid ourselves of the little failings or big errors that come from following the dictates of personal will. God gave us freedom of will, the power to decide whether we want the happiness and peace that result from following His way, or the unhappiness and restlessness inherent in the human way.

Clara Beranger, *Peace Begins At Home*, 1954, pp. 13-14. Copyrighted material reprinted with permission of Unity, Unity.org.

January 20

PRAYER

It is not enough to pray. Prayer is one step that you take, but you need other steps. You need to think of God, the all-powerful Healer, as being already within you, in every part of your mind, heart, and body. To keep one's attention and prayers in the spiritual realm of mind, without letting them work out into the soul's expression and into the actual physical doing of that which corresponds with what the mind and heart has thought and spoken and prayed, is to court trouble. To keep declaring love and power and life and substance, and yet unconsciously, perhaps, assuming limitations and living them, will cause explosions and congestion that work out in the physical. We need to harmonize our thinking and our prayers with actual living experiences.

Sometimes we pray to a God outside of ourselves. It is the God in the midst of us that frees and heals.

With our eye of faith we must see God in our flesh, see that wholeness for which we are praying in every part of the body temple. "Do you not know that your body is a temple of the Holy Spirit within you?... Glorify God in your body." I Corinthians 6:19, 20

Myrtle Fillmore, *Letters of Myrtle Fillmore*, (ed. Foulks), 1936, pp. 26-27. Copyrighted material reprinted with permission of Unity, Unity.org.

January 21

ONE'S HIGHER SELF

One's higher self, which is the true self, is divine, spiritual. It is this self that is Divine Mind's perfect idea, the same self that in Genesis is spoken of as the image and likeness of God. In the New Testament, this self is represented by the Christ, the only begotten Son of God.

Thus, we are all children of God, and the qualities of God are inherent in us. Humankind, of course, is not all that God is, for God is the life of all living things as well as the law governing the mighty cosmos. This truth that we are God's highest creation and that we partake of God's nature is one that is most important to recognize. When we recognize and acknowledge this truth, we can exercise the divine powers that assure us of peace of mind, health of body, love that inspires service, and prosperity. This higher self, this indwelling presence, is the "mystery" revealed by Paul as "Christ in you, the hope of glory." Colossians 1:27

The precious gift of Christ is born of and given of God's love. "For God so loved the world that he gave his only Son, that whoever believes in him should not perish but have eternal life." John 3:16

It is our high privilege to know Christ; our great mission to let Christ have expression through us so that we, too, may "bear witness to the truth." John 18:37

Elizabeth Sand Turner, *What Unity Teaches*, 1954, pp. 7-8. Copyrighted material reprinted with permission of Unity, Unity.org.

January 22

THE LIGHT OF LIFE

"And God said, Let there be light," and light came into being. Man walks in the darkness of ignorance, stumbling along and struggling against obstacles that impede his progress and make painful his way. His eyes are not opened and lifted to the light that illumines the pathway of life. Plodding along in the lowlands, he misses the wider vision of the hills, and his days indeed seem monotonous with tasks to be done and trials to be endured, without real joy to lighten his burdens. The days go by until a time comes when something hitherto unknown stirs within him – something to which he perforce gives heed. He then raises his eyes from the circumscribed reach of his narrow life and beholds a light playing upon the hillside before him. Its rays seem to enfold him. An unfamiliar warmth pervades his being, and his soul awakes to a startlingly new impulse that demands expression.

What is this new impelling force that animates him? No previous experience can give him answer; he must find the solution for himself. This is the beginning of man's rise from blind acceptance of mortal limitations into an understanding of the divine possibilities and potentialities within him. The inner voice, the "and God said," bids the creative spirit to come forth and become active in manifesting this new and rare material abiding in man's soul. During the process of recreation going on in his consciousness man becomes aware of his undeveloped mental and spiritual powers, his own divine nature, his inheritance from God. Without this knowledge man is not really alive. When he possesses this knowledge it is as if God were repeating Himself in the individual and breathing into his nostrils the breath of life until he becomes a "living soul," conscious of an indwelling activity, which Jesus said was the light of man, "the *light* which lighteth every man coming into the world."

Someone has said that a person must be uplifted before he can uplift others, he must live the "life" if he would teach it, he must be a veritable "light" on the path if he would have others walk in the way of the Lord.

"I, if I be lifted from the earth, will draw all men unto myself."

Jennie H. Croft, published in *Unity*, June 1930, pp. 15-16. Copyrighted material reprinted with permission of Unity, Unity.org.

January 23

THE OPEN DOOR

Behold, I have set before thee an open door and no man can shut it.
Revelation 3:8

The doorway of the Absolute stands open at the center of our intuitive perception. *The Science of Mind,* p. 112.

Do we fully appreciate what the word "absolute" means? It is important that we do. When we read certain words frequently we sometimes don't register their true value. If we are to understand God's spiritual laws we must realize and thoroughly grasp the fact that absolute means forever, never-changing, something that is and always will be.

During meditation we enter the Absolute and forsake the relative. In other words, we enter that which is invincible, certain, and never failing. We leave behind the ever-changing, uncertain, and unpredictable things of the relative world. This is where we enter into the security of God's provision. Here, God's love and care are forever. Here, God's creative law is completely dependable. Here, we can rest safely and use God's laws in full confidence.

Raymond Charles Barker said: "The answer to every problem is in our knowledge of God and in our ability to let divine ideas lead us to the correct solution." We have knowledge of God when we understand the Absolute. When our faith and trust are strong we go through the door to all the richness of life that is available to us.

Our knowledge and faith are the means by which we knock on the door. Our knock opens the door and we enter into that special place of security, love, peace, and plenty of which we have been dreaming.

The more I dwell upon the Absolute, the stronger grows my faith. As the door opens, I enter in with joy and thanksgiving. I feel that at last I am coming home.

Norah Boyd, *Science of Mind,* May 2000, p. 71. Copyrighted material reprinted with permission of SOM Publishing.

January 24

A CLEAN SLATE

Ready for a clean slate? Does everyone have one of the stones we have today from Israel? Their use is based on a ritual from back in Jesus' day. When someone was freed from prison they were given a white stone with which a new name could be written. We celebrate this every year in the white stone ceremony where we get to put a new name or a new quality of our consciousness at the forefront of our awareness.

It takes a lot of courage in order to do this, to have a clean slate. It takes a lot of courage. What's one of the things you have to give up when you want to have a clean slate? Old stuff, fear, everything.

One of the things we have to give up is the thought that sometimes when we've written a "story" on our slate, that's the truth. Right?...

And what we do then, that we don't even know we do, is to start to add "stories" to it and treat them as the truth. Why? Because we don't consciously stay in a place of awareness….When you or I make up a story we have now fed into energy that is not of the highest vibration. Can I get an Amen?

What we're talking about in Unity is living in a place of high vibration. I'm not talking about living in a place of good or bad, right or wrong, gets it or doesn't get it or health or unhealthy. I'm talking about a high vibration that says it doesn't matter what's happening in my life: I know who I Am and I Am a beloved expression of the Divine. It is the power of Love, it is the power of God, it is the power of Health that moves through my body.

Do you know that about yourself? You are a divine expression that does not change.

Jennifer Holder, from her lesson delivered at Unity of Gaithersburg, Maryland, January 4, 2015. Transcribed and printed with permission of her family.

January 25

THE OAK AND THE LEAVES

A mighty oak on the hillside grew,
A monarch among trees:
In winter it knew the voice of the storm,
And in June the hum of bees.
But a little leaf on the end of a bough
Sighed "Alas, how small am I;
I really will not be missed at all
If I shrivel up and die."
And so in a qualm of self-pity
It fell to the grass below.
And one by one the other leaves said
"I'm so small I too will go."
But as they rested on the ground
A sad sight met their eye
For the oak they had thought mighty
Was surely beginning to die.
And so the leaves held a convention
And said "It is plain to see
That we really are very important
    To the life of that great big tree."
And straightway they chartered a south wind
And back to their places they stole.
Having learned one of Life's great lessons,
That each is a part of the Whole.

Helen Van Slyke, published in *Religious Science Monthly*, October 1927, p. 32. Copyrighted material reprinted with permission of SOM Publishing.

January 26

THOUGHTS OF PEACE

* We can all spend our lives going about doing good. Every time you meet a person, think of something encouraging to say – a kind word, a helpful suggestion, an expression of admiration. Every time you come into a situation, think of some good thing to bring – a thoughtful gift, a considerate attitude, a helping hand.

* If you love people enough, they will respond lovingly. If I offend people, I blame myself, for I know that if my conduct had been correct, they would not have been offended, even though they did not agree with me. "Before the tongue can speak, it must have lost the power to wound."

* In our spiritual development we are often required to pull up roots and to close many chapters of our lives until we are no longer attached to any material thing and can love all people without any attachment to them.

* You cannot leave a situation without spiritual injury unless you leave it lovingly.

* The spiritual life is the real life – all else is illusion and deception. Only those who are attached to God alone are truly free. Only those who live up to the highest light they have find their lives in harmony. Those who act on their highest motivations become a power for good. It is not important that others be noticeably affected. Results should never be sought or desired. Know that every right thing you do – every good word you say – every positive thought you think – has good effect.

* All difficulties in your life have a purpose. They are pushing you toward harmony with God's will.

Peace Pilgrim, *Steps Toward Inner Peace*, 1983, pp.17, 19-20. No known copyright in effect.

January 27

BAPTISM OF SPIRIT

Listen to the voice of Spirit. Thy life is Myself, I Am thy Mind, Will and Faith. I Am thy Love, Truth, and Wisdom, and thou hast no other. I Am the only Creator, Maker of all things. I Am everywhere under all circumstances; in Me are all worlds seated, and I pervade them all. There is nothing real in all the universe but Me.

Come unto Me. Claim Me for thyself. Believe that there is no Being but Me, and thou wilt do My will and act as I act, and thou wilt find rest in Me. There is no life in thought not born of Me or which does not represent my Divine Being. Impersonal thought, word and deed are born of me. I recognize no other. I know no lack of perfection, knowledge, power; I Am Wholeness to all, and they who see as I see and think My thoughts come unto Me, and are glorified in My Truth – "for he that believeth" shall do the things that I do. Dear child, thou art radiant with My Being, for thou art one with Me. Thou art free, peaceful, and harmonious – thy work is finished, thou hast returned in consciousness and understanding from thy journeying through the land of effects, ignorance and doubt. The Sabbath day is come, thou art at rest in the full consciousness that the kingdom is within thee and that thou art in the kingdom, power and glory – drinking the blessed Truth of thy perfect Being in Me.

Malinda Elliott Cramer, (1890), published in *Present At The Beginning*, (Mercer), 2014, p. 19.

January 28

THE THRONE ROOM

My child, at the very center of your being there is a golden throne where Divinity dwells. Here you can come and meet your Lord in the quietness of your own soul. Come each day, My child, set apart some special time; come, knock on that door of your heart and it shall swing open and you shall come in and hold sweet communion with the Lord of your Life.

I know, My child, it is often hard to steal away alone, the cares and duties of life press so closely and bind so surely; but if you will but try, if you will but make the effort, all these cares and duties shall fall into their proper relationship and you shall find such renewal of strength and beauty and calmness of spirit that as you leave that sacred spot and go again about the daily tasks, you shall find every care lightened and the path of every duty made plain.

But, you say, how shall I find this throne room of my heart, how can I come close to this Divine Presence? And I say unto you, it is only by becoming very still that you can find the path, and when you find it the door shall open and flood your whole being with a glory of which you have never dreamed before. This being still does not mean a blank stillness, but rather a constant sense of inner quiet which you shall achieve when you have the firm knowledge that your God is on His Throne, not in some far off sky, but at the center of your own being.

And so you shall come to that Great Stillness, and there shall awaken in you the realization that you stand before a door that has long been closed and as you knock, the door surely opens and you shall kneel before your Christ, sitting on the throne therein....

My words shall fit every need as you journey on the path of peace, and you shall have a sense of fellowship and know that the hand of the loving Master of men holds your hand and leads you on and up, every step of the way.

Eva Bell Werber. *Quiet Talks With the Master*, 1936, pp. 11-12. Reproduced from QUIET TALKS WITH THE MASTER by Eva Bell Werber 9780875161044 DeVorss Publications, www.devorss.com.

January 29

REJOICE! GOD REIGNS

Two thousand years ago, a babe was born in humble circumstances. He grew to adulthood and became the *greatest* Teacher in the world! He didn't write a book, didn't have a home, didn't build a church. He traveled, was scorned, flogged, his friends left him – he even borrowed a grave! Yet, his laws are greater than *all* science today! Science is still trying to understand substance, yet He spoke, and substance was created, bodies came back from death.

There is only One Mind, One Power, One Substance. Archaeological discoveries prove our Bible, just as scientific discoveries do. As told in the Bible, Moses struck a rock and produced water. Energy researchers are extracting water from rocks today. Moses acted as if God were acting *as* him, and God did! Not God *and...!*

We *see* bodies, but not Mind, *and* Spirit and emotion. Nobody sees YOU! We get a glimpse, as in the eyes of love. We are threefold– Spirit, thinking and emotions – Mind, Power and Substance. "I hope, I want, I will, I won't" are words of *challenge* that we must never use. We must take our invisible self, and turn it *up* to God. If not, *we* are submerged!

All we need is to declare, *God as All there is!* God never sets the clock back for any of us! Life is an escalator. If we look back, we become cross-eyed. Look forward! The clock is set right *out there* on the *same* vibration when we could have started.

The New Testament is a complete book of psychiatry. The chapters on taints of earth, which tell the things *not to do* are a must! The submerged part of anyone who obeys the Laws of God is turned upward to God, but they must have a burning Desire *of* God and a burning Desire to see God first.

Put Him into *all* you do! Praise everything you want increased. Joy, Beauty will follow you all the rest of your life when you praise and put God first! The submerged part is turned upward. Stay in Heaven first, and God will reward you.

Edna M. Lister, from the opening of the 49th INTA Congress, Seattle, Washington, June 5, 1964. Reprinted with permission.

January 30

MAKE YOUR LIFE SUCCESSFUL

When Jesus spoke to the multitudes, he told them that when they prayed they should believe that their prayers were answered. This represents the reality that if you can turn away from the effect of failure and initiate a new idea of success, a change for the better will take place in your life, because there is a law of life that operates on your beliefs as you believe them – not as you hope them to be, but what you actually believe them to be.

You can experience more successful living, better living, because you have been endowed with a creative mind, and you have been given the privilege of free choice. Regardless of financial problems, health problems, social problems or environmental problems, you can choose to do something to help yourself to find success.

Your thought of success, backed by faith and conviction, is the start of your experience. Remember, whatever is planted firmly in your mind in absolute belief is acted upon by the law of mind and has to come forth in your world of experience....

Since there is only one Law of Mind in action and It reacts for you at the level of perception, declare only thoughts of success in your life now.

Clara M. Wright, *Prayer in Action*, 1973, pp. 43-44. Copyrighted material reprinted with permission of SOM Publishing.

January 31

LIFE IN PARADOX

The paradoxes of life keep us on the quest for our own truth. This is an individual quest. We cannot just accept external answers to our internal questions. There is no one or nothing that has the answers to our personal life questions. We are responsible for our own life map. This spiritual map must be exposed through self-realization. We can use the wonderful examples of paradox as we build our personal belief system. I believe we can find them helpful.

Let's look at *The Sermon on the Mount* found in the gospel of Matthew. This section of the Gospels has been labeled in many different ways. Each person interprets it through his or her own point of view. As we read it, we can accept any point from the outer, or we can go to our inner knower, and find a part of our personal map for spiritual growth. This is our choice. All life is choice; therefore, the paradox.

Choosing an open-minded process of assimilating another's opinion will lead us to our own awareness of how to apply this to our spiritual growth. I believe that this approach expands our questions into possibilities. It may help us to move in a certain direction, but it is not the answer. I believe that we cannot make another person's opinion our Truth.

We are each on the journey to unfolding our potential, our possibilities as human beings evolving our spiritual essence. We are moving forward to expand our spiritual selves and create healthy, happy and prosperous lives.

Nancy Purcell, *A Flow Chart of Life*, 2012, pp. 35-36. Reproduced from A FLOW CHART OF LIFE by Nancy Purcell, 9781466966765 Trafford Publishing, www.trafford.com.

FEBRUARY

February 1

STRENGTH

STRENGTH is not necessarily the ability to push or pull; it is not proven by fighting energy; material wealth is not an indication of real strength.

STRENGTH is best indicated by sustained force; by intensity and vigor; by a maintained supply of things needful.

STRENGTH is known to the student as his own ability to persist or endure; his capacity for intense and maintained activity; his willingness to press forward on a given course.

STRENGTH in the Mind of God is His unlimited Power to sustain the activity of Creation; the continued movement and unfolding of Creation; the constant supply of all things required for the development of the plan.

STRENGTH in the Mind of God is an idea of endurance, continuity.

STRENGTH in man is his ability to hold to his selected course, to sustain his own efforts.

Ella Pomeroy, *Powers of the Soul*, 1948, p. 131. No known copyright in effect.

February 2

KNOW THE TRUTH

Jesus said, *"Ye shall know the truth and the truth shall make you free."*
There are, therefore, two phases to be considered. Jesus' promise that we shall know the truth is sufficient proof that it is something within our reach – not merely a visionary idea.

These words caught my attention this morning: "Knowing the truth of our Oneness with the Father unites with the Source of all good."

That gives us something with which to start, "the truth of our Oneness with the Father." Surely that is the perfect union. We are no longer two; we have become one. In some measure we partake of the God qualities, share the Father's powers and privileges and manifest in our body and affairs the advantages of a son-ship so intimate that we are not aware of any dividing line. We are partakers so completely unified with the Father that we think His thoughts, speak His words, and do His works.

Annie S. Greenwood, *How to Know the Truth*, Unity pamphlet, 1957, pp. 4-5. Copyrighted material reprinted with permission of Unity, Unity.org.

February 3

BLESSED WITH TRUE PROSPERITY

Prosperity is not always money. The tither may or may not receive an increase in income, but he always receives an increase in satisfaction and peace of mind.

Let us pray to give more, and to express and share the abilities with which we have been blessed. Let us not withhold our abilities or our time. When freely given, they will bring us true prosperity. It may come as increases in varied and unexpected ways, but surely we will be prospered in the ways we need to be prospered.

Our prosperity and success come through us. We have something to give and to share. As we make use of our gifts, we discover other gifts and abilities within us. As we open our minds and hearts to divine ideas, we are rich in spirit and in manifestation. We can sing our song of prosperity, "I am blessed with true prosperity! I see abundance everywhere."

Then you shall make your way prosperous, and then you shall be successful.
Joshua 1:8

Christina Knox-Walthall, (1998), published in *Daily Inspiration*, Copyright 2014, *Daily Inspiration for Better Living.* Reprinted with permission of the Universal Foundation for Better Living (UFBL) Press, July 2014, p. 39.

February 4

LIFE AS A RIVER

The river of my life
Flows with a constant current.
It has its shallows…
It has its deeps,
But always keeps
The constant current.
One way it flows,
From summit's snows
To expanding sea;
Endless, boundless,
Joyous, free!
God is the source –
The river,
The sea,
And me.

Dorothy M. Pierson, *Daily Word,* from Unity's Facebook page, September 5, 2013. Copyrighted material reprinted with permission of Unity, Unity.org.

February 5

THE SCIENCE OF SPIRIT

We teach the Science of Spirit, Being or God in Creation.

Science is exact knowledge, and knowledge is a certain perception of Truth; and Truth is unalterable principle, so there can be no Science that is not based on unchanging principle, nor can we have knowledge but of that which is exact or unchanging Truth. Therefore, it is true that Science or Knowledge is a perception of First and Final Truth, which is God or Principle. That which is highest, first, and from which anything proceeds is Principle; as in the Science of Mathematics the principle is the highest and first, and is that from which all problems and examples proceed. So the Spirit of God or Goodness is Principle, is highest and first, and is that from which all creation, visible and invisible proceeds. A mathematical demonstration is one which accords with unchanging Truth and Principle; therefore it is true that there is an unchanging Truth and Principle underlying all Mathematical demonstration – a correct solution and truthful conclusion of the problem of life and harmonious expression are those that are in exact accord with the Spirit of God or Goodness.

Therefore it is true that there is the Spirit of God or Goodness underlying all correct, truthful solutions or conclusions and harmonious expression. As there is but one Infinite there is but one method of demonstration, one law of expression or creation.

We begin our reasoning from the abstract to the concrete, from the invisible Principle to the visible example, from "Being" to visible form, by which method only, are we sure of a correct solution to the problem of life and we are certain if we commence, where all things commence, we shall work in unison with God and work as the All works.

Malinda Elliott Cramer, (1890), published in *Present At The Beginning*, (Mercer), 2014, pp. 20-21.

February 6

THE OBJECT OF THE GAME OF LIFE

The object of the game of life is to see clearly one's good and to obliterate all mental pictures of evil. This must be done by impressing the subconscious mind with a realization of good. A very brilliant man, who has attained great success, told me he had suddenly erased all fear from his consciousness by reading a sign which hung in a room. He saw printed, in large letters this statement – "Why worry, it will probably never happen." These words were stamped indelibly upon his subconscious mind, and he has now a firm conviction that only good can come into his life, therefore only *good can manifest.*

Florence Scovel Shinn, *The Game Of Life and How to Play It*, 1925, p. 12. No known copyright in effect.

February 7

ATONEMENT

Atonement is the exemplification of man's unity with God, whereby man reflects divine Truth, Life, and Love. Jesus of Nazareth taught and demonstrated man's oneness with the Father, and for this we owe him endless homage. His mission was both individual and collective. He did life's work aright not only in justice to himself, but in mercy to mortals, -- to show them how to do theirs, but not to do it for them nor to relieve them of a single responsibility. Jesus acted boldly, against the accredited evidence of the senses, against Pharisaical creeds and practices, and he refuted all opponents with his healing power.

The atonement of Christ reconciles man to God, not God to man; for the divine Principle of Christ is God, and how can God propitiate Himself? Christ is Truth, which reaches no higher than itself. The fountain can rise no higher than its source. Christ, Truth, could conciliate no nature above His own, derived from eternal Love. It was therefore Christ's purpose to reconcile man to God, not God to man. Love and Truth are not at war with God's image and likeness. Man cannot exceed divine Love, and so atone for himself. Even Christ cannot reconcile Truth to error, for Truth and error are irreconcilable. Jesus aided in reconciling man to God by giving man a truer sense of Love, the divine Principle of Jesus' teachings, and this truer sense of Love redeems man from the law of matter, sin, and death by the law of Spirit -- the law of divine Love.

Mary Baker Eddy, *Science and Health*, 1875, pp. 18-19. No known copyright in effect.

February 8

NO LIMIT TO WHAT GOD CAN DO IN YOU

There is no limit to what God will do for those who believe.

This is the Law: "Whatsoever things you desire When You Pray, Believe that you receive them Now, and you shall have them.

Therefore I say unto you pray and believe; do it the first thing in the morning when you wake up, and the last thing at night when you go to sleep. Between times forget all about it if you can; but when you just can't help thinking about the health problem, then repeat the Prayer of Faith. Make your prayer something like this:

Thou, God, are my life and my perfect health.
In spirit and in truth I am whole now.
My flesh is perfect.
All my tissues are strong and are knit together where they belong.
This is true to my real self.
This is true in spirit and in truth now.
I Am whole Now.
I Am pure spirit, and God is my health now and forever.
My body is already reflecting God's wholeness.
I thank Thee, oh God, for my perfect health, happiness and abundance of life.
I rejoice in Thy wholeness now and evermore.

Elizabeth Towne, published in *Washington News Letter*, (ed. Sabin), November 1919, p. 52. No known copyright in effect.

February 9

NINETEEN WORDS

Just before Jesus said,
"Seek ye first the kingdom of God,
and his righteousness;
and all these things shall be added unto you."
He had been telling His listeners that man
cannot serve two masters, God and mammon.
In alluding to the birds of the air
and the lilies of the field,
which neither toil nor spin but are sustained by God,
He was not implying that we should not
work to satisfy our material and physical needs.
He was saying that we should reverse our priorities.
He was saying that
if God takes care of the birds and the lilies,
He will take care of His children.

In nineteen words
we were given the secret of life eternal
through Self-realization.
In our journey toward the kingdom consciousness
we move from self to Self.

F. Bernadette Turner, published in *At-One-Ment*, November-December 2006, p. 4. Copyrighted material reprinted with permission of Divine Science Federation International.

February 10

I AM SPIRITUAL ENERGY

Today is a nice day for me. I accept and use spiritual energy to go into my Father's house, the house of All-good.

The prodigal son used his spiritual energy to return to his Father's house. I have the same energy of Spirit. Therefore, I recognize that I am meant to use it to have a healthy, wealthy, and harmonious life.

God has given me energy plus the love and wisdom to use it. I am empowered by the Spirit of God in me, my Christ self, to rise above every undesirable circumstance.

In Divine Order, I express a new experience today, as I live in the understanding that I am using spiritual energy to move out of problems and into my Father's house of fulfillment and joy.

I use my spiritual energy to activate the love of God and achieve loving relationships.

I will arise and go to my Father…
Luke 15:15

Judith G. Weekes, (1990), published in *Daily Inspiration*, Copyright 2015, *Daily Inspiration for Better Living.* Reprinted with permission of the Universal Foundation for Better Living (UFBL) Press, September 2015, p. 23.

February 11

GIVING THANKS VS. COMPLAINING

We should not forget that we make a magnet of ourselves to attract whatever corresponds with our habitual state of mind. Thus the cheerful, grateful soul that appreciates the omnipresent bounty, health, strength and freedom, and acknowledging it with praise and thanksgiving, is attracting more of the good things that minister to our profit and pleasure on this plane of existence. It is *here* and *now* that we are to concern ourselves about; it is always now and always will be; yesterday is not, and tomorrow is unborn, and when born it will be *now*.

The worry and forebodings about what *might be* is a fruitful source of discomfort and even dis-ease. The soul that is perpetually in a state of anxiety, dread and apprehension cannot realize what the kingdom of heaven *within* means. It is the mortal, carnal self that indulges such fantasies, and we are proving daily that carnal ways lead to death, as it is written. All complaints and morbid anticipations must give place to confidence in the divine love that makes the heaven within. Ella Wheeler Wilcox has said in one of her pithy poems, "Heaven is a realm by loving souls created, and hell was fashioned by the hearts that hated." It is the loving souls that find both profit and pleasure in thanksgiving, and the loving souls that find the heaven within radiating a corresponding influence, as the rose sheds its perfume.

Jane Yarnall, published in *Washington News Letter*, (ed. Sabin), August 1902, p. 726. No known copyright in effect.

February 12

CONTEMPLATION

Contemplation, together with meditation, is the activity that leads us to Self-awareness. We evolve through human consciousness and realize our oneness with God. No longer does the mystic search for an answer to the questions: "What is truth?" "What is God?" "Why am I here?" The mystic does not ask these questions any longer because he knows that *he* is the answer – the answer to every question that he has ever asked. "I AM" is the answer to my own question, always….

The mystical journey is the journey through our own being to that experience known as cosmic consciousness, cosmic reality, or oneness with God. The principles and stages of this journey are not new…

The mystical journey takes many paths, but all paths lead to the same Truth. Eventually, the student begins to hear a message, and the message is, "You are the answer that you are searching for. The Truth, the Reality, the God that you are looking for is inside of you now."

Helen Brungardt, *Contemplation*, 1975, pp.16-17. No known copyright in effect.

February 13

SILENCE SELF, AND LISTEN

Be still, and know that I am God. I am Mind, Idea, Consciousness.
Colossians 2:9

In him dwelleth the fullness of the God head bodily;
and of his fullness, have all we received, and grace for grace.
John 1:16

I am the fullness of the Godhead bodily.

In Source I am Life, Strength, Intelligence, Love, Wholeness, Freedom, Fullness, Goodness, and Truth.

In Source I have power to *express* Life, Strength, Wholeness, Goodness, etc.

In Source I am *conscious* of having power to express my Wholeness, Strength, Life, etc.

I know the Truth of Being Whole.

"In him ye are complete."

I think of my freedom and peace.

I declare now my strength and completeness.

By the Law Divine, as I recognize and declare my Peace, Plenty, and Satisfaction, the Truth of Peace, Plenty and Satisfaction resounds through all my existence.

The One Only Voice that speaks. "I am Peace," is God. My soul and body echo that voice and say "I am Peace."

Fannie Brooks James, *Divine Science: New Light Upon Old Truths*, 1896, p. 55. No known copyright in effect.

February 14

DIVINE LOVE

Love is an inherent power that, if allowed to be expressed in one's life, will transform every inharmony, will heal every disease, will transmute every negative condition into part of the harmonious whole. The results of love are always good. But do not confuse sentiment and sympathy with love. I am speaking of the purified, transcendent power of divine love that expresses itself through you and me when we open our hearts and minds to it, when we recognize and encourage it.

May Rowland, *The Irresistible Power of Divine Love*, Unity pamphlet, 1969, p. 4. Copyrighted material reprinted with permission of Unity, Unity.org.

February 15

PRACTICE PRAISING GOD

In the Old Testament stories, we find that whenever the people got into trouble of any kind, they praised God. Moderns do not use spiritual power enough, and we find that when we do use it, it is regenerative.

In Paul's letter to the Thessalonians, he said this: "Always be joyful. Always keep on praying. No matter what happens, always be thankful, for this is God's will for you who belong to Christ Jesus." If you will begin to practice praising and thanking God for everything in your life, you'll soon find that you can't be low or depressed. As you turn to God in thanksgiving and praise, your spirits will begin to rise, and you will see opportunities and possibilities where none had seemed to exist before you began your expression of gratitude. If you think you need more money in order to be secure, your real need is to know God as your only source and supply….

Sometimes, when we are so intent on learning the new mental and spiritual attitudes which are stepping stones to our new prosperity, we forget to practice the art of appreciation. All forms of life respond to appreciation, expressed and demonstrated.…You know how children, animals, and even flowers and plants respond to warmth, love and praise. All life responds in one way or another. Harshness, criticism and lack of appreciation tend to shrivel and stifle all forms of life, from people to plants, while praise, love and appreciation evoke the same emotions and actions from people who are the recipients of such attention. Don't forget to say "Thank you" at the slightest provocation. Those two words are magic: they can melt the hardest heart and bring out the best in anyone.

Margaret M. Stevens, *PROSPERITY is God's Idea*, 1978, pp. 71, 74. Reproduced from PROSPERITY IS GOD'S IDEA by Margaret M. Stevens, 9780875162645 DeVorss Publications, www.devorss.com.

February 16

SPIRITUAL PRINCIPLE

Spiritual principle is embodied in the sacred books of the world's living religions. Christians hold to the Bible as the supreme exponent of spiritual principle. They believe that the Bible is the greatest and most deeply spiritual of all the scriptures, though they realize that other scriptures, such as the Zend-Avesta and the Upanishads, as well as the teachings of Buddha, the Koran, and the Tao of Lao-tse, and the writings on Confucius, contain expressions of eminent spiritual truths. A study of comparative religion shows a marked similarity among the ideas expounded by the founders of religions, revealing that there is one ultimate Truth, some phase of which each has perceived. The differences in religions seem to be due primarily to the different interpretations put upon spiritual truths by the leaders of each, and to forms of worship, which unfortunately often tend to obscure the beauty and simplicity of the original principles.

Elizabeth Sand Turner, *What Unity Teaches*, 1954, pp. 4-5. Copyrighted material reprinted with permission of Unity, Unity.org.

February 17

HAPPINESS

All through the ages man has been seeking happiness through material establishment of our at-one-ment with the Indwelling Spirit, and thus all through material means; but he has never found it there, and thus with God the Father do we find that peace and harmony which never change; that spiritual contentment and love which satisfy. When we come to that place of understanding where we know that God the Good is all there is and can rise in our consciousness to a realization of our Oneness with Spirit then do we partake of the Divine Nature of which we are an individualized part.

Spiritual growth always takes place when the Truth is realized. Happiness and contentment, therefore, come through the expression of that which is within oneself, and it is knowing and realizing the Truth about ourselves and our fellow men that enriches the consciousness and sets us free from all sense of separation from that which eternally is the One Unchangeable, Indivisible Reality. Happiness should be the best portion of everyone's life, for it is that through which God's love is expressed. It is necessary to understand the Divine Law in order that it may operate in our human affairs.

Right thinking is the keynote to right living. We need to consciously contact happiness and when we strike the key of love and peace within ourselves. Then will our lives manifest harmony. True happiness is not obtained in the possession of worldly things; but rather in the possession of self. There is only one way to obtain this full realization -- the way of the Indwelling Christ -- Unity with the Whole. Let us know, therefore, that we are in tune with the Infinite Harmony of the Universe.

Alberta Smith, published in *Religious Science Monthly*, October 1927, pp. 30-31. Copyrighted material reprinted with permission of SOM Publishing.

February 18

IT WORKS IF YOU WORK IT

At Christ Universal Temple (Chicago), the mantra is, 'It works if you work it.' What does that mean?

I work with Johnnie Colemon all the time and any lesson, prayer or any sermon that I'm giving, I'm not really giving to the people sitting out there -- I'm teaching Johnnie Colemon. One day as I was praying, that statement came -- it works if you work it. It comes from within you and if you are not meditating and have your attention stayed on God, you miss it. But, I heard the Father say, "It works if you work it." It can't work unless you work it. If it's not working, it's not God's fault it is your fault. In order for prosperity, health and peace to work, you've got to get rid of some things. You've got to let go of some things. You've got to stop gossiping. You've got to stop being jealous. You have got to let all of that go and realize that the same God that is within me is within you, and can do for you the same things He has done for me.

You are the thinker that thinks the thought that makes the thing. Please explain that statement.

Once again, I am a metaphysician, which means I deal with the mind. Everything begins in the mind. And, if it begins in the mind, whatever the effects are in your world, life and affairs, you must find the cause. There's a cause for every effect. You've got to think the right thoughts because every thought comes back to you. Whatever you think, you have made it. How does it come back? It comes back from the substance of God. And, the substance of God is like a big piece of dough; with no form and no shape — just a huge piece of dough waiting for you to use the cutter to make an incision out of this big piece of dough. Your thoughts happen to be the cookie cutter; so, whatever you think say, "I am the thinker that thinks the thought that makes the thing." Therefore, you must be very careful about what you think, what you say and what you feel. Because what I think will not hurt you—it will only hurt me.

Johnnie Colemon, from a transcribed interview with Philippe Matthews, Chicago, 2001. Reprinted with permission.

February 19

DIVINE LOVE

The Christ has still the desire to gather everyone under the protecting wings of Divine Love, but those who have not found the Inner Light or heard the "still small voice," the protecting Presence within the soul, are "they who would not" – they for whom the Christ still weeps. The Spirit within you is to save the world, waiting for you to invite all mankind. The "bride" is a type of divine love. It is yours to give the invitation to come to the "Marriage Supper." Sit down to the feast of good things which the Father has prepared for everyone who will partake. "Joy unspeakable and full of glory" shall be yours, now and forevermore.

The life that Jesus lived saves those who live the same life.

Agnes J. Galer, published in *The TRUTH*, (ed. A. Grier with F. Holmes and E. Holmes), June 1918, p. 11.

February 20

SERENITY

FATHER, I am well pleased with You and with everything You do – in silence, or equilibrium, or in activity.

I am well pleased with all things. I see that all expression is Yours, in endless variety of manifestation.

The tides of Your Life move through my being in harmony and order and tranquility. The flow of Your life is peaceful and satisfying.

I am indeed well pleased to be in this flow. I seek no other life. Do with me as You Will. I am Your Life, and You are my Life – Eternally.

Vida Reed Stone, *Come Now Into Your Freedom*, 1946, p. 90. No known copyright in effect.

February 21

FINDING THE CHRIST IN OURSELVES

Throughout all His teaching Jesus tried to show those who listened to Him how He was related to the Father, and to teach them that they were related to the same Father in exactly the same way. Over and over again He tried in different ways to explain to them that God lived within them, that He was "not *the God* of the dead, but of the living." And never once did He assume to do anything as of Himself, always saying: "I can of myself do nothing." "The Father abiding in me doeth his works." But it was very hard then for people to understand, just as it is very hard for us to understand today.

There were, in the person of Jesus, two distinct regions. There was the fleshly, mortal part that was Jesus, the son of man; then there was the central, living, real part that was Spirit, the Son of God -- that was the Christ, the Anointed. So each one of us has two regions of being -- one the fleshly, mortal part, which is always feeling its weakness and insufficiency in all things, always saying, "I can't." Then at the very center of our being there is something that, in our highest moments, knows itself more than conqueror over all things; it always says, "I can, and I will." It is the Christ child, the Son of God, the Anointed in us. "Call no man your father on the earth," said Jesus, "for one is your Father, even He who is in heaven."

H. Emilie Cady, *How I Used Truth*, 1939, p. 17-18. Copyrighted material reprinted with permission of Unity, Unity.org.

February 22

LEARNING TO KNOW GOD

Know that the Lord is God! It is He that made us, and not we ourselves.
Psalms 100:3

Learning to know God is the purpose and the privilege of our life on this plane. Jesus knew God intimately. His mission was to teach all men His way. Not only did He speak the Truth, He demonstrated it with miracles of healing, and by His mastery of natural forces. He raised others from the dead, and finally resurrected His own body to prove the power of the Father and the reality of eternal Life.

He took no personal credit, but said over and over that it was the Father who did the work, through Him. He also said that each son of God could do likewise. He even said we were to do greater works than He did. At this stage of our development we find this nearly impossible to believe. But this is our destiny.

I remember the words and the work of Jesus the Christ. I follow His way to the best of my present understanding. Miracles come to pass as I grow in consciousness.

Barbara L. Wolfe, published in *Daily Studies in Divine Science*, 2010, p. 116. Copyrighted material reprinted with permission of Divine Science Federation International.

February 23

THE MAGIC OF BELIEVING

Let us refresh our minds as to what we believe. We believe that we are true children of God and that we are placed here as channels through which God can express. We believe that there is only one Mind, the great universal Mind of God, which is Spirit. We believe that all manifestations in the material world are made of this Spirit. We believe that we, as true children of God, can demonstrate anything we wish in our lives and if we do not the responsibility is entirely our own. That we do not may be due to a lack of understanding, a matter of indifference, or, most telling of all, it may be because our faith is shaky. If our faith is absolute, then we are One with the Father and nothing is impossible to us....

Man, meaning each of us, is an individual manifestation of the One Great Universal God Mind for the purpose of expressing and bringing forth God ideas. Within man there are two states of consciousness: the conscious mind where we express our will and desire because of our free will, and the subconscious mind which manages all of the automatic detail required to keep our marvelous and complex bodies in operation – and which also takes orders from the conscious mind and brings them to fruition in the material world. Man has within himself the power to control; he has dominion, he can carve out his own destiny, he can make his own fortune. You have control, you have dominion and you can carve out your own destiny – and this you either do consciously or unconsciously. You are the master of the creative force working within you and demonstrating through you.

Cora B. Mayo, from the lesson she delivered at First Institute of Religious Science in Denver, Sunday, February 6, 1949. No known copyright in effect.

February 24

AFFIRMATIONS

For Prosperity: God is my unfailing supply, and large sums of money come to me quickly, under grace, in a perfect way.

For Right Conditions: Only that which is true of God is true for me, for the Father and I are ONE.

For Faith: As I am one with God, I am one with my good, for God is both the *Giver* and *Gift.* I cannot separate the *Giver* from the gift.

For Health: Divine Love floods my consciousness with health, and every cell in my body is filled with light.

For Eyesight: My eyes are God's eyes, I see with the eyes of Spirit. I see clearly the open way; there are no obstacles on my pathway. I see clearly the perfect plan.

For Guidance: I am divinely sensitive to my intuitive leads, and give instant obedience to Thy will.

For Hearing: My ears are God's ears. I hear with the ears of Spirit. I am non-resistant and am willing to be led. I hear glad tidings of great joy.

For Right Work: I have perfect work in a perfect way; I give perfect service for perfect pay.

For Freedom from all Bondage: I cast this burden on the Christ within, and I go free!

Florence Scovel Shinn, *The Game Of Life and How to Play It*, 1925, pp. 78-79. No known copyright in effect.

February 25

A BELOVED MINISTER'S WISDOM

It is done unto you as you believe.
Right where the pain is -- God is.
Short prayers pierce Heaven.
Celebrate your epiphanies!
God don't make no junk.
Do not "futurize" your good!
Clarify before you Unify.
Harmony is Heaven's first law.
That which I am seeking is seeking me.
Act like a bouncer at the gate of your thoughts.
Argue for your limitations and that is what you'll get.
The Spirit that has brought me this far will take me the rest of the way.
Don't tell God how big your problems are –
tell your problems how big your God is.
There is not a disease to be healed, but a perfect being to be revealed.
We learn through inspiration or desperation. It is up to us.
There is not something to do, there is something to know.
Everything that comes to you, comes to bless you.
Do not ask for success and prepare for failure.
God is always home, it is we who take a walk.
Thought + Feeling = Demonstration.

Marguerite Lewis, *Memorial Program,* New Thought Spiritual Center of Eastern Long Island, April 4, 2008. Reprinted with permission.

February 26

IMMORTALITY – THE CELEBRATION OF LIFE

We are One with God now. We shall remain One with God no matter where we go. There are beings beyond us in evolution, even as we are beyond the tadpole, and we too shall gain these lofty mountains of evolution and go from there to more. We can never become less than we now are. The whole road ahead of us is one of expansion. So let us say of all of our friends who have left this world that they have but passed through a door to a larger life. You and I stand on this side of that doorway seeing it open and close behind them. We say that they have left this room, but those on the other side will say that they have entered.

For every death there is a resurrection. For every resurrection something must be discarded. We are all children of the Light, and in that Light there is no darkness. We are all children of Life, and in that Life there is no death. We are born out of Love, and in that Love there is no fear. We all belong to Eternal Peace, and in that Peace there is no confusion.

I know that the Law of Good surrounds each person with love and friendship. I permit this love and friendship to flow out to all things, to all people, everywhere.

I let it radiate in the environment, bless everything that is touched, make whole that which is weak, turn fear into faith, and accomplish the miracle of healing through love.

We live, move and have our being in wholeness. Peace, poise and power belong in the Kingdom of God. We give joy and love to all, knowing that the gift of Life is not of each one alone. We share their good.

Each one welcomes the opportunity to love fully, completely and joyfully. We celebrate Life and Life is everlasting. This is the celebration of life.

Betty Jean House, from her brother's memorial service. Copyrighted material reprinted with permission.

February 27

OLD UNWANTED HABITS CANNOT BIND ME

Thank you, God, for revealing to me the Truth that is constant and eternal. The Truth about me is that I am pure and divine. I have the ability to think right, and through my right thinking my life is blessed.

Thank you, God, for the knowledge of Truth, the knowledge of knowing that I am one with Thee. This knowledge keeps me centered in Thee and I am free from frustration, fear and doubt. I experience a deep feeling of love, freedom and peace, as I follow the Truth that you reveal to me.

"Ye are the light of the world," the Master, Jesus, said. It is the Light of Truth in you that lights the world. It is the Light of Truth in you that lights *your* world.

The Truth is revealed to me through the Christ that indwells me. "The true light which lighteth every man that cometh into the world" was the way it was revealed to John, the gospel writer. Today I accept that light, that Truth which is revealed to me through the Christ in me.

I accept the Truth, the whole Truth and nothing but the Truth as the way to better living for me. Thank you, Father.

And ye shall know the truth, and the truth shall make you free.
John 8:32

Olga Una Barker, published in *Daily Inspiration*, Copyright 1980, *Daily Inspiration for Better Living*. Reprinted with permission of the Universal Foundation for Better Living (UFBL) Press, November 1980, p. 22.

February 28

MY MEDITATION

Be still, my body…rest…relax
Let go…let go…
Breathe in God's love,
Breathe out tiredness and strain.
I'm resting, Lord…take charge.

Be still, my heart…cease to worry, fret, or care.
Beat steady, slow and sure.
I feel nothing, God…You are All.
"Thy will be done."

Be still, my mind…be quiet and know
God is…all is well.
O God, Infinite Intelligence,
I'm listening now…quietly listening.
Speak, O Lord!

Be still, my soul…I'm empty now of me,
Ready for the Presence and the Power.
Fill this empty vessel, Lord.
Yes, Lord, now I hear:
"Be still and know that I am God."
Still…deep, deep still…
Now I KNOW
You are here…within…without;
I in You and You in me – life of endless unity,
One with your Light…your Life…your Love…
Your Joy…your Peace…your Power.
All that I am is You.
I AM THAT I AM.
-- So it is. Thank you, God!

Elizabeth R. McClellan, published in *Aspire*, August 1979, pp. 12-13. Copyrighted material reprinted with permission of Divine Science Federation International.

February 29 (Leap Year Bonus Day)

LIFE'S REVERIE

Today I was awake very early and decided to walk on the beach. It was a beautiful morning. The early mist arising from the sea evaporated into the sparkling seashore. As I wandered down the beach, I became so involved in the world around me – the sun, the sea, the gulls, the sandpipers – that for a time the world let go of its hold on me. I became immersed in life, and it came to me that perhaps this is what the experience we call death really is, a time when we let go of the world or the world releases us, when we merge mind, ego, body and soul into life until that moment when we are ready to begin again. Truly, there is only life, changing, moving life, a series of endings and beginnings. If I look back on what I remember with my conscious mind to the person I was thirty, twenty, or even ten years ago, it is almost like viewing a stranger. How I reacted to life yesterday was from my consciousness of yesterday, how I react today is from my consciousness of today. When I am rehearsing the past, I am robbing myself of now.

Why are we so hard on ourselves? If I had a friend, whom I really cared about, and I knew that friend had made mistakes in the past and had caused pain for himself and others, if I loved my friend would I continually and forevermore shake my finger at him and say, "You're bad, you're guilty, and I will never let you forget."? Oh no, if I loved my friend I would say, "Sure, you made some mistakes, but they are in the past. Try to learn what you can from them, but remember, my friend, you acted then from where you were at that time; but you are different now, and how you act today is what is important. Forgive yourself, be free, let go, it is past." If I feel this for a friend, then surely I can give the same compassion and understanding to myself.

Rosemary Fillmore Rhea, *That's Just How My Spirit Travels*, 2003, pp. 228-229. Copyrighted material reprinted with permission of Unity, Unity.org.

MARCH

March 1

DEVELOPING OUR FACULTIES

The only way to abide in cosmic consciousness is to develop Christ consciousness, the abiding realization of oneness with God-Mind and of its ideas as directing all the faculties in fulfilling the divine purpose in being.

All true followers of Jesus Christ are required to discipline the human self in the journey from the personal to the Christ consciousness. The human part of us wants to cling to things visible and to other people, but as the impersonal, spiritual Christ finds expression we gradually cease to lean upon these material limitations. Our spiritual faculties become so strong, vital, and substantial that we are able to contact the great invisible through them. When these faculties are well developed, the invisible reality becomes to us even more real and substantial and enduring than material things are to the senses.

We study God as mind, and people as mind; and we find that in the expression of divine ideas people have definite centers of consciousness, which the soul has built through its effort to use divine ideas or qualities of being. We have found that there are twelve central or basic centers of consciousness, which are the result of the soul's use of the God qualities of life, love, wisdom, power, and substance. These centers of consciousness are centers of God-Mind; but they have built the physical organism through which they express. We have twelve locations in the body, where the soul expresses definite qualities, which go to make up the Christ consciousness–at least we term it Christ consciousness when the individual is expressing himself under divine law. Developing these latent powers and capacities of the inner person is the key that will open to us the kingdom and give us Christ mastery. When we do this we shall succeed in whatever we undertake.

Myrtle Fillmore, *Letters of Myrtle Fillmore*, (ed. Foulks), 1936, pp. 79-80. Copyrighted material reprinted with permission of Unity, Unity.org.

March 2

GOD'S HAND

There is but one hand in the universe. It is God's hand. Whenever you have felt that your hand was empty, it has been because you have believed yourself something separate from God. Have you not felt, at times, great desire to give to others something that they needed or wanted, yet have not been able so to give? Have you not said many times within yourself, "Oh, if I only had money, how I would relieve anxiety and distress! If it were only in my power, how quickly would I give a lucrative position to this one needing work, freedom to that one wanting release from material bondage," and so forth? Have you not often said, "if I could only afford it, I would so gladly give my time and service to others with no thought of return"?

Whence, suppose you, comes this desire to give? Is it from the mortal of you? Nay, nay. It is the voice of the Giver of all good gifts crying out through you. It is God's desire to give through you. Cannot He afford to give whenever and wherever He will, and not be made poorer, but richer, thereby? Your hand is God's hand. My hand is God's hand. Our Father reaches out through these, His only hands, to give His gifts….So this conscious consecration of our hands to God, helps us to recognize them as God's hands in which is (no longer "shall be") the fullness of all things.

H. Emilie Cady, *How I Used Truth*, 1939, pp. 65-66. Copyrighted material reprinted with permission of Unity, Unity.org.

March 3

EXPERIMENT IN PRAYER

When we ask for the indwelling of God's Holy Spirit in the body, let us think of that part of the body that most needs His life. Let us imagine his light and life glowing there like a fire, shining there like a light. Then through the rest of the day let us continually give thanks that His life is at work in us accomplishing his perfect will and recreating us after His image and likeness, which is perfection. If we have sought God for a simple thing such as healing a cold in the head, we may find that healing perfected in a few minutes. If we have sought Him for the rebuilding of bones and nerves or sinuses, the process may require more time. In this prayer we can ask for a renewal of God's healing power, remembering always to thank Him for what he already has done, and is continuing to do.

How long should we continue to pray for healing? Until the healing is accomplished. Sometimes prayer once or twice a day is sufficient, but sometimes we need to "pray without ceasing," to keep ourselves open to the continuous inflow of God's power. We do this, not by saying over and over again, "Oh, please, Lord," for that sounds as though we do not believe He is really working. It is much better to keep the power flowing by continuing to give thanks for it. Every time we think of a condition within ourselves that needs healing we can say, "Thank you, Lord, that your power is making me well." And we can look ahead and see ourselves well and strong.

Agnes Sanford, *The Healing Light*, 1947, p. 28. No known copyright in effect.

March 4

DEEDS NOT RESULTS

Let us talk quietly for a few moments. You are coming to see how I AM guiding and directing you every moment of your day. I AM sending to you those who desire you to help. Do not look beyond the moment of the helping or try to see the result; that is in the hands of your Father. It might give you joy to see the awakening and full flower of your work and in time it shall be so, but now you are to work in faith. It is one of the ways to grow, and part of the Divine Plan for you.

As I see you are ready, I shall from time to time lift the veil and give you the greatest joy known -- the joy of seeing the fulfillment of your work in My Service. Go now, not seeking to see results, but to do deeds and ever shall you be guided to those who need a word of help and cheer.

You are blessed to be chosen an instrument in My Creative Service.

Eva Bell Werber. *Quiet Talks With the Master*, 1936, p. 21. Reproduced from QUIET TALKS WITH THE MASTER by Eva Bell Werber 9780875161044 DeVorss Publications, www.devorss.com.

March 5

PEACE

Peace is not speaking with bated breath,
A lowering of voice as in presence of death.
Peace is not standing with folded hands
Enduring insults and lash and bands.
Peace is not turning the other cheek.
Peace is not numbered with the meek.
Peace is not letting the world go by,
Renouncing the Earth while for Heaven we sigh.
Peace is vital, a vibrant thing –
Self caught up in the Cosmic Swing.
Peace is knowing there is only the Whole,
Not in trying to save a soul.
Peace is not knowing a soul is lost –
Christ rising above the waves storm-tossed.
Peace is Oneness, One Life, My Own –
The Sureness that stays after words have flown.
Peace is the union of grass and sod –
Peace is the Power at the Heart of God.

Helen Van Slyke, published in *Religious Science Monthly*, December 1927, p. 17. Copyrighted material reprinted with permission of SOM Publishing.

March 6

LOVE: THE KEYNOTE OF JESUS' TEACHING

Jesus made Love the keynote of His teaching. He attempted to get across to His listeners the various meanings and shadings of the word *Love*, using practically every style of teaching. Sometimes He spoke directly, commanding His followers to "Love your enemies, bless them that curse you, do good to them that hate you." At other times He taught in the parables of the "Good Samaritan," the "Prodigal Son," and others. He set forth in the Beatitudes distinctive ways in which love must be expressed to obtain heavenly rewards today.

When asked how to pray He answered by delivering the greatest prayer ever spoken by man. In every phrase of this prayer He emphasizes the interplay of the great love existing between the ideal father and son.

Jesus reached the peak of His oral teaching with the statements: *"Thou shalt love the Lord thy God with all thy heart, and with all thy soul, and with all thy mind. This is the first and great commandment. And the second is like unto it, Thou shalt love thy neighbor as thyself. On these two commandments hang all the law and the prophets."*

Grace L. Faus, published in *Aspire*, July 1956, p. 4-5. Copyrighted material reprinted with permission of Divine Science Federation International.

March 7

GODLINESS AND THE SUBSTANCE OF RICHES

He shall be like a tree planted by the streams of water,
That bringeth forth its fruit in its season,
Whose leaf also doth not wither;
And whatsoever he doeth shall prosper.
Psalm 1:3

Thus is the godly man described as regards his good fortune.

There are some of us who did not come into this existence "with a silver spoon in our mouth." It seems to us that all our goodness has been fruitless, that fate is against us, and that there is no use in trying.

If we have started this life as bankrupt men, then the more must we have resolution and determination and a courage that knows no defeat.

The law of Christ removes the past burdens and debts that may have been loaded upon our shoulders. No matter what bad luck may seem to have been ours from birth, this day we come under the law of our Christ self, and believe in the God promise that our good shall take tangible form here and now.

Exercise a patience that is one with absolute trust and never, even in the secrecy of your own chamber, acknowledge any slowness of manifestation or any failure as real or lasting.

The treasures that you have laid up in heaven – the within – are destined to take form as the treasures on earth. You do not need to wait for another incarnation, but your good of today can be expressed here and now as overflowing plenteousness of the world's goods.

Annie Rix Militz, *Both Riches and Honor*, 1945, pp. 79-80. Copyrighted material reprinted with permission of Unity, Unity.org.

March 8

WISDOM

WISDOM does not consist in using all knowledge for personal ends; does not consist of the accumulation of facts, ideas, or things; nor is its main purpose provision against future contingencies.

WISDOM consists in the advantageous use of knowledge; in the ability to perceive and utilize accuracy, rightness, precision; in a quick and precise rejection of unrighteousness in favor of right balance, right action, "an understanding heart."

WISDOM is the Power to discern real values, real and continuing interests. It indicates the ways to adapt means to ends. It produces efficient foresight by immediate correctness of observation and conclusion.

WISDOM in the Mind of God is His precise discrimination, discernment of outcome, His infallible judgment of the present and the future. His immediate and right use of all available means for the achievement of His ends is constant, inflexible, successful. He is the "Providence" working good to and for all men, the Resource inexhaustible, eternal, and wholly right.

WISDOM in the Mind of God is an idea of choice.

WISDOM in man is the ability to discern rightness, accuracy, balance, judgment.

Ella Pomeroy, *Powers of the Soul*, 1948, p. 132. No known copyright in effect.

March 9

THE INFERIORITY COMPLEX

The definition of inferior is given as "lower in quality" and that of superior as "surpassing in quality." An "inferiority complex," then, is the acceptance of the belief that one is lacking in the qualities which make for a normal expression of life. This state of mind brings that sense of being unsuccessful and incapable of coping with conditions resulting in a self-conscious condition which causes one to withdraw from people and become introspective, inhibiting free action or normal expression.

"To be or not to be; that is the question." Are we, through reliance upon our own objective reasoning, to feel a sense of lack or inferiority? Or, are we, by the recognition of the God within us, to realize that we are the channel through which all power manifests and thus feel superior to any incident which may come into our lives? Here we must make a conscious choice, and having done so, proceed on one or the other of these lines of thought, following it to its logical conclusion.

If we recognize At-One-Ment with Infinite Mind, we realize that we have at our command the power, the Intelligence, and all the strength of the Universe. This sense of At-One-Ment gives us that confidence which we lack when we rely entirely upon our own objective minds, and, by so doing, cut off the source of inspiration. Jesus said, "It is not I, but the Father who dwelleth in me, He doeth the works." This brings us the assurance that, if we will recognize that Father as the Source of life, and ourselves as the channel for its expression, then we have but to "be" in order that we may "become." This would so fortify us with a consciousness of power that it would automatically destroy any thought of inferiority.

Augusta E. Rundel, *Science of Mind*, March 1930, p. 59. Copyrighted material reprinted with permission of SOM Publishing.

March 10

MEDITATION ON GOD'S LOVE

We take words with us unto Jehovah. Our words today are: I build my life on the firm foundation of God's Love." God is love, perfect, pure and ever-present love. As we let God's love become the guiding force for our lives, we lay a firm foundation on which to build happy, successful, love-filled lives. With God's firm foundation of love supporting and sustaining us, God's Truths become the building blocks for our every activity and relationship. This sturdy foundation of love gives us peace of mind, for we know that God's love enfolds us and our loved ones in security.

When we build our lives on the firm foundation of God's love we know and feel that we are safe and protected. We are calm and serene. In God's love we express health and perfection in spirit, mind and body. The more we put God's loving truths into practice, the stronger is our foundation of love. As we continue to grow in God's love, we live in harmony with all life and express God's love in all our relations. God's firm foundation stands. I build my life on the firm foundation of God's love.

Jane Paulson, from a recorded meditation offered at the Golden Pyramid, Unity of Houston, Texas, about 1981. No known copyright in effect.

March 11

FATHER, I'M TRUSTING

The Master often said that He, of Himself, could do nothing. He knew the futility of forcing matters, of trying to accomplish things by means of personal will and human reasoning, and He knew the truth that it always is the Father within who does the works. He told his followers this, and He told them only to believe, to trust, to know that the Father knew their needs and their desires and purposes better than they themselves.

This is still His advice to you and me today; namely to trust God's power above the power of man. This is what we do when we say, *"Father, I'm trusting!"* All the most poetic and beautiful prayers in the world cannot bring us any closer to the Father than our speaking this simple prayer directly from our heart.

Mary L. Kupferle, *The Simple Prayer*, Unity pamphlet, 1956, p. 5.
Copyrighted material reprinted with permission of Unity, Unity.org.

March 12

THE ETERNAL RHYTHM

It takes the action and inaction of all things
To bring forth thought anew –
Realization waits upon the hour
Of three-dimensional crossing of events.

In the Eternal Rhythm there is Silence;
Thoughts wait upon the stir of life;
The tides moving out in action
Create the cross-section of events.

At these intersections of the shadow-world,
Events, circumstances, and thoughts are born.
He who is One with the Eternal Rhythm
Recognizes the Truth within them all.

Vida Reed Stone, *Come Now Into Your Freedom*, 1946, p. 85. No known copyright in effect.

March 13

ONENESS WITH GOD

Prayer that craves a particular commodity, anything less than all good, is vicious. Prayer is the contemplation of the facts of life from the highest point of view. It is the soliloquy of a beholding and jubilant soul. It is the Spirit of God pronouncing His works good. But prayer as a means to effect a private end is meanness and theft. It supposes dualism and not unity in nature and consciousness. As soon as the man is consciously at one with God, he will not beg.
Ralph Waldo Emerson

True Prayer, then, is just a continual recognition and thanksgiving that all is good, and that all good is ours now as much as it ever can be. Oh, when will our faith become strong and steadfast enough to take possession of our inheritance here? The Israelites entered not into the Promised Land because of their unbelief. Their inheritance was real and was awaiting them then and there, but it could not do them any good nor give any enjoyment until they took hold of it by faith, after which and as a result of which, would have come the reality. It is this taking by faith that brings anything into actuality and visibility.

Why will this mortal mind of ours forever postpone the acceptance of all good as our rightful inheritance for this life?... All things are ours now, fullness of love, of life, of wisdom, of power -- aye, more than these, fullness of all good, which means abundance of all things, material as well as spiritual. *"Every good gift and every perfect gift is from above, coming down from the Father of lights, with whom can be no variation, neither shadow that is cast by turning."*

H. Emilie Cady, *How I Used Truth*, 1939, pp. 104-105. Copyrighted material reprinted with permission of Unity, Unity.org.

March 14

WORLD CREATED BY THE WORD OF GOD

The world was created by the word of God, Hebrews 11:3, and surely our world is "created" by our words. When we learn to think the God-thought and say words of truth and love, our world will become a happier and better one in which to live.

Evil is the result of our disobedience to divine law. It does not exist as an entity in and of itself. The basis for our belief that disobedience gives rise to evil is to be found in the allegory of the fall of man. The Lord God told Adam that he might *"eat of every tree of the garden; but of the tree of the knowledge of good and evil you shall not eat."* Genesis 2:16-17

We all know why Adam disobeyed God; the arguments of Eve (the feeling nature) were too strong for him! Metaphysically interpreted, this signifies that everyone's human inclination is to yield to temptation. The command is *"You shall worship the Lord your God and Him only shall you serve."* Matthew 4:10

When Adam and Eve disregarded this, they were driven from the Garden and thenceforth knew hardship and sorrow. Their fate has been shared by humanity throughout the ages.

Elizabeth Sand Turner, *What Unity Teaches*, 1954, p. 15. Copyrighted material reprinted with permission of Unity, Unity.org.

March 15

HEAVEN'S FIRST LAW

"Order is heaven's first law." Order is the result of love and wisdom working together in perfect conjunction and harmony. It reveals the rulership of God.

Let us then bless the weather with a thought of divine order, saying, *Divine order is established in the atmospheric conditions, producing the kind of weather needed for the earth to bring forth its bountiful harvest.*

As the rich harvest appears let us work consistently in the Spirit of divine justice and order so that the crops may be righteously shared and distributed, lest God be mocked by man's greed and infidelity.

The perfect equalizing, adjusting power of the Holy Spirit is active in the atmosphere. In all parts of the world, in every phase of climate and weather, peace, order, and harmony are now established.

Clara A. Palmer, *Heaven's First Law*, Unity pamphlet, 1937, pp. 1, 6.
Copyrighted material reprinted with permission of Unity, Unity.org.

March 16

JESUS CHRIST: RICH OR POOR?

Jesus Christ was the wealthiest man who ever trod this earth. He needed not to exercise any effort to maintain Himself. He sent His disciples forth, telling them not to provide two coats, or shoes, or to take scrip with them, for, as He said, "The man I send forth is worthy of his hire," that is, he will be maintained by a Divine Law. After a time He said to them, "When I sent you without purse and scrip, lacked ye anything?" and they said, "Nay, Lord, we lacked nothing."

Jesus Christ was not poor. Would you be poor if you could heal every disease that came to you? *Would you be poor?* Would you be poor if you could raise a dead man from the tomb? Would you be poor if you could turn weak water into rich wine? *Would you be poor or would you be rich?* Be sensible! Was Jesus Christ poor? Why, He had the miracle working Mind – the Mind that increases through rich thinking, rich knowledge. And so my Christ is not a poor Christ. *I wish I were as wealthy.* What were a million dollars in your hand to that power He possessed? Which would you take? Not one of you would hesitate a second if you are sensible. You would be wealthy with that knowledge.

Paul says that whereas Christ was rich, He took upon himself poverty that we might be rich. That is, He took upon Himself the appearance of poverty and He proved that *having* is not prosperity, but if he thinks richly he is indeed the wealthiest of men.

Harriet Hale Rix, *The Rich Mentality*, 1916, pp. 22-23. No known copyright in effect.

March 17

WHAT KIND OF A GOD DO YOU HAVE?

To many people, such a question as this would seem completely sacrilegious. They would assure you that they believe in God as the One Supreme Ruler of the Universe, Who has created all and sustains all. They would tell you all the attributes of God in which they believe. They would tell you they believe in the Omnipotence and Omniscience of God working through their lives and affairs. They would give you all the answers they have heard from ministers, lecturers and books. They would protest that is the kind of God they have, that is what they live by. But – do they?

The kind of God you have is not necessarily the one to which you pay lip-service, but the one in which *you believe* – the one in which you have perfect trust and confidence. And you can easily see what that is by watching, not what you say, but what you actually think and feel and do….

If you *really* believe that God is all-powerful there will be no fear in your heart. If you think God, Who has made all, can change anything at a moment's notice, there will be no time limits on your demonstrations. They will be instantaneous. If you really think God is Love, you can never be hurt by another human being, and there will be no criticism in you. If you really believe that God is Intelligence, there will be no doubt in your heart about your ability to find your place in life.

The Bible tells us, "Thou shalt not limit the Holy One of Israel," but we do limit Him every day of our lives. And then we wonder why we fail to make more progress. Jesus told us, *"Whatsoever* ye ask, BELIEVING, that shall be done unto you." It could not be plainer or simpler. Until we begin to remove the limitations in our own minds, we will worship a very limited God. As you push back the mental frontiers your God comes closer to you, and all that you intellectually perceive now becomes a living reality.

Mildred Mann, *Become What You Believe, Volume I*, 1970, p. 3. No known copyright in effect.

March 18

WINTER-SPRING DROPS OF GOLD

* Logic is good, but dry. So season yours with knowledge of spiritual laws. This is your text: *My Words are Spirit and Life.*

* What made your feet and head pain you was intellectual reasoning. Only a knowledge of Spiritual Truth will heal you. Learn to believe this affirmation of Jesus Christ: *Ye shall know the Truth, and the Truth shall make you free.*

* Your intentions are good. When you seem to be stubborn it is really an instinctive self protection you are exercising. Stand by your intuitions. Repeat these words: *God is my judge.*

* Seek not the world's applause. To yield to public opinion when you know the true principle of action would cause you to cry: *Would God I had never been born.* Keep this for your text: *He leadeth me.*

* When you look on the body of people your eyes burn with the controlling fires. Have you learned to train those eyes by affirming every morning: *I will guide thee with mine eyes.*

* You know how to deal with humanity along mercantile lines. You will keep yourself healthy by declaring that: *No evil can come near me. God is my health.*

* Loving-hearted are you. Home is your joy. Prove this by the living text: *God is love.*

Emma Curtis Hopkins, (1891), *Drops of Gold*, 1970, pp. 6, 9-10, 18, 26-27. No known copyright in effect.

March 19

REMEMBER

Remember to love and to love abundantly and freely. Love purifies, cleanses and heals. Love inspires you to press on and achieve.

Remember to be grateful and to express your gratitude. If you fail to express your love and your gratitude to those who have pointed the Way to you and to those who have helped you, you are like the plant that has not yet blossomed but still selfishly holds its perfume in the undeveloped bud.

Remember that all that loves rightly, manifests divine love; all that lives rightly, manifests the One Life; all that thinks rightly, manifests the true Mind.

Remember to lay down all sense of burden, for infinite and adorable Life is not a burden bearer. Love your work and it becomes play.

Remember that you are a link in this great chain of infinite Being. Life would not be complete without you.

Remember that the unfoldment of your soul is the only growth worthwhile. Life will become a success to you when you become a success to yourself.

Remember that thinking good, speaking good, is true prayer. As Emerson says, *"Prayer is the contemplation of the facts of life from the highest point of view; It is the soliloquy of a beholding and jubilant Soul; It is the Spirit of God pronouncing his works good."*

Remember to love right thought and become inspired with its wonder and power. "My words (thoughts) shall never pass away." Right thoughts are the active force of Mind (God), use them freely and thus love for right thinking will become natural and spontaneous.

Remember the harder the lesson the greater the need for strong faith, a pure love and a clear understanding; and also the greater is the blessing when we have succeeded.

Remember that some feet will tread all heights now unattained. Why not thine own? Press on! Achieve! Your dominion is ever within thee, waiting your command to set you free.

Lillian DeWaters, *How To Have Dominion*, 1921, pp. 33-35. No known copyright in effect.

March 20

REALIZE CHRIST WITHIN

I am the light of the world. Ye are the light of the world.
Not my will, but thine be done.
Blessed are my eyes, for they see clearly, distinctly, and perfectly.
I am God's loving and obedient child. Blessed are my ears for they hear easily, clearly, and distinctly.
All power is given unto me in mind and in body.
I am not bound in personal consciousness, I am free with the freedom of Spirit.
My yoke is easy, and my burden is light.
I am strong in the Lord and in the power of His might.
There is nothing to fear. I breathe the breath of life freely and easily.
The forgiving love of Jesus Christ sets me free from mistakes of the past, and the results of mistakes of the past.
God's cleansing, healing, purifying love flows freely through every part of my body, renewing and restoring me.
Divine order is established in my mind, body, and in all my affairs.
I am the ever-renewing, the ever-unfolding expression of infinite life.

May Rowland, excerpts from *Come Ye Apart Awhile*, 1957, p. 9. Copyrighted material reprinted with permission of Unity, Unity.org.

March 21

I AM A CHILD OF THE LIVING GOD

If we can *believe* that we are children of the Living God, then we know that we are never alone. We cannot want for anything if our Eternal Father, in Whom is all richness, sustains us, now and always, in the fullness of his wisdom and guidance. Surely, if we approach Him as a little child, He will answer our prayer. Why is the child-like approach so magical? Because the child is confident and not yet daunted or hurt by circumstances and it asks for what it wants, simply, in faith, believing. If we can become sufficiently child-like to surrender our sense of responsibility, of anxiety and pressure, and with a heart free and at peace, pray, or ask what we want, then we are making it possible for God to give us that for which we ask. In prayer we must abandon ourselves to God, sure in our belief that He does indwell us and answers even the simplest prayer.

There is a secret place within us to which we can retire in silence and peace. Into this sacred place we need take nothing but the thoughts we wish. In this place we pray whether our prayer is audible or silent, whether it is phrased in lofty terminology or simple word. But if we take all of the anxiety, the fear and strife of experience in with our thought, then our prayer is colored by that burden. *All that takes place in the moving panorama which we call the objective life and experience, has been created by man's thought and activity and will be maintained by man or will be changed by man when he wishes to think and act differently.* We are not saying that man's personal determination has made and sustained the objective world. Man of himself can do nothing – but man is never *of* himself, alone. It is the Father who dwelleth in man – He doeth the works. It is man's thought, working in, with and through the Mind of God, which creates.

Josephine Holmes Curtis, *How To Get The Most Out Of Life*, 1937, pp. 106-107. Copyrighted material reprinted with permission of SOM Publishing.

March 22

APPLIED TRUTH

The thing that deters many from realizing prosperity and permits them to suffer today from world disturbances is that they have not applied their understanding of Truth definitely and concretely enough to the problem of finance, to demonstrating along that line. Poverty is just as great a mistake as disease. I like to tell the story in II Kings, fourth chapter: A widow appeals to Elisha for help. She is very poor and her two boys are to be taken for debt. This was not unusual in those days. The prophet asks what she has in the house. She has only a pot of oil. She is told to borrow from her neighbors every jar that she can get. To shut herself and her sons in and to pour the oil into the empty jars. The woman did as she was told and the oil poured *"until it filled every jar that she had set."* Life is always doing this; it always meets our every positive expectation; every jar that we set is filled.

In the early days I set my jar for health and got it. Now I set many jars – for supply, joy, companionship and many other God-given blessings.

Nona L. Brooks, published in *Divine Science Monthly*, September 1932, p. 4. Copyrighted material reprinted with permission of Divine Science Federation International.

March 23

HOW TO REALIZE ILLUMINATION, OR UNDERSTANDING

First, realize what I am.
I am Strength and Understanding. I am Light, I am that I am. I am Mind, I am Idea.
I am Consciousness. I am all Wisdom within myself, for my *self* is God's Divine Idea.
There is no lack in the universe. God fills it all. There is no need of anything. There is no ignorance.
Mind has no lack in It, and All is Mind.
There is no Mind of darkness or misunderstanding – no Mind of fear or error.
There is no fear. There is no cause of fear. There is nothing to be afraid of.
Light fills all – for Light is God.
Understanding is all in all.
I live, move and have my being in Light. I express perfect understanding.
I am Light, in Mind, in thought and in body. I am all Light. I am complete. I am satisfied now.
I am filled full of the Fullness that filleth all.
Life, Truth, Light, Love and Understanding are all mine in God.

Fannie Brooks James, *Divine Science: New Light Upon Old Truths*, 1896, p. 126. No known copyright in effect.

March 24

JOY

A great deal has been said and written about peace, and probably more about love, until we have quite a clear idea of the value and power of these qualities. But joy has been the subject of many false concepts. Certainly in the Old Thought, joy is postponed to a time and place called heaven, and people regard suffering and misery as a necessary part of life on the earth plane. And sometimes people in the New Thought forget that joy and happiness are inherent elements of true life and are to be known and experienced now. Is it not significant that the advent of Christ was announced with a proclamation of joy? *"Behold I bring you good tidings of great joy, which shall be to all people."* Are we not justified, therefore, in emphasizing this note of joy in the beginning of our study of Truth? Surely joy and happiness should be a part of our experience now and always….

Joy is the fullness of divine content. It sees its own creation as perfect, harmonious, divine. Joy is complete satisfaction here and now, so that we do not long continually for all manner of external things to make us happy and joyous. It is a state of serene consciousness, not created by any act of the will, but entered into through unfoldment, through constant thought and study of truth. We find it when we absolutely know our unity with the Spirit, which is universal Joy. *"I too partake of that great invisible Spirit, which is perfect, divine, abiding Joy."*

Daisy Baum, *Studies in Divine Science*, 1909, pp.105-107. Copyrighted material reprinted with permission of Divine Science Federation International.

March 25

POWER

POWER is not merely a mental or physical driving force. Its exercise is not confined to physical or mental authority; its expression is not spasmodic or irregular.

POWER is latent capacity for motion; an unexpressed capacity for achievement, completion; it is always present, always unremitting.

POWER is astir in the individual who is compelled mentally or physically toward action; it demands the exercise of all the faculties and functions of the human being; it begets an instinctive respect and admiration for great force, great magnitude, great volume.

POWER enables the Creator to sustain Creation without pause; in God, Power acts of itself, without compulsion; the activities of the Creator are continuous, varied and immediate.

POWER in the Mind of God is an idea of motion.

POWER in man is the ability to initiate, to start things.

Ella Pomeroy, *Powers of the Soul*, 1948, p. 134. No known copyright in effect.

March 26

THE POWER OF INVOCATION

Every man has the ability to invoke the power of God because of the law of response that operates through the universe. The law of response is Principle and it is through this law of response that man may draw into his world of experience the Almighty Power of God. His mercy, His love, and all that He is. This is the most wonderful love that could be possibly given mankind – that he would be given the power within himself to invoke God to manifest, not only in his life, but in the lives of others. We do not use this Power of Invocation to the extent we should. Perhaps we do not think much about it. Perhaps we are not very much aware of God's great power indwelling man through our own Power of Invocation. In the very plan of things there would have to be a way that the Will of God could be brought forth into the world of men – that the kingdom of Heaven could be established on earth. It is through the Power of Invocation that this is accomplished.

Every time a farmer plants a seed in the ground, he has invoked the Creative Power of the universe to feed him, to bring forth what he needs in the world of men so that he might live. He has invoked the Power of God to feed the world when he plants a seed, for within one grain of wheat is food for millions of people – enough to feed the world over and over and over again, through the replanting of that seed. Through the replanting, the same Power of Invocation is at work and the same response is made to that call to feed mankind, to take care of everyone. This is mentioned in Psalm 145 at verse 15 where it says, "Thou givest them their meat in good season." This is a statement of the power of seedtime and harvest, the Power of Invocation.

You are God's child of Light!

Ethel Barnhart, from her lesson at The Santa Anita Church, Arcadia, California, (est. 1950), Volume 3, No. 9, p. 1. Reprinted with permission of The Santa Anita Church.

March 27

IN HIS NAME

Has it ever occurred to you that you are almost daily taking God's name in vain? Unless you are very watchful, very careful, you are doing so.

When God called Moses to lead the Children of Israel out of Egypt, "Moses said unto God, Behold, when I come unto the children of Israel, and shall say unto them, The God of your fathers hath sent me unto you; and they shall say to me, What is His name? What shall I say unto them?

And God said unto Moses, I AM THAT I AM: and He said, Thus shall thou say unto the children of Israel, I AM hath sent Me unto you....

This is my name forever, and this is my memorial unto all generations.

"I AM," then, is God's name. Every time you say, "I am sick," "I am weak," "I am discouraged," are you not speaking God's name in vain, falsely?

I AM cannot be sick; I AM cannot be weary, or faint, or powerless; for I AM is all-life, all-power, All-Good.

"I AM," spoken with a downward tendency, is always false, always "in vain." A commandment says, *Thou shalt not take the name of Jehovah thy God in vain; for Jehovah will not hold him guiltless that taketh his name in vain.* And Jesus said, *"By thy words thou shalt be justified, and by thy words thou shalt be condemned."*

If you speak the "I AM" falsely, you will get the result of false speaking. If you say, "I am sick," you will get sickness; if you say, "I am poor," you will get poverty; for the law is, *"Whatsoever a man soweth, that shall he also reap."* "I AM," spoken upward, toward the good, the true, is sure to out-picture in visible good, in success, in happiness.

H. Emilie Cady, *How I Used Truth*, 1939, pp. 41-42. Copyrighted material reprinted with permission of Unity, Unity.org.

March 28

BEATITUDES (1)

Blessed are the poor in spirit, for theirs is the kingdom of heaven.
The "poor in spirit" are people who relinquish their human concepts that they may learn from God. The intellect of humankind is marvelous indeed; yet, if we are to attain divine wisdom we must be humble (poor in spirit) toward Him and willing and eager to hear His words and follow them….

Blessed are those who mourn, for they shall be comforted.
Trials and tribulations cause us to mourn. Yet it is true that "man's extremity is God's opportunity," and when woes beset us we turn to Him and receive comfort.

Blessed are the meek, for they shall inherit the earth.
Meekness, spiritually considered, is an attitude of receptivity to the divine will. Meekness is a willingness to surrender to God and a confidence that His way is the better way. When the Christ expresses through us, we have power over external conditions (the earth).

Blessed are those who hunger and thirst for righteousness, for they shall be satisfied.
Righteousness is the right or spiritual use of mental, physical, and spiritual faculties, which are manifested as right action. When our desire to express the Christ is more powerful than our desire for personal gain or for personal power, we are hungering and thirsting after righteousness.

Blessed are the merciful, for they shall obtain mercy.
The merciful are those who are kind in thought and in deed. On occasion we may feel impelled to help someone but we do it reluctantly. Such acts fall short of true mercy because thought and deed are at variance. We are only merciful when we realize that we are all brothers and sisters and that the good of one is the good of all, and act accordingly….

Elizabeth Sand Turner, *Your Hope of Glory*, 1959, pp. 91-92. Copyrighted material reprinted with permission of Unity, Unity.org.

March 29

BEATITUDES (2)

Blessed are the pure in heart, for they shall see God.
Pure means unmixed, chaste, and free from defilement. A person whose heart is pure directs his whole attention to God, to good. Purity is one-pointed vision, the "single" eye.... When the consciousness is so purified that we perceive only one Presence and one Power, we are, in reality, seeing God.

Blessed are the peacemakers, for they shalt be called sons of God.
The peacemakers are those who make peace outwardly because they have attained an inner peace. Since they are at peace with God they are also at peace with others, and they bring peace to all the conditions in which they are involved. We are sons and daughters of God, but our kinship is merely an inherent potentiality until we gain peace of mind and express it. Then we are His sons and daughters in actuality.

Blessed are those who are persecuted for righteousness' sake, for theirs is the kingdom of heaven. Blessed are you when men revile you and persecute you and utter all kinds of evil against you falsely on my account. Rejoice and be glad, for your reward is great in heaven.
Persons who are persecuted for righteousness' sake are ones who have spiritual ideals and yet encounter within themselves states of consciousness that oppose their ideals. These adverse states of consciousness belong to the race thought, much of which is still in each of us...When people do not understand our spiritual convictions they are apt to misjudge and condemn us. This beatitude promises that we shall be blessed if we maintain our ideals in the face of inner and outer persecution. We should actually rejoice and be glad, for our steadfastness will bring great spiritual advancement.

Elizabeth Sand Turner, *Your Hope of Glory*, 1959, pp. 92-93. Copyrighted material reprinted with permission of Unity, Unity.org.

March 30

KEYS TO PROSPERITY

Twenty dynamic ideas you can use to attract more money into your life!
1. Get rid of fear with denial and affirmation, and everything else will come along in due order.
2. Realize that everything you need exists at this present moment....
3. List the number of things you want to reverse each day....
4. Reverse the belief in a mind other than God.
5. Reverse the false economic beliefs of the race.
6. Reverse the belief in competition....
7. Reverse the belief that money, itself, has power....
8. Reverse the belief that man has to earn his own living....
9. There is no unemployment....
10. Reverse the fear of expenditure....
11. Bring a sense of interest and of joy into your spiritual treatment or your prayer....
12. Do not break the rhythm of daily prayer....
13. Act as though your good is at hand and it will be so.
14. Never look upon any person, place or thing as your financial support – not even yourself or your own efforts....
15. Revel in the joyous assurance that God's guidance is all there is and God is the only worker.
16. Do not put your desires in the future....
17. Learn to break problematic sentences in two different parts...Break it with a denial like this: as the thought "I don't believe I'm going to be able to pay this bill" comes, immediately assert, "Not a word of Truth is in it; it is *already* paid in Divine Mind."
18. Associate yourself with persons who are prosperous....
19. Always rejoice in success wherever you find it....
20. Remember that this law of abundance applies to relationships and achievements as well as to money....
Remember: In this universe, there is no virtue in not having what you need for a joyous, healthy life. Be done with lack!

Elizabeth Carrick-Cook, published in *Science of Mind*, October 1983, pp. 26-28. Copyrighted material reprinted with permission of SOM Publishing.

March 31

THE SUBCONSCIOUS

Wherever beliefs in materiality, in the power of disease, or in adversity of any sort have been allowed to settle into mind and result in formations of flesh or in functional activity, it takes great illumination -- and not only illumination but earnest, constant identification of ourselves with Jesus Christ and His wonderful humility and obedience, and with the spiritual knowledge of mastering the physical elements -- to dissolve these beliefs. But as long as there is in our subconscious minds (our memory and habits of thinking) that which does not accord with Truth (God, good, the only presence and power in all and through all), we keep meeting it in some form or other, and we shall be obliged to keep using Truth and the power God has given us to change our minds if we are to cast out the old and establish a new order.

So long as we remember experiences that were unhappy, as we saw them once and still see them and speak of them, we will be unable to demonstrate joy and prosperity and health in our lives. Because of lack of understanding, these seemingly unkind things have made negative impressions upon our souls. Whatever has been impressed upon our souls will work out in our bodies and affairs. Because the activities of the mind in its contacts with Divine Mind and also with the world of appearances and the minds of others, build the soul, which in turn forms the body through which it carries out its impressions and the urge from within; the soul's desires and impressions also make the conditions under which we live.

Understanding this law of mind action will help us to see why we have the experiences we have, and why we react to them, and why it is important to go to God-Mind for more light and love and life and substance. We have the power to change our soul's impressions, our subconscious, through the indwelling Christ Mind, and so change our bodies and their functioning and also the conditions about us.

Myrtle Fillmore, *Letters of Myrtle Fillmore*, (ed. Foulks), 1936, pp. 67-68.
Copyrighted material reprinted with permission of Unity, Unity.org.

APRIL

April 1

GIVE AND RECEIVE

Give, and thou shalt receive. Give thoughts of cheer,
  Of courage and success, to friend and stranger.
And from a thousand sources, far and near,
  Strength will be sent thee in thy hour of danger.

Give words of comfort, of defense, and hope,
  To mortals crushed by sorrow and by error.
And though thy feet through shadowy paths may grope,
  Thou shalt not walk in loneliness or terror.

Give of thy gold, though small thy portion be.
  Gold rusts and shrivels in the hand that keeps it.
It grows in one that opens wide and free.
  Who sows his harvest is the one who reaps it.

Give of thy love, nor wait to know the worth
  Of what thou lovest; and ask no returning.
And wheresoe'er thy pathway leads on earth,
  There thou shalt find the lamp of love-light burning.

Ella Wheeler Wilcox, published in *The Nautilus*, (ed. Towne), June 1906, p. 21. No known copyright in effect.

April 2

GOD IS ALL IN ALL

God is All in All. God in me is unlimited. I accept this and proceed to demonstrate it. My troubles are no longer stumbling blocks but become stepping stones. There is always a way out of trouble.

The way is spiritual and mental, not material. I have to struggle with conditions, but I demonstrate with Mind. I have a way out and a way upward. The way is joyous and loving.

The solution to my situation makes me a better person. I am victorious over my troubles. In quietness my purpose becomes clear.

The way of Truth is mine today. There is nothing to oppose me, and all of God is working for me and my solution.

Thank you God for I know you hear me and answer all my Treatments. I accept my need is fulfilled now.

I release this Treatment into Law with Love.

Betty Jean House, June 2000, Copyrighted material reprinted with permission.

April 3

WHAT IS MAN?

What is man? What is that Power which has made him "a little lower than the angels," – that has given him dominion over all creation?

Having personally experienced this great Universal Power, inspired men of old have named it Jehovah, Allah, Brahma, God. Jesus called this Universal Power *Father*. "I and my Father are one," he stated. *"The Father in me, He doeth the works. Of mine own self I can do nothing."*

Whatever it may please us to call it, it is this Supreme Power that unifies the universe and all mankind, making all one with all. …We call this Supreme Power Omnipresence; Truth, God; God being synonymous with *Good.*

This Omnipresent Good we call God has given man of his spirit. Individual man has been given the inherencies, the qualities of God. Man has intelligence; man has consciousness.

Grace L. Faus, published in *Grace and Truth*, (Zevgolis), 1985, pp. 175-176.
No known copyright in effect.

April 4

DIVINE LOVE HEALS ME

*Then shall thy light break forth as the morning,
and thine health shall spring forth speedily.*
Isaiah 58:8.

    God is love, and love is infinitely healing. Divine Love is flowing through my mind and my emotions, dissolving in my consciousness all hard thought and hard feelings toward others and healing the resultant manifestations in my body. If any part of my body needs healing, Divine Love is now restoring it to wholeness. Love purifies whatever needs cleansing, banishes infection, completely dissolves any false growth. Divine Love fills me with harmony, health and vigor.

    The warmth of Divine Love permeates my affairs, melting away all obstructions to the perfect circulation of God's good. The creative power of God is now flowing freely in my life, healing me of lack and frustration. Divine Love heals me of fear, anxiety, confusion and doubt. It makes my faith strong and unswerving.

    God is light and in Him is no darkness. Therefore, I trust the Light of Pure Love to guide me safely, serenely, steadily. I do not need to see the way ahead, for God knows it. God is my security.

Claudine Whitaker, published in *Creative Thought* for February 21, 1965.
Copyrighted material reprinted with permission of SOM Publishing.

April 5

CONQUERING FAITH

When everything in life is going well, it is easy enough to say, and to believe, that a loving Father is at the helm and all is well. But perhaps a difficult experience suddenly looms, one that tests our knowledge and our faith. We "pray and pray" and "nothing happens." Has God forgotten us? Did God send this experience to us?

It is then that we should ask ourselves: Am I so problem-centered that I cannot drop it? Am I judging wholly from the self-conscious plane? Do I really know that beyond, above, within, is that Something that is whole, perfect, and eternal? If I believe this, why do I not know it as a certainty.

The Creator of the universe is perfect Being, changeless and eternal, always acting as perfect Law and literally bringing forth the universe from within. This is the first and great Truth of Being.

Caroline Munz, published in *Aspire*, February 1954, pp. 4-5. Copyrighted material reprinted with permission of Divine Science Federation International.

April 6

IN ALL THE WORKS OF THY HANDS

If you find yourself becoming discouraged because of the seeming unimportance of your place in life, the routine of your daily activities, and the apparent dullness of hour-by-hour responsibilities, turn your thoughts to the promise, *"the Lord thy God shall bless thee…in all the works of thine hands, therefore then thou shalt surely rejoice."* Deuteronomy 16:15

As you begin your task this day, take with you the words, "God is blessing me in all the work of my hands, and I am altogether joyful." Remember that everything you do today is vitally important to God since you, His beloved child, are vitally important to Him. Remember that in your Father's sight deeds and works are neither large nor small, and that He looks as lovingly and joyfully upon the humblest, quietest service as upon the most glorious and outstanding feat or attainment.

Mary L. Kupferle, published in *Aspire*, July 1954, p. 8. Copyrighted material reprinted with permission of Divine Science Federation International.

April 7

THE ESSENTIAL DORIS JONES

Our lives evolve because it is the nature of the Universe;
So, get out of the way and allow yourself to develop.
Out of doubt comes great wisdom.
Feelings are built-in guides.
Race consciousness is mostly unconscious;
To the degree we buy into it, it affects our beliefs.
We get what we want when we're ready to receive it.
To make changes, we must own our life the way it is.
Oneness: Think of a pot of stew that needs more salt;
Your old beliefs have run your life long enough!
All spiritual truths give us permission to trust.
Don't ignore fear; it is there for a reason.
Substitute consciousness for chemicals!
What was that fear intending to show you?
There is no way you can salt part of the stew.
God is not finished with me and I am not finished with God.

Doris Jones, from her *Memorial Program*, December 2008. Reprinted with permission of her family.

April 8

LETTING GO

Many cling to old memory and behavior patterns that interfere with their peace of mind. If we are reluctant in letting go of past hurts, misunderstandings and painful memories we live as though these were a part of who we are. These memories and beliefs become the barnacles that build up in the subconscious. We may know these interfere with our happiness yet not realize we can let them go.

Unless we understand that we are greater than our experiences we assume that these are part of our make-up -- something we cannot change. This belief holds us in bondage to the past.

Dr. Raymond Charles Barker wrote: *"Old hurts and old rejections arrive at the threshold of consciousness in order to get out."* It is time to release them and move on. If we would stop reviewing and rehearsing these we could do that and experience greater freedom. This is an opportunity to see the experience for what it is -- one that is finished and over and then be willing to let it go.

We decide to continue in the old pattern or move on. It no longer has power over us unless we give it a place in our consciousness.

Affirm: *I choose to let go of old memory patterns and live in the "now."*

Marian G. Moon, *Lessons of Truth*, 2012 p. 13. Reprinted with permission of her family.

April 9

TWENTY-THIRD PSALM

The Lord is my shepherd; I shall not want.
No good thing shall be withheld from them who walk uprightly.

He maketh me to lie down in green pastures; He leadeth me beside the still waters.
God is love. Love never faileth.

He restoreth my soul: He leadeth me in the paths of righteousness for His name's sake.
He satisfieth the longing soul, he filleth the hungry soul with goodness.

Yea, though I walk through the valley of the shadow of death, I will fear no evil; for Thou art with me; Thy rod and Thy staff they comfort me.
My presence shall go with thee and I will give thee rest.

Thou preparest a table before me in the presence of mine enemies; thou anointest my head with oil; my cup runneth over.
I will strengthen thee; yea, I will help thee.

Surely goodness and mercy shall follow me all the days of my life: and I will dwell in the house of the Lord forever.
Lo, I am with you always.

O Lord, my God, in Thee do I put my trust.
Come unto Me, all thee that labor and are heavy laden, and I will give you rest.

Ruth B. Smith, published in *Divine Science Monthly*, June 1933, p. 11. Copyrighted material reprinted with permission of Divine Science Federation International.

April 10

MIND VS. MENTAL

Intuition is perception of the possibility of Mind.
    Intellect is perception of the possibility of the Mental.
Knowledge is inherent in Mind.
    Reason belongs to the Mental.
Perception is inherent in Mind.
    Seeing is Mental.
Consciousness is inherent in Mind.
    Feeling is confined to the Mental.
Idea is the possibility of Mind.
    Intent or motive is the possibility of the Mental.

    The Science of Expression is a Trinity in Unity from Spirit to nature. Spirit is the only Expressor, the mental is the medium of expression and nature the effect; or in an individual sense, Spirit the Thinker, thought the expression of Spirit and word Its outward appearance.

    Thought must be representative of Being if sensation be agreeable to Consciousness. Intellect is sense culture relative to things, unless illumined by intuition.

    We cannot use Truth, but can adjust all things to Truth. Truth is eternal, error only seems to be, where Truth is unrecognized. If we think thoughts of love there is nothing between our thought and God, between the mental and that which it images.

    Mistake in the example is not born of Principle -- God cannot recognize Himself in the opposite of His attributes. Perversity is a self-notion.

Malinda Elliott Cramer, (1890), published in *Present At The Beginning*, (Mercer), 2014, p. 32.

April 11

FATHER, THE HOUR IS COME

*Father, the hour is come; glorify Thy Son,
that Thy Son also may glorify Thee.*
John 17:1

Either we are immortal now or we never can be. Death can't be a necessary door to eternal life. We must accept this and get on with it, living accordingly. Now, we are aware that we shall never cease to be, think, do, feel, love, for in God we live and move and have our being. The moment we wrestle this into real *knowing,* we enter the Christ-consciousness. "I am the way, the truth, and the life," Jesus said. Approaching the glorified symbols of Easter, we too can say "I am." Can't we? *What* life? Who beats our hearts? Who gave us also power over all flesh if we will but learn to use that power? Who set the great pattern of the science Jesus revealed? A loving Father. Then the Life that I am must glorify me as His child and Him as my Father. The hour *is* come. It comes to us daily.

Would the Son be glorified if he ended in defeat on the cross or in pain, anguish, despair, and frustration? Would the Father be glorified by a Son left there wearing a crown of thorns in his last appearance among the men he came to teach life eternal? We accept the tender love expressed by the voluntary laying down of his earthly life by Jesus. But we know that to glorify and be glorified he must move on to prove the immortality of life, that which is good, beautiful, and above suffering.

Father, the hour *is* come. I am glorified with Thy Grace and share again the teaching and the experiments that lead me step by step to the wisdom of the Christ-consciousness. This is always that hour. I now rise above all that is unlike Thee.

"Jesus stands alone as a man who knew himself and was cognizant of his relationship to the perfect whole. In the ecstasy of self-realization, he proclaimed the truth to be working through him." *The Science of Mind,* p. 366.

Adela Rogers St. Johns, published in *Science of Mind*, April 1958, p. 55.
Copyrighted material reprinted with permission of SOM Publishing.

April 12

I AM WHERE I AM BY LAW, NOT BY CHANCE

When we acknowledge that we are where we are by law, not by chance, we want to remember to be thankful for this law whose operation has brought us to our present blessings. Too often do people repeat the meditation statement given above and then look dejected, remembering only some difficult situation in their present environment.

Back of our lives today is the law and integrity of the Father by whose will we are here at this time. We are born of Spirit; we are here in accordance with the will of Spirit; we are where we are by law, the law of the One Perfect Mind.

All goes well with us when we keep ourselves mentally in tune with Spirit and adhere to Its will and law. If we become mentally detached, through non-recognition, fear and doubt, we lose, temporarily, our conscious connection with our power to succeed, to progress, to be peaceful, well and joyous.

Our part is to make most of the opportunities for advancement in the place where we find ourselves, to do gladly whatever we find to do, to render our most efficient service to others and to have faith in the law of progress.

Study: Romans 8:28-31 and John 5:17-22

Alice R. Ritchie, published in *Divine Science Monthly*, October 1933, p. 25. Copyrighted material reprinted with permission of Divine Science Federation International.

April 13

THE SAVIOR'S MISSION

If there is no reality in evil, why did the Messiah come to the world, and from what evils was it his purpose to save humankind? How, indeed, is he a Savior, if the evils from which he saves are nonentities?

Jesus came to earth; but the Christ (that is, the divine idea of the divine Principle which made heaven and earth) was never absent from the earth and heaven; hence the phraseology of Jesus, who spoke of the Christ as one who came down from heaven, yet as *"the Son of man which is in heaven."* John 3:13 By this we understand Christ to be the divine idea brought to the flesh in the son of Mary.

Salvation is as eternal as God. To mortal thought Jesus appeared as a child, and grew to manhood, to suffer before Pilate and on Calvary, because he could reach and teach mankind only through this conformity to mortal conditions; but Soul never saw the Savior come and go, because the divine idea is always present.

Jesus came to rescue men from these very illusions to which he seemed to conform: from the illusion which calls sin real, and man a sinner, needing a Savior; the illusion which calls sickness real, and man an invalid, needing a physician; the illusion that death is as real as Life. From such thoughts -- mortal inventions, one and all -- Christ Jesus came to save men, through ever-present and eternal good.

Mary Baker Eddy, *Unity of Good*, 1887, pp. 59-60. No known copyright in effect.

April 14

I RESOLVE TO GROW

...We beseech you, brethren, that ye increase more and more.
I Thessalonians 4:10

Yesterday is gone, and with it the former standard. The benevolent passage of the day, the month, the year, paves the way for the new day, the greater challenge, the more abundant life.

I release yesterday to history, and joyfully embrace the new day and the advancing standard. Only one resolution do I make: *to grow*. Knowing that all growth takes place first in consciousness, I embark daily on the exciting venture of raising my consciousness to a new level. This I achieve by expanding my awareness that I am made in the image of God, the Infinite.

From the center of my heightening consciousness, my experience takes on greater and greater dimensions. I function more and more effectively because I am more and more in tune with Divine Intelligence. I progress in all areas because I have increasing access to the spiritual power of my indwelling God-presence.

I welcome the greater good, the fuller life, the finer self which are the divine potentials of this new day.

Elena Goforth Whitehead, published in *Creative Thought*, February 1965, p. 23. Copyrighted material reprinted with permission of SOM Publishing.

April 15

THE DRAMA OF LIFE

There was a time in my development when I thought that Truth was to be applied to health alone; the light increased and I came to see that Principle was all inclusive and was to be demonstrated in every phase of my existence, in my environment and my relationships as well as in my body.

The light continued to expand and now I realized that nothing was to be excluded from my consciousness. I had been denying certain external processes, they did not seem good to me or they seemed not to be consistent with the fundamental principles I had learned. So I said, "This is delusion, it does not exist in reality." Often we form our decisions, even after very thorough study of advanced thought, from personal prejudices. In my childhood I had been taught to reject evolution as a device of the devil's, a clever scheme to divert us from the true concept of the creative fiat of an all-powerful God. It took me some years to get over this view of this great life process. Then it began to dawn on me that evolution, with its evidence of law, order and power, was God's method of creating a marvelous Life process. Not to be eliminated from our thought-world but to be understood and interpreted aright.

By such gradual unfoldment, my individual consciousness has been greatly enriched. The universe in which I live is larger, more wonderful than I had conceived possible. The experiences of the day are much more significant and vital. My realization of companionship has extended far, far out beyond the confines of those earliest days. I live in a universe that is alive, conscious at every point. A universe that responds to my every call, that fulfills my every need.

Nona L. Brooks, published in *Divine Science Monthly*, October 1932, pp. 42-43. Copyrighted material reprinted with permission of Divine Science Federation International.

April 16

LIFE A MINISTRY

Whosoever would become great among you shall be your minister, and whosoever would be first among you shall be your servant: even as the Son of man came not to be ministered unto, but to minister, and to give his life as a ransom for many.
Jesus

Looked at from a purely commercial standpoint, the life of Jesus Christ was a failure. His place in the world was obscure, His occupation a humble one. The work of His hands commanded only the usual recompense. From the world's point of view His contribution was merely that of an average man.

Even after His public life began He seemingly failed just as signally as before. He made Himself of no reputation among men. In the field where His greatest visible success lay, the delivering of men from sorrow and trouble, He sometimes failed. "He saved others; himself he cannot save," they cried when deriding Him. All the way to His ignominious death He stood before self-satisfied men, chief priests and Pharisees, as a failure. Why? Because He and these men were living from entirely different standpoints. Men were living largely from the external; Jesus was living from within. Men were reckoning success then as the world reckons success today, largely in terms of numbers and figures and the possession of external things.

After two thousand years we can see that the life of Jesus Christ, lived so obscurely, so unostentatiously, really was not the failure that it seemed; that He was living a life that in the long run was the only successful one. For today, when His contemporaries have passed away and are forgotten, His life stands forth among men and within men as the inspiration of all love and all goodness, the inspiration of all success.

H. Emilie Cady, *God, A Present Help*, 1938, pp. 105-106. Copyrighted material reprinted with permission of Unity, Unity.org.

April 17

I SHALL SUCCEED

Though everything looks dark and drear,
    I SHALL SUCCEED.
Though failure's voice speaks in my ear,
    I SHALL SUCCEED.
I do not fear misfortune's blow,
I tower with strength above each foe,
I stand erect, because I KNOW
    I SHALL SUCCEED.

Though others' doubts are built 'round me,
    I SHALL SUCCEED.
Though Fortune's ship I cannot see,
    I SHALL SUCCEED.
Through mist and rain I left my eyes,
I see the sunlight in the skies,
And, seeing it, my glad heart cries
    I SHALL SUCCEED.

Night swoops on me with blackest wings,
    BUT I'LL SUCCEED.
I see the stars that darkness brings,
    AND I'LL SUCCEED.
No force on earth can make me cower,
Because, each moment and each hour,
I still affirm, with strength and power,
    I SHALL SUCCEED.

Evelyn Whitell, *Service and Smiles*, 1934, p. 5. Copyrighted material reprinted with permission of Unity, Unity.org.

April 18

ONENESS

There is one body, and one Spirit...One Lord, one faith...One God and Father of all, who is above all, and through all, and in you all.
Ephesians 4:4-6

We could not have a more definite statement of oneness of all life than in these words of Paul. The lines are like a hymn or poem, with their reiteration of "one, one" and "all, all."

As we let these words sink into our consciousness we become more deeply aware of the feeling of this oneness of all life. Gradually our daily living comes more and more into alignment with the truth of Oneness.

What are some of the keynotes of a way of life based upon acceptance of this truth? First, we delight in

expressing universal love toward all men. In every experience of life, every decision that faces us, we choose

the way of love. We desire the highest good for all concerned. We do not judge others, but wait for time to

reveal that which is righteous and true. To judge "righteous judgment" is to judge on the basis of spiritual

understanding rather than prejudice or limited views. We do not criticize or condemn -- even in thought -- but seek only to let God's love live in and through us.

We walk humbly with Thee, O God, and reverence the Christ-Self in our fellowmen.

Vida Reed Stone, published in *Daily Studies In Divine Science*, 2010, p. 349. Copyrighted material reprinted with permission of Divine Science Federation International.

April 19

IMAGINATION

IMAGINATION is not mere fancy; nor is it a vain ability to picture or create fantasies without relation to life; it is not necessarily unreasonable, nor does it always produce idols and other types of stupidity.

IMAGINATION is the ability to conceive (draw together), to inspire the mind with a sense of newness. It is the mind's exercise in foreseeing results in material form. It is the gift with which man combines separated bits of information or feeling into wholes and brings forth formed ideas, formed lives, policies and philosophies.

IMAGINATION reveals that a thought planted in mind is like a seed. It is an inner Power which brings vague ideas of future matters into clear outlines – an invisible process of gathering together which takes place on the inner side of life before a conception can be born.

IMAGINATION is God's Power to conceive form in infinite variety; to bring such conceptions to birth; to combine conceived forms into new and different forms and so fill the world with shapes and materials adapted to His own purposes.

IMAGINATION in the Mind of God is an idea of form.

IMAGINATION in man is the Power to exercise, control and achieve conception.

Ella Pomeroy, *Powers of the Soul*, 1948, p. 135. No known copyright in effect.

April 20

OMNIPRESENCE OF SPIRIT

Living with a constant thought of the omnipresence of Spirit, we must, as a logical consequence, cast out fear. We cannot fear anything or anybody if we have the full realization that God is everywhere, that God is Love and that Love is the great power of life. Here it may be said…that it is well to read often and to remember the wonderful thirteenth chapter of First Corinthians and make our daily life according to its teaching.

If we follow the rule of right thinking we shall obey the command, "Pray without ceasing." Our whole life will be a prayer, a song of praise to the giver of all life, a joyous, happy realization of Oneness with the Holy Spirit. That is the true prayer.

Prayer is the food of the soul and is more necessary to us than physical food.

This teaching, while called New Thought, is not new. It is as old as thought. It has been practiced in the oldest religions. The only new thing is that it has been made to fit the needs of our new, modern life. It is a simple, practical Christianity, and like everything else taught by Jesus is easily clear to our understanding.

The fruits of this teaching we may acquire only by effort, by constant daily practice. If we fall short of our ideals, let us not be discouraged. Instead of groaning when we fail, let us begin again with the thought that there is always progress made with every renewed effort, even if the gain is not always apparent.

Kathleen M. H. Besly, *The Divine Art of Living*, 1917, pp. 7-8. No known copyright in effect.

April 21

THE ETERNAL NOW

"The kingdom of God is at hand." We need not wait to achieve eternal life for we are in the midst of it. We need not pass through the curtain called death to reach the happy land. We need but capture the wonderful Now, the challenging Now, and live it hopefully, gratefully, and courageously.

*Thus saith the high and lofty One that inhabits eternity,
whose name is Holy: I dwell in the high and holy place.*
Isaiah 57:15

Let us reside in the "high and holy place," in the consciousness of the Omnipresence, and face each day with a joyful heart, while eternity unfolds before us like a river, continuing on endlessly. Through self-discipline and patience we will abide in the Presence of our Lord.

Today may be likened to putty in our hands. May we shape it according to Thy will, Father, and make it a thing of beauty. Today is the Eternal Now.

May this day bring us increased understanding of the "unchanging state of good," which is the definition of *eternity*. "And God saw the light, that it was good....God saw everything that He had made, and, behold, it was very good." Genesis 1:4, 31

F. Bernadette Turner, published in *Aspire*, August 1975, p. 26. Copyrighted material reprinted with permission of Divine Science Federation International.

April 22

THE HIGHROAD OF PROSPERITY

"Come now, and let us reason together." God is the true source of all the riches in the earth. "The silver is mine, and the gold is mine, saith Jehovah of hosts." You are the offspring of the Most High, heir of all the richness of God, and you are here to express that richness through this body and in this world.

There is a highway of prosperity, a king's highway, a road up the mountain of supreme success, and it is an easy grade, the travel is ever smooth, and they that walk therein know no more worry nor fear, nor strife, nor hard times, nor slavish work, nor failure. They live and let live, and they are consciously secure forever from all sense of deprivation or lack.

The uninstructed follow bypaths in seeking their wealth where there is much stumbling and blindness of chance, where burdens pile up, and the travelers never reach the heights. All these side roads end in gullies and pits, for all that is gained must eventually be given up. Men enter them as shortcuts to wealth, and though some of them cross the real road, so intoxicated are these wanderers that they know not this road even when their feet press its fair track, long miles at a time.

The right view of prosperity as God's own presence, which is not to be refused or despised but to be seen as the legitimate expression of the spiritual life, comes to the man whose eyes are open and who seeks understanding so as to think and feel, speak and act according to the law that operates to make bodies healthy and circumstances wealthy, who sees that it is all one and the same work. The body is wealthy that has health, and the circumstances are healthy that have wealth.

Annie Rix Militz, *Both Riches and Honor*, 1945, pp. 85-86. Copyrighted material reprinted with permission of Unity, Unity.org.

April 23

ILLUMINATION — UNDERSTANDING

When the disciples had associated with the Risen Christ long enough to sense that He had been wounded for the transgressions of a world, and by the acknowledgement of the same the world might go free – *"then opened He their understanding that they might understand the Scriptures."*
Luke 24: 25

And the "Scriptures" He gave them was His own name: *"The Holy Ghost whom the Father will send in my name shall teach you all things."*
John 14:26

This name constitutes the most remarkable book ever mentioned on earth, *"for the Spirit of Truth it wakens shall guide into all truth, and show mankind of things to come."*
John 16:13

Every man's name conveys his qualities. If he is a strong intellect, the repetition of his name, especially the calling of his name earnestly, imbues the caller with new intellectual strength. If he is heroic in battle, a certain accession of heroism stirs the caller. Cruden, in his immortal *Concordance*, under the head of "Call," declares that things that had no existence may come into sight by strong words of calling, *"I have made thee like unto Him, even God, who quickeneth the dead, and calleth those things which be not as though they were."*
Romans 4: 17

And, *"Who hath God so nigh unto them as the Lord our God is in all things that we call unto Him for?"*
Deuteronomy 4:7

Isaiah lamented that *"no man called for justice."*
Isaiah 59:4

Emma Curtis Hopkins, *Resume*, 1928, pp. 55-56. No known copyright in effect.

April 24

COURAGE IN SEEKING GOD

Lord Jesus Christ, Son of God, have mercy upon me, a sinner.
Prayer of the Heart (Jesus' Prayer)

Courage in the face of seeking God is imperative because the goal is remote and the sense of Oneness tends to disappear repeatedly, causing frustration, anxiety, and despair. Tillich has defined this quality of courage as "the self-affirmation of being in spite of non-being"....As Kierkegaard brilliantly describes it, this courage must be the principle of faith moving forward without expectation of good results.

Whether conceptualized by Tillich or Kierkegaard; whether exemplified in the life of Buddha, Abraham, or the drama of Jesus, this special brand of courage is necessary and its qualities are fourfold:

1. to express courage in the face of worldly trials;
2. to carry the conviction that the Divine lives in every situation and life form;
3. to share courage as a dauntless joy standing impervious in the midst of pain and pleasure; and
4. to exemplify courage, not as an expectation of good results, but as a statement of love for God in spite of results.

Carol Ruth Knox, *The Prayer of the Heart*, 1992, p. 22. No known copyright in effect.

April 25

DEMONSTRATION

People often ask how long it will take to make a desired demonstration. The time element does not enter into spiritual healing. There is no time in Spirit, and all answer to prayer is instantaneous. *"Before they call, I will answer, and while they are yet speaking, I will hear."* However, time enters into man's mortal concept of things; therefore the time required to bring about the healing in the outer depends upon one's ability to realize Truth and to bring it into manifestation through faith and the spoken word.

Myrtle Fillmore, published in *Myrtle Fillmore, Mother of Unity* (Witherspoon), 1977, p. 273. Copyrighted material reprinted with permission of Unity, Unity.org.

April 26

WHAT IS GOD, METAPHYSICALLY CONSIDERED?

All spiritual unfoldment must of necessity start with the conception of God as Spirit. The mind must completely let go of all pre-conceived ideas of God as a Super-man, a sort of king, doling out to his people both favors and punishments. With the conception of God as Spirit there naturally follows a clearer understanding of Omnipresence. The student grows in the tremendous realization of God, Spirit, as the invisible Life and Intelligence underlying all physical things, and immediately the whole universe becomes transformed and takes on a new meaning.

Jesus not only defined God as Spirit and the Father but also described Him when he said, "God is Love." Perfect love is perfect harmony. Perfect harmony is inclusive of wisdom and power, so in his description of God as Love, Jesus ascribed to him omnipresence and omnipotence. In those three words, "God is Love" he recognized the All-wisdom and All-power working together for the All-good.

When he described God as Spirit (John 4:24) he claimed the Omnipresence or Every-whereness of the Love that God is, for Spirit is limitless and indivisible -- the Universal Mind in all and through all.

In beholding God as Spirit, or the invisible Life, Intelligence, Harmony and Power of the Universe we recognize him as Creative Principle -- that which is the Cause and Source of all that is; pure Being; all Law and all Truth; Primordial Substance; Ultimate Cause, or more simply phrased, "that from which all proceeds."

Georgiana Tree West, from her Unity ordination application submitted on June 10, 1935. No known copyright in effect.

April 27

TODAY, I AM SHOWN

Good morning, God! I turn to you in prayer and prepare myself to live the best day of my life. I open my mind to divine ideas and divine wisdom, and my way is clear.

Good morning, God! I clear my thoughts of all that might separate me in consciousness from my Christ Self. With my mind at peace, I am filled with life, strength, and health.

Good morning, God! I rid my heart of all un-forgiveness so that your great love can flow in and through me to harmonize every relationship, everywhere.

Good morning, God! I turn to you for the solution to every situation I do not quite understand. I turn to you for the supply that is needed in all areas of my life.

Dear God, thank you for being with me all through this day as my directive power. Make me and mold me through all this day.

...be of good cheer. I have overcome the world.
John 16:13

Christina Knox-Walthall, (1985), published in *Daily Inspiration*, Copyright 2015, *Daily Inspiration for Better Living*. Reprinted with permission of the Universal Foundation for Better Living (UFBL) Press, September 2015, p. 14.

April 28

SUPPLICATION VS. ACKNOWLEDGEMENT

In giving a false estimate to Being, man has established in his consciousness an untrue relationship between himself and God. Thus he thinks of himself as "a worm in the dust," imperfect and mortal, one who must approach God in a begging, pleading attitude. Such a foundation can never uphold the science of right thinking. It reminds us of one who foolishly pulls down all the curtains of a room and then longs for the light and warmth of the sun.

If your prayers have not been answered, if they have not been brought you the highest result, do not stop praying, but learn to pray correctly. There is a right and wrong way of doing everything and this is true of prayer. It is Phillips Brooks who reminds us that "Prayer is not the beseeching of a reluctant God, but the opening of ourselves to God's willingness," and James says, "The effectual, fervent prayer of a righteous man availeth much" (James 5:16), which statement cannot be understood to mean a virtuous, moral man in any limited sense, since such often confess great failure, and cannot even heal a headache with prayer, but it must mean a right-thinking man or one of scientific-spiritual understanding.

God may be looked upon as our great Banker in the bank of life, love and truth, health and prosperity. As we would not approach the cashier of an ordinary bank with a cry and supplication for money provided we held the credentials, but with confidence and dignity would present our authority for a demand on the bank, so in this spirit let us approach our great Good, ready to prove our Son-ship by right thinking. Our demand will thus be honored.

Harriet Hale Rix, *Christian Mind Healing*, 1914, pp. 48-49. No known copyright in effect.

April 29

OUR FATHER NEVER FAILETH

Our Father never faileth
To give his children bread;
They only need to hunger,
More richly to be fed.
For love's abundant table
Most graciously supplies
Each earnest aspiration,
That hourly doth rise.

Our Father never faileth
To give His offspring strength;
They need but lean, to measure
Its height and breadth and length.
"Lo, I am with you always!"
This is the promise true,
That knows no shade or turning,
Beloved, meant for you.

Our Father, God, the Only,
Is 'round and in us all,
Sustaining and embracing,
That none need ever fall.
He's light and joy and healing,
Oh, come and taste and see:
Our Father faileth never
Throughout eternity.

Hannah More Kohaus, published in *Unity Song Selections*, 1947, Hymn 118. Tune: "The Church's One Foundation." Copyrighted material reprinted with permission of Unity, Unity.org.

April 30

GOD AND LOVE

The tide of love swells in me with such force
  It sweeps away all hate and all distrust,
  As eddying straws and particles of dust
Are lost by some swift river in its course.

Love is a plant which we can cultivate
  To grace and fragrance sweeter than the rose,
  Or leave neglected while our heart soil grows
Rank with that vile and poison nettle – hate.

Love is a joyous thrush, that we can teach
  To sing sweet lute-like songs, which all may hear,
  Or we can silence him, and tune the ear
To caw of crows, or to the vulture's screech.

Love is a feast; and if the guests divide
  With all who pass, though thousands swell the van,
  There shall be food and drink for every man;
The loaves and fishes will be multiplied.

Love is the law; but yield to its control
  And thou shalt find all things work for the best.
  And in the calm, still heaven of thy breast
That God Himself sits talking with thy soul.

Ella Wheeler Wilcox, published in *Washington News Letter*, (ed. Sabin), July 1902, p. 690. No known copyright in effect.

MAY

May 1

PRAYER

Oh, Thou All-seeing, and All-knowing One,
Whom we call "Father," "God," "Creator," -- to Thee
We pray, not as of old when ignorance of
Thy laws and Thee, did bid us supplicate, entreat,
Implore for things we most desired.
But in the higher understanding
With which our great Teacher bade us pray;
He who said: 'When thou prayest, *believe*
That things desired by thee, *are thine!*
For thy Father knoweth *all thy heart*,
And gives thee all good blessings, *e'er thy prayer
Is uttered!* God is perfection, law itself,
And *He* no changing needs. But we, His children,
Heirs by birth and inheritance, have lived
So long *in doubt* of our estate, cannot receive;
Our spiritual ears, eyes and thoughts are silent;
So *we the changing need*,
Now when we pray, we will not say:
"Dear Father, hear our prayer;" but know
That Thou *dost hear*, and answer!
We will not plead, "Be near us,"
But *know* that space *filled* by Thee alone!
And surely Thou art here as *everywhere*.
We will not *plead* that Spirit's power,
May us encompass and protect,
We *know* that spirit never leaves us day or night.
We'll let each breath, and thought, and word,
A *recognition* be, our lives be hid in Thee.
Content in Thee, we find our heaven *now*,
And *nothing* have we to fear,
Since God is "All in All," and God is *good*.

Fannie Brooks James, *Divine Science: New Light Upon Old Truths*, 1896, p. 87. No known copyright in effect.

May 2

COURAGE

The truly courageous man is afraid of nothing, and least of all is he afraid of himself. He believes in himself and believing in himself believes in the perfection of the Law [of Opulence]. He may not put this in words, may not say to himself, "I believe in the Law of Opulence," but he nevertheless acts upon such belief. He says, "I will succeed," he takes the Law into partnership, he plans, and he executes because he has courage.

It may not even have occurred to such a man to think of himself as being courageous. His courage is so much a part of him that he does not give it a name separate from himself. He says, "I," I will do so and so, and goes and does it without once thinking there is any reason why he should not succeed, whereas a man of less courage would approach the purpose of his desires haltingly, wondering if, possibly, he was wise in undertaking it, and how he ever had the courage to undertake it. And the difference in the way in which each approached the object of his desires is often the difference between success and failure.

The timid man is ever at a disadvantage both before his fellows and before the Law through which success is attained.

Confidence in self breeds confidence in others, and fear weakens both the brain that plans and the hand that executes.

Helen Wilmans, *The Conquest of Poverty*, 1901, pp. 143-144. No known copyright in effect.

May 3

RICHES THE GIFT OF GOD

The laws of spiritual prosperity are the very reverse of the laws of worldly prosperity. In the divine economy you do not gain by saving up for a rainy day; you do not lose by spending; the more you can give away the more you have. You do not "earn" divine riches; therefore you do not have to work hard for them either mentally or physically.

It belongs to your creative consciousness to love to work, and by fearlessness as regards supply and support you can gravitate to your congenial work, which will be valued highly by the world because art will enter into it.

"Art is love for one's work."

We come out of Egypt by ceasing "to work for a living" in our mind. Whatever work you are engaged in now, put your soul into service and become an artist in it.

Educate yourself to find divinity in your work and in your associates, whether employer or employee. When you have learned your lesson, you will graduate easily into a congenial, because your own, vocation.

Spirit knows Spirit only, and in its realm there is no bargaining, no buying and selling, no wages, no hirelings, no laborers, no rewards or punishments, no merit or demerit, no deserving and no unworthy persons.

All is love, and everything is done for love, and all the fruits of love are gifts.

Annie Rix Militz, *Both Riches and Honor*, 1945, pp. 91-92. Copyrighted material reprinted with permission of Unity, Unity.org.

May 4

THE WAY OF LOVE

Love cannot be taught. Jesus said that we are to love God. He said, "The Lord our God is one Lord; and thou shalt love the Lord thy God with all your heart, and with all thy soul, and with all thy mind, and with all thy strength: this is the first commandment."
Mark 12:30

To love God is to seek Him, to seek Truth within ourselves first. We know that what we love is that to which we give our attention. To what do we give our attention?...

We give our attention...to the clothes we wear,... jobs,... relationships,...the thoughts we think. We give our attention to the mistakes that we have made....We give it to money, vacations, achievement, success, relationships. Yet we do not seem to hear the basic message, and that is: "Love God first." Let us devote our attention to God within *first*....

When we turn within and direct our attention to Truth, Truth flows into our minds and hearts. The Truth always seeks to express itself....As we give our attention to God, we acknowledge the Truth within us and recognize that this Truth is the answer to everything. God becomes our companion.

Truth personifies Itself when we can recognize it – as though some new friend...

When you "put God *first*," then Love personifies itself through all whom you meet....That love may be personified in some person who comes into your life and loves you as God does, totally.

Helen Brungardt, *Contemplation*, 1975, pp. 69-71. No known copyright in effect.

May 5

UNITING WITH GOD

The prayer process of seeking and becoming one with God is a subtle experience in which you become involved in a totally different approach to mind, emotions, and body. As a direct result of the prayer work, many life activities, attitudes and reflections, gradually disappear.

There may be difficult periods where you feel a distance from your usual life patterns and responses, but clarity emerges. Certain attitudes towards life, such as psychological interpretations, treating yourself as the object or creator of events, disregarding or repressing your rich humanity, are gradually dissolved.

You begin to recognize and affirm that any physical, mental, emotional or external occurrence is only the activity of Spirit. This recognition becomes your living faith. As a result, your relationship with life shifts from an attitude of action to one of silence, from external motivation to internal beingness, from fear to trust. Prayer becomes the motivation for all thought and action. Gradually, life begins to move from *inside out*. As understanding grows, surrender begins to be a way of life.

Carol Ruth Knox, *The Prayer Of The Heart,* 1992, pp. 73-74. No known copyright in effect.

May 6

CHOICES

The last of the human freedoms – to choose one's attitude in any given set of circumstances, to choose one's own way.
Viktor Frankl

How free are we to make choices in our lives? Although we have unlimited freedom of choice, we appear to never be free of the conditions or circumstances or consequences of those choices. Pure and simple, then, we experience the result of the choices that we've made in the past. If we continue making choices as we have up until now our future will be a multiplication of what we're experiencing, or as Ernest Holmes said, we will continue to create with monotonous regularity.

There's no reason to feel guilty about the choices we've made. We made those choices out of an ignorance of who we are…. We forget that we are whole perfect and complete. We forget this and make choices that are not very fulfilling. As Deepak Chopra said, "We are where we are because we have made a premature cognitive commitment to who we are." Only we can make a change in how we make choices, by changing our internal definition of who we are. To do this, we must remember that we are made of the substance of God, with full omniscience and omnipotence omnipresent in our lives. Our own conditioning is in our way. We must let it go. We can no longer compromise Spirit within us. Our decisions were made out of an erroneous idea of who we are.

We must have the courage to learn to make choices and decisions that resonate with the divinity within us….Our decisions must resonate with us, challenge us, and have us living on our edge. That is what our lives are meant to be.

We must affirm our true nature, refuse to be immobilized by our past decisions and be free to choose to reorient ourselves and turn in a new direction.

Peggy Bassett, from her lesson at Huntington Beach Church of Religious Science, July 1990. Transcribed and printed with permission of Huntington Beach Center for Spiritual Living, Huntington Beach, California.

May 7

TEN OF JESUS' COMMANDMENTS

I. Thou shalt love the Lord thy God with all thy heart, and with all thy soul, and with all thy mind. This is the first great commandment. And the second is like unto it.

II. Thou shalt love thy neighbor as thyself. On these two commandments hang all the law and prophets.

III. Seek ye first the kingdom of God and His righteousness and all these things will be added.

IV. Be ye therefore perfect, even as your Father which is in heaven is perfect.

V. Resist not evil.

VI. Sin no more, lest a worse thing come unto thee.

VII. Take my yoke upon you; my yoke is easy and my burden is light.

VIII. Love your enemies.

IX. Let the dead bury their dead; go thou and preach the kingdom of God.

X. Be of good cheer; I have overcome the world.

Ada B. Fay, *The Evolution of the Ten Commandments*, 1937, p. 21. No known copyright in effect.

May 8

RESOLUTIONS TO RESULTS

GOAL SETTING -- A resolution is a declaration. I am clear. This who I am, this is what I want. What is that saying? "If I can conceive it, I can believe it and I can achieve it or receive it." We are getting in touch with the truth about our heart's desire….

We're not talking about "how do we put a magic penny in the machine" and get what we want. We're talking about a resolution within ourselves. So as we learn to be bold, to be accountable, to be loved, and as we return to those tools, we can achieve our heart's desire….

We have to have faith to trust in our journey. We get to trust that faith and listen to that Guidance…I've got to give up my good to make room for my better.

GOAL AWAKENING -- Awakening occurs when we're willing to do the work. Several weeks ago we lost a great Unity leader, Rev. Dr. Johnnie Colemon. And she used to say, "It works if you work it." It works if you work it. It's about our individual journey of working it and whether we are willing to also broaden our perspective to see how it affects our family, our friends and spiritual community. Because if it works when we work it as an individual, how is it going to be when we work it as a whole church?

There's no limit. There is no limitation. In that no limitation is peace, not right or wrong, not good or bad, just peace.

Jennifer Holder, from her lesson at Unity of Gaithersburg, Maryland, January 11, 2015. Transcribed and printed with permission of her family.

May 9

WHO ARE GOD'S TEACHERS?

A teacher of God is anyone who chooses to be one. His qualifications consist solely in this; somehow, somewhere he has made a deliberate choice in which he did not see his interests as apart from someone else's. Once he has done that, his road is established and his direction is sure. A light has entered the darkness. It may be a single light, but that is enough. He has entered an agreement with God even if he does not yet believe in Him. He has become a bringer of salvation. He has become a teacher of God.

They come from all over the world. They come from all religions and from no religion. They are the ones who have answered. The Call is universal. It goes on all the time everywhere. It calls for teachers to speak for it and redeem the world. Many hear it, but few will answer. Yet it is all a matter of time. Everyone will answer in the end, but the end can be a long, long way off. It is because of this that the plan of the teachers was established. Their function is to save time. Each one begins as a single light, but with the Call at its center it is a light that cannot be limited. And each one saves a thousand years of time as the world judges it. To the Call Itself time has no meaning.

Helen Schucman, *A Course In Miracles*, 1975, Manual For Teachers, p. 3. No known copyright in effect.

May 10

INFINITE SPIRIT OF SUBSTANCE

QUESTION — We find our finances in very bad shape, mortgage about to be foreclosed, daughter ill and mother-in-law very discordant and fault finding. I feel so confused, can't make decisions. Is my confused state of mind the result of chaotic conditions of our life, because, when these things began to happen I was poised and happy? I can't feel they are the result of my thought.

ANSWER — You will be caught in the picture just so long as you permit the conditions you mention to have weight in your mind. You must close your mental door to them all, and realize that the Infinite Spirit of Substance is the very center of your life, and that no condition or circumstance can affect It. Your work lies wholly within yourself, and should exclude all appearances on the objective. Know that that which formerly made your decisions and kept you wholesome and happy is active at this moment, keeping you positive and dominant; that no situation exists on the objective level which It cannot handle to your satisfaction. Keep yourself in this impregnable mental stronghold and no outward conflict can affect you. After all, making a decision is only making a choice. Choose to believe that no matter what the appearance may be to the contrary, you occupy and are protected in your own Impregnable Point of Good, wherein right action alone can obtain. Know that Divine Intelligence within you compels you by your full cooperation, to say and do the right thing at the right time, and rest your case in God, the All Good. Then wait, watchfully and with certainty. Avenues will open automatically, once you convince yourself it is true for there is no obstruction to the harmonious action of your life if you set in motion definite laws which, when used and understood, produce definite results. Be steady, persistent and faithful in your work and you will win.

Alberta Smith, published in *Science of Mind*, July 1932, pp. 66-67.
Copyrighted material reprinted with permission of SOM Publishing.

May 11

I AM DIVINELY PROTECTED

I am safe and secure because I am in my Father's world. Sometimes there is an underlying feeling of fear, a restlessness for which I can find no reason.

Today, I remind myself that I can depend on God, who, according to the scriptures and my own experiences, always honors promises. The promise I keep uppermost in my mind is "He that dwelleth…shall abide. No evil shall befall you." Psalm 61:7

I accept this promise and keep my side of the contract: I abide, which means I am constantly conscious that I am in the Presence of Pure Being, God. I am safe and secure.

The realization that I am never separated from the protecting presence of God is reassuring. Knowing that whatever I am, God is, frees me from fear. I experience a beautiful day of peace. Thank you God!

No evil shall befall you.
Psalm 91:13

Judith G. Weekes, (1990), published in *Daily Inspiration*, Copyright 2015, *Daily Inspiration for Better Living*. Reprinted with permission of the Universal Foundation for Better Living (UFBL) Press, September 2015, p. 26.

May 12

THE LAW OF PROSPERITY

We are not here to work for anything less than to unfold our God nature, our Divine Self, and this is not possible when we concentrate on money alone. What is money? Why, you are the creator and maker of money. You put into it all that makes it of value and you can withdraw that and it is not worth any more than sand. God did not make money valuable; to Him there is no difference between a pebble and a diamond.

You must give if you would get; the man who forgets to give, forgets how to receive. He closes the door of receptivity; he closes the door of life and is like a lake which, unless opened at both ends, becomes stagnant. Many people are planting disease, physical poverty and misery of all kinds through not maintaining the other half of the law of Prosperity. They want to receive only, but the law is not a hemisphere, it is a sphere. It is only as you bring the two parts together and recognize that giving and receiving should be equal, that you can weld them into a unit and have the law work for you. "With what measure you give, it shall be measured back to you."

Harriet Hale Rix, *The Rich Mentality*, 1916, pp. 24-25. No known copyright in effect.

May 13

HOW WE FIND GOD

*Ye shall seek me, and find me,
when ye shall search for me with all your heart.*
Jeremiah 29:13

How do we find God? Sometimes we are told to "feel out" after God. Perhaps this is the wrong direction. While it is true that God is everywhere, all about us, we find Him most easily by seeking Him within ourselves.

But what do we mean by "within"? We know that God must be within our bodies; they are His temple. However, the body is only one level of our being, the envelope in which we live on earth. We have a mind, too, in which we feel the movement of thought forces, which we can control and direct in right ways. Surely God is in mind.

But what moves the body, and what directs the thoughts? "I do," we reply. "I." "I AM." This is the control center, the "within," where we find God in ourselves. I am not merely a body. Nor am I only a mind. I am spirit. And even as I glimpse this truth, the impression slips away. Spirit cannot be held even in thought. But we do know it. We each say, "I am." No one can say it for us. I remember that I AM one with the Father, even as Jesus said. Here I find God.

Barbara L. Wolfe, published in *Daily Studies In Divine Science*, 2010, p. 153. Copyrighted material reprinted with permission of Divine Science Federation International.

May 14

I RESPOND WITH JOY TODAY

Joy is a spirit-lifter, a life-giver, a hope-saver! If I seem to feel no inner joy on this day, I call it forth. I affirm joy: "God's presence surrounds me with joy."

"Reality, the truth about life, and the mystery of beauty are all the same, and they are the first concern of everyone," says Agnes Martin [artist mystic]. And again, "We are in the midst of reality responding with joy." The creative part of her is speaking about life and about art; she is speaking to all of us. We can respond to the reality of our lives with joy. If we doubt this, we need to take a new look at our lives. We need to see them as proving grounds for faith, as being centered in our identity as children of God. Thus our lives are outpourings of His expression through us.

"Joy is the most infallible sign of the presence of God," writes Pierre Teilhard de Chardin. But if we lack joy, it is not that God is not with us, but that we have lost our sense, our awareness, of that Presence. To regain it, we need only to open our hearts and let our minds and spirits receive His Spirit.

This joy, this perfect joy, is now mine.
John 3:29

Elizabeth Searle Lamb, published in *Daily Studies in Divine Science*, 2010, p. 194. Copyrighted material reprinted with permission of Divine Science Federation International.

May 15

LIFE TURNS TO US AS WE TURN TO IT

As we turn in consciousness to life, it turns to us and gives us of its bounty, all that we are able to take. It does not limit us, but we have to set our own limitation. Life is waiting at the door of our minds to fill us, when we open the door, with whatever the need is. It makes no charges, but it does make a demand, and that is, that you open the door, and your work is over. "Behold I stand at the door and knock; any man that will open, I will come in and sup with him, and He with Me." The fullness of life doesn't come as the result of a search, but as an awakening. Awake thou that sleepest.

Pearl C. Wood, *Thinking With God: Daily Thoughts*, March 1940, p. 2. Copyrighted material reprinted with permission of Triangular Church.

May 16

PRAYER

We pray to change our mind, not to change God Mind. For us prayer is not supplication to a God who is withholding our good from us. Prayer instead is an affirmation of that truth about us that eternally exists in God Mind; but which has not yet come into our minds, and therefore not into our lives.

Prayer, then, is the most highly accelerated mind action known. It steps up our mental activity to synchronize with the Truth that is in God Mind; and it creates through us a channel through which that Truth, existing in God Mind, of life, health, wholeness and harmony can demonstrate it first in our mind and then in full manifestation.

For us prayer is not something we do to God but something we do to ourselves. It is not a position but more a disposition. It is not doubting but knowing. It is not just words but feelings. It's not our will but our willingness. In the Gospel of John, talking to the woman at the well, Jesus said, "God is Spirit, and they that worship Him must worship Him in Spirit and in Truth."

Sallye Taylor, transcribed from her recorded introduction to Soul Food Unity, a website prayer ministry. Posted on YouTube, January 12, 2015. No known copyright in effect.

May 17

INTELLIGENCE

I affirm: I will let this mind be in me which also was in Christ Jesus.

Eternally coexistent with Life is Intelligence. The wonder of the intelligent activity of our universe never fades. The intelligence of growing things -- the constant adjustment to new conditions, the overcoming of obstacles in order to complete the life cycle -- fills us with amazement.

We are aware of a great Intelligence within ourselves that helps us climb the hills of life, that gives us wisdom to solve problems, that helps us to adjust our lives to our environment. How grateful we are for this inexhaustible Source of Wisdom that is always sharing Itself with Its manifestation.

To be alone, to open ourselves to Infinite Mind, is one of our greatest privileges. Do you realize how quietly the great forces of life perform their work? Here a mighty oak tree comes forth; a star is born; a flower unfolds, stem, leaves, bloom, color—but no sound is heard. In the same way, the harmonious, intelligent activity in man beats his heart, digests his food, builds his nerves and bones, and does hundreds of other things silently, powerfully, intelligently.

There is no place where Intelligence is not.

Caroline Munz, published in *Daily Studies In Divine Science*, 2010, p.185.
Copyrighted material reprinted with permission of Divine Science Federation International.

May 18

GROWING IN SPIRITUAL UNDERSTANDING

WATCHWORD – I resolve to grow in spiritual understanding.

Now we have received, not the spirit of the world, but the Spirit which is of God, that we might know the things that are freely given to us of God.
II Corinthians. 2:12

How are we to grow in spiritual understanding but to turn to our Source, which is Spirit, and to follow after the Divine Instruction?

We are to know the things that are so freely given to us: Eternal Life, unlimited intelligence, the fullness of Love, abundance of supply and all the joy, peace and harmony we desire.

Then why be down-hearted, discouraged, and blue; remember if you can't be happy when you feel miserable you can't be happy at all, for our feelings have no real power and as we become happy within, the outer living is changed.

True satisfaction comes from a contented mind and a serene outlook; we may be satisfied and happy with no material possessions or we may lack satisfaction with the whole world of things at our command.

Daisy Baum, *Individual Responsibility*, 1918, p. 25. Copyrighted material reprinted with permission of Divine Science Federation International.

May 19

OMNIPRESENT LIFE

Emerson says there is but one mind, and that we are all different expressions of it.

The Mental Science student means the same thing when he says there is but one Life, of which we are but individual manifestations.

If there is but one Life, then life is omnipresent--it fills all space. There is nothing outside of it. Indeed, there is no outside. There is but one Life. This Life is the universal Principle of Being that men call God.

There is a Life Principle, and it is unlimited; it is one. It holds the visible universe in place, though it is invisible. It is a self-existent principle. It underlies universal law. It is the one Law -- the Law of Attraction -- and beside it there is no other law. It is also the very essence of love; and the recognition of it as love is expressed by us in love for each other.

All the races of men have felt the presence and the power of this Law of Attraction, whose ultimate expression is love, or life, in a myriad of different forms.

The undeviating Law has never been violated, and never will be. And this is our hope. It is unchanging, diseaseless, deathless; and a knowledge of it conforms us to it in a way that renders us diseaseless and deathless.

For the law does permeate all visible forms. It is one with all substance. And no doubt that an expanded and spiritual interpretation of the word "God" has been the foundation for the expression that "God and man are one."

Helen Wilmans, *Home Course in Mental Science*, 1914, p. 1. No known copyright in effect.

May 20

THE BODY TEMPLE

As you come to know your body as the living temple of God, a temple that God never has deserted, one that He never will forsake, you appreciate it more and more. You pattern your thoughts after God's thought of life. You work with Him to keep His temple radiant, pure, strong, and lovely in every part.

Let us work lovingly, unitedly, joyously together with God for the perfect body temple, for eyes filled with His light, for hands adept in His service, for feet fleet and free in bearing His glad tidings of wholeness, for strong, courageous, loving hearts, for Truth in every organ, every cell. All are related in some form of expression to the inner work of the Holy Spirit. Let us bless them every one, day by day. Then the years will yield us the blessing of growth and development in the perfect temple of the perfect being God intends us to be. "We are a temple of the living God; even as God said."

Clara A. Palmer, *The Eternal Temple*, Unity pamphlet, 1965, pp. 3, 4.
Copyrighted material reprinted with permission of Unity, Unity.org.

May 21

OLD UNWANTED HABITS CANNOT BIND ME

If I have ever been burdened with old, unwanted habits, now is the time I pray for freedom from these habits. I am a spiritual being having power to free myself. Prayer is a tool to be used in overcoming any problem, and I now use it to free myself. Knowing myself to be a spiritual being, having power from God to overcome, I am free to claim perfect freedom right now. I am not bound or burdened by cares. The truth is that nothing can bind or limit me; I am free in Christ. As I affirm my freedom in Christ, I feel the burden or bondage dropping away. I feel light, happy and enthusiastic.

This joy and newness of life comes to me because I have gotten rid of old, unwanted habits and replaced them with new, desirable habits. I am now free to make prayer a habit, to make thanksgiving a habit, to make giving a habit, and to make loving a habit. My whole life has changed for the better because I've chosen to free myself of the undesirable to make room for the desirable.

I am a spiritual being, free to express my true nature of light, life and love. I am a spiritual being, free to be happy, joyous, prosperous and peaceful. Praise God, I am free and free, indeed!

For freedom, Christ has made us free.
Galatians 5:1

Olga Una Barker, published in *Daily Inspiration*, Copyright 1980, *Daily Inspiration for Better Living.* Reprinted with permission of the Universal Foundation for Better Living (UFBL) Press, November 1980, p. 23.

May 22

THE PAST IS PRESENT

A wise Frenchman once said, "The past is always present," And this is true. Out of the past we are built. Out of the past we grow and unfold.

Our past has been a process of unfoldment. We unfold physically and mentally from children to adults. We unfold in spiritual consciousness. We have to get to know God and rise above limitations. You are a child of God, and you can restore the past. You can see all of your past life in its proper light. Do not try to run away from past experiences. Just try to put them in their right place. They were experiences that you came through. Put away anxiety and condemnation of yourself just as children grown to adulthood put away their toys.

It does not matter what the past has been or what you believe about it or what you think about it, today it is being restored as a part of God unfolding in and through you. Nothing that occurred in the past can possibly separate you from God. It is never too late to be forgiven; it is never too late to be healed; it is never too late to be prospered; it is never too late to pray; it is never too late to receive your good; it is never too late to grow.

You can restore the past. God is in you; God is your path; God is your power. And He can "restore to you the years that the locust hath eaten."

Sue Sikking, *The Years That The Locust Hath Eaten*, Unity pamphlet, 1966, pp. 3-4. Copyrighted material reprinted with permission of Unity, Unity.org.

May 23

THE PEARL OF GREAT PRICE

Acquaint now thyself with Him, and be at peace.
Job 22:21

The attainment of peace, poise, balance is the pearl of great price. No one enters a higher realization while he indulges in anger, worry, or resentment. One of the quickest and surest means of overcoming these baneful thoughts and emotions is by working definitely for the realization of peace.

We live in a universe wherein peaceful activity is the creative Power. Think how silently, yet how powerfully, everything from atom to planet is brought forth. Think how harmoniously and powerfully the creative Intelligence within you is replacing worn-out cells, how easily your thoughts come to you, how quickly your muscles respond to your will, all so peacefully done.

When we recognize the Spirit of Peace -- here and now, within and without -- we have taken our first step in the realization of I Am Peace.

Our foundation for living depends upon the changelessness of that which God is and His Law of Action. God is Peace. God-activity is peaceful. I lift my thought to Eternal Truth every day.

My peace I give unto you.
John 14:27

Caroline Munz, published in *Daily Studies in Divine Science*, 2010, p. 283. Copyrighted material reprinted with permission of Divine Science Federation International.

May 24

THE DIVINE PLAN FOR YOUR LIFE

There is a wonderful, beautiful plan for your life. Your destiny is divine! As your consciousness of the Christ indwelling is quickened through daily life, you find yourself fitting into the divine plan easily. You come to know that you are a part of a great universal plan of spiritual growth and unfoldment.

When you enter into the feeling that you are a part of the good of the world, you are at ease. Frustration vanishes. You live your life in harmony. A hymn in *Unity Song Selections* expresses this thought.

"We are a part of all that's good, and good shall be victorious."

You are eternally a part of the good in the world. Know this and be at peace. All is working well in your life and affairs because you are a part of the divine plan for good for every man.

Relax. Be at ease. There is no need to struggle hard to find the good. You are a part of all that is good.

May Rowland, *The Magic of the Word*, 1972, p. 81. Copyrighted material reprinted with permission of Unity, Unity.org.

May 25

LET US LEARN

Let us learn to have faith in the master power of the Soul Self within and then address the Master after this manner:

Indwelling Master, thou knowest me. Thou art able to fulfill my need and I ask Thee while in sleep and while in work that You go forth to bring for me the wisdom and intelligence of God that will work through me to manifest the harmony, life, love and joy that I do so much desire. Indwelling Master, I have faith in Thee and I leave this request trusting that Thou wilt reveal to me the perfect way.

Anna L. Palmer, published in *Divine Science Monthly*, June 1933, p. 58. Copyrighted material reprinted with permission of Divine Science Federation International.

May 26

GOD

God is both within and without us. He is the source of all life; creator of universe behind universe; and of unimaginable depths of inter-stellar space and of light-years without end. But He is also the indwelling life of our own little selves. And just as the whole world full of electricity will not light a house unless the house itself is prepared to receive that electricity, so the infinite and eternal life of God cannot help us unless we are prepared to receive that life within ourselves. *Only the amount of God we can get in us will work for us.*

"*The kingdom of God is within you,*" said Jesus. And it is the indwelling light, the secret place of the consciousness of the Most High that is the kingdom of Heaven in its present manifestation on this earth. Learning to live in the kingdom of Heaven is learning to turn on the light of God within.

We must learn that God is not an unreasonable and impulsive sovereign who breaks His own laws at will. As soon as we learn that God does things *through* us (not *for* us), the matter becomes as simple as breathing, as inevitable as sunrise.

Agnes Sanford, *The Healing Light*, 1947, p. 19. No known copyright in effect.

May 27

WISDOM

When a person is faced with vital issues, when he is reduced to his own loneliness and failure, then only will he see that the wisdom and judgment of God alone can save the day, and then only is he likely to become very meek and humble and seek earnestly for the inner light....

Every soul has free access to the source of wisdom within. As we approach the divine source of wisdom and begin to realize our oneness with it, we find that we are evolving a higher intelligence than that of intellect alone and that we are moving toward a greater science, the science of intuition and wisdom working through the mind. We find ourselves touched and moved by the more primal energies and principles of Being. These may be called pure ideas, and such ideas express themselves through the mind in the form of clear words and thoughts. Divine wisdom, Divine judgment, has in itself the essence of profound goodness. When we really live in deep relation to Divine wisdom, we shall have much greater power to combine words and actions effectively and so manifest greater wholeness and perfection in mind and body.

In all wisdom man must consciously control and work with his body. In fact he must not only consciously but also subconsciously be in command of his body. This ability is attained through continuous care and wise development of the twelve spiritual faculties.

Cora Dedrick Fillmore, *Christ Enthroned in Man*, 1937, pp. 33, 35-36.
Copyrighted material reprinted with permission of Unity, Unity.org.

May 28

MYSTICISM

To be a mystic is simply to participate here and now in that real and eternal life; in the fullest, deepest sense which is possible to man. It is to share, as a free and conscious agent – not a servant, but a son – in the joyous travail of the Universe: its mighty onward sweep through pain and glory toward its home in God. This gift of "sonship," this power of free cooperation in the world process, is man's greatest honor. The ordered sequence of states, the organic development, whereby his consciousness is detached from illusion and rises to the mystic freedom which conditions, instead of being conditioned by, its normal world, is the way he must tread if that sonship is to be realized. Only by this fostering of his deeper self, this transmutation of the elements of his character, can he reach those levels of consciousness upon which he hears, and responds to, the measure "whereto the worlds keep time" on their great pilgrimage toward the Father's heart. The mystic act of union, that joyous loss of the transfigured self in God, which is the crown of man's conscious ascent towards the Absolute, is the contribution of the individual to this, the destiny of the Cosmos.

Evelyn Underhill, *Mysticism*, 1955, p. 447. No known copyright in effect.

May 29

SPRING - SUMMER DROPS OF GOLD

* Be constant in friendship, faithful in marriage, diligent in business. Resist your temptation to inconstancy. Bear these words in mind: *"I am the Lord, I change not."*

* Keep steady courage. Be cheerful in principle. There is no credit to you for smiling when there is plenty to smile at – no; smile in spite of fate. So you will be great and beloved. This is your life text: *"The Lord God will help me; therefore have I set my face like a flint."*

* You may do faithfully each day what belongs to you whether you like it or not, for it is the only way you can earn the fruit of your life. Be cheerful by determining to be cheerful. This is labor that conquers. Keep this motto: *"Blessed is he that waiteth."*

* There is a lovely talent hiding within your nature. Let it shine forth by spreading abroad this word continually: *"God is my Light and my inspiration."*

* There is a Christ way of healing the sick which you can learn very readily because you heart is kind and tender. These words spoken by you will accomplish much: *"I love all the world."*

* There is a quality about you that will make you successful without anxiety. Therefore, "trust in the Lord and…verily thou shalt be fed." Keep this word: *"In righteousness shall thou be established."*

* Who is that one who wins your heart? Trust in that one as guided by the love of righteousness 'til there is absolute safety in all the friendship – all the confidence. This is your life text: *"God, thy God, has anointed thee with the oil of gladness."*

* You are strong in Spirit. You are bold in Truth. You are great in Goodness. Demonstrate all this by believing this: *"Jesus Christ is my friend."*

Emma Curtis Hopkins, (1891), *Drops of Gold*, 1970, pp. 35-36, 39-40, 47, 53. No known copyright in effect.

May 30

SKEPTICISM

There are many persons who are in the state of wanting to believe but who cannot entirely eliminate old doubts. The lifelong habit of believing only in the evidence of the senses makes it difficult for them to believe anything invisible or intangible. And they cannot see or touch God. Neither can they see or touch electricity; but they feel free to use and trust its power, because they have found that it works.

If they would only start with trust in God, they could prove His power and make it work as surely and effectively as they make electricity work. But to use electricity they must turn it on by pushing a button or flipping a dial – by connecting the current with a physical instrument designed to conduct it, such a light bulb, a vacuum cleaner, or a radio.

The same is true with the power of God. We must connect ourselves with Him if we would bring His Spirit into active manifestation within our lives. Those who have had enough faith to make the initial effort, even so some unbelief is lodged in their minds, have had demonstrations that *God is;* and in thousands of cases, whole lives have been changed by faith. Faith is the switch that releases God's power and makes it ever available for our use.

Clara Beranger, *Peace Begins At Home*, 1954, p. 38. Copyrighted material reprinted with permission of Unity, Unity.org.

May 31

PURE POTENTIALITY

There is something within every person that is absolutely unlimited – a part of us that is never bound. That is the Real Self, our divinity, our spiritual wholeness. What we are and what we can do is beyond human comprehension. There are no limits to our creativity. Our consciousness is ever expanding, which means that our ability to be creative can never stop. What mind can conceive, and believe possible, it can achieve.

Each of us in on a path of self-discovery. Although some are not as yet aware of this, all are seeking to release themselves for greater self-expression and creativity. The part of us that is absolutely unlimited can never run out of ideas for expression. The Real Self or Spirit is all complete and always perfect. The power within us is greater than we understand, yet it is ready for our use and direction.

By expanding our consciousness of Self we can draw upon this power for infinite creative expression. There are no limits to possibilities but each of us must claim these for greater creative expression.

Deepak Chopra wrote: "Pure consciousness is pure potentiality, it is the field of all possibilities, it is infinite creativity." We should realize that we are all a part of this potential, which needs us for Its expression.

Marian G. Moon, *Lessons of Truth*, 2012, p. 9. Reprinted with permission of her family.

JUNE

June 1

THAT SECRET PLACE

*He that dwelleth in the secret place of the most High
shall abide under the shadow of the Almighty.*
Psalm 91:1

What is that secret place and how shall we attain unto it? I believe that it is that deep, satisfying, confident feeling that we are attuned to God, trusting Him, and relying on His protection, love, and guidance. This is not an intellectual attainment; it is an inner awareness of peace and trust which defies definition but is the most real experience anyone can have. When it has been reached, there is no doubt in the mind of the person who experiences it, even if he cannot put it into words. Thought beyond explanation, it is precious and enduring to all who have attained it.

How are we to gain this experience? Possibly in as many ways as there are persons seeking it, but always plain to the earnest seeker even though no one else may find it in the same way. It is the result of the surrender of the little self to the divine will – a letting go of anything that would hinder the full blessing of the God-Presence in one's heart and life. It is thinking, feeling, saying, and acting "Thy will be done."

And the reward? We shall consciously live in a realm of *knowing* that we are safe, led, provided for and kept from wrong actions and wrong results. It is the conviction that enables us to say with Jesus, "The Father and I are one." It is security; it is peace, power, and happiness; it is success in the work of helping establish the kingdom of God on earth.

Father, I would attain to this security, peace, and power today, as I seek to become constantly aware of Thy Presence.

Annie S. Greenwood, published in *Aspire*, March 1954, p. 30. Copyrighted material reprinted with permission of Divine Science Federation International.

June 2

SEEK AND YE SHALL FIND

Asking, searching, knocking are for one purpose only: that man may awaken to his divine potentialities and bring these realities into daily expression, thereby broadening and deepening his life in inner consciousness and outer activity.

There is no joy in life that is comparable to that awakening of man to his inner self. A new heaven and a new earth indeed appear to him; he becomes aware of inner planes of life of which he has hitherto been unaware; those ideas that have been difficult to comprehend now are clear; all that is fine and beautiful in his life, in his world is accentuated; he sees new beauty in his fellow man; a keener appreciation of the majesty and power of the world comes to him and he rises into a new consciousness that love rules the universe, himself included.

And still he asks, searches and knocks! For he knows the limitlessness of the Infinite and always It seems to beckon him onward, he is to search and find even more of the treasures of life. He knows they are for him.

Caroline Munz, published in *Divine Science Monthly*, February 1932, p. 42. Copyrighted material reprinted with permission of Divine Science Federation International.

June 3

HER FINAL LESSON

We are told clearly in Matthew 4:4, "Man shall live not by bread alone, but by every word that proceedeth from the mouth of God." What suddenly swept over me was our bumbling human interpretation of those clear directions. The true staff of life is not some concoction of wheat and water and corn meal, but the living word of God that directs our souls to our own infinite provision, and divine nature. Didn't Moses say "The word is very nigh thee, even in thy mouth"?

The word of God is the creative word that supplies our every need. Far more basic than bread -- but likened unto that commodity because even the most deprived and doltish among us knows that without some sustenance life on this plane ceases. But oh, my dears, the Bible is an allegory -- look how long it's taken for the lit bulb to go on in <u>my</u> head, and I have given these subjects thirty-two years of study and contemplation as an adult!

The "word of God" sealed in our soul and listened for, and obeyed, will meet our every need and then some! Bread, because it is a universal need, was the nearest ancient equivalent available everywhere to sustain life. So also is a constant awareness of the Presence and Availability of our God; and even more essential. The word of God enthroned in the soul of man or woman, becomes a channel -- direct to the All Good, or fountain of God's gifts filling our lives.

Marguerite Lewis, from her final undelivered lesson, New Thought Spiritual Center of Eastern Long Island, March 2, 2008. Printed with permission.

June 4

IN THE NAME OF JESUS CHRIST

"Whatever ye shall ask in my name, that will I do."

Jesus Christ expresses God. The name of Jesus Christ contains the nature of Jesus Christ. When we ask in His name, Jesus Christ does for us that which is in His name…

Life is in Jesus Christ. The life in Him is God's life. If we ask life of Jesus Christ, He will give it to us, even the more abundant life which He expressed in Galilee, and which He now expresses in those who ask life through Him – His name.

The peace which passes understanding is in Jesus Christ. If we ask Him to give us peace, as it is contained in His name He will give it to us.

Joy is in Jesus Christ. If in His name we ask for joy, He will give us the joy that no man can take from us.

In Jesus Christ are health, understanding, supply, love. If we ask in His name, for any or all of these, He will give them to us.

If we ask him for a revelation of the treasures hidden in His name, He will give us that.

If we ask in His name to be taut how to ask, He will give us the knowledge that we seek.

"Lord Jesus Christ, expresser of our Father's goodness, in Thy name we ask Thee to make known to us the nature of Thy name, that throu it we may become like Thee. Amen."

Imelda Octavia Shanklin, *In the Name of Jesus Christ,* Unity pamphlet, 1962, pp. 1, 3. Copyrighted material reprinted with permission of Unity, Unity.org.

June 5

MEDITATION OF A PROSPERED CONSCIOUSNESS

I praise Thee and give thanks, O Giver of gifts, for the inner realization of Thine omnipresence, for the consciousness of Thine omnipotence and Thine omniscience. I thank Thee for the measure of Thine abundance now poured out upon me. I rejoice in an outer sign of an inner covenant of faith between Thee and me. Thou hast fulfilled the covenant and made me exceedingly fruitful; Thou hast multiplied the good on my path until all sorrow and sighing have flown away, and I have entered into the place of everlasting gladness.

As I walk and talk with Thee in the garden of my soul, I am released from all thought of labor, for Thou hast given me the power to speak of Thine invisible substance so that it takes form from my spoken word. Everything and everybody in my world is enriched because of my companionship with Thee, and every act of my life has become a joyous service of love to Thee and to my fellow man.

Throughout eternity I shall be Thine and Thou shalt be mine. For my ever-increasing consciousness of the Christ presence, leading me into fuller and higher expressions of His perfection, I give thanks, my Father-Mother God. In this inner richness I abide, in this glory I truly live.

Frances W. Foulks, *The Prospered Consciousness,* undated Unity pamphlet, pp. 2-3. Copyrighted material reprinted with permission of Unity, Unity.org.

June 6

OMNIPRESENCE

Always with me! I can never stray beyond His tender care,
For our God is omnipresent, Here and there and everywhere…

Always with me! Love so tender, Feels each trembling breath of prayer,
For our God is ever listening, and His love is everywhere…

Always with me! In His treasures, Free, abundant, I may share,
For He holds them ever ready, For His children everywhere…

Always with me! Every burden, His strong arm will help me bear,
For our God is omnipresent, With his children everywhere…

Refrain:
Yes, everywhere, and everywhere, Here and there and everywhere.

Clara H. Scott (1895), published in *Divine Science Church School Hymnal*, 1925, Hymn 1; and *Unity Song Selections*, 1947, Hymn 190. Copyrighted material reprinted with permission of Divine Science Federation International and Unity, Unity.org.

June 7

MEDITATION

Whenever you stand praying, forgive, if you have anything against anyone; so that your Father in heaven may also forgive you your trespasses.
Mark 11:25

Father-Mother God, thank you for revealing to me the power of forgiveness. I have not always understood it, but I see now that forgiveness is the key to living a healthy, happy and prosperous life. My elder brother and way shower Jesus demonstrated that forgiveness gave him mastery, authority and dominion in the face of seemingly insurmountable odds. He told me that I could do the same. So I choose, right now, so I release those right now that I bound to me by my refusal to forgive. I rejoice in the knowledge that forgiving them releases me; releases me to move on to bigger and better experiences. I forgive myself and I release me from the bondage of guilt. Your grace allows me to begin again. I can no longer afford to stand in the way of the greatness You have prepared for me. I forgive and I am free. Thank you, Father-Mother God for the liberating power of forgiveness. And so it is.

Mary A. Tumpkin, *Before You Pray – Forgive*, p. 29. Copyright 2005 by Mary Tumpkin Presentations. Reprinted with permission of the estate of Mary A. Tumpkin.

June 8

SUCCESS

Let those who will, believe the old world Law
  That men were born to suffer length on length.
It is a lie! The God within us speaks;
  We lift our thoughts and feel a new-born strength.

Our human life is part of a Great Whole
  All life was given to use for truth and right
Each man may claim the freedom of his soul
  He is a King, and rules with power and might.

We are the lords of all this lower world;
  We make the laws by which our life has might;
And as the thoughts of freedom forth are hurled,
  We build a world of peace and truth and right.

Oh, man! A kingdom is within your soul!
  A king enthroned with sceptre in his hand!
Why slumber on in grief and tears untold?
  Awake! God calls you; rise and understand!

Julia Seton Sears, *The Science of Success*, 1914. No known copyright in effect.

June 9

BIBLE STUDY

Bible study will never cease to be vital to those who desire to reach spiritual heights of attainment and accomplishment. We awaken on a spiritual staircase that we seem to have climbed. This is the stairway the race has climbed and we inherit the fruits of their labor. There are yet stairs above us reaching into infinity. We are the surer of our present position and the better equipped for the journey ahead if the essential steps below us are firmly imbedded in our consciousness. History has a fashion of repeating itself and in the light shed by past attainment, our decisions are the wiser and surer.

Agnes M. Lawson, *Hints to Bible Study*, 1920, p. 7. Copyrighted material reprinted with permission of Divine Science Federation International.

June 10

WE ARE LIFE

We are living in life, we are moving in life, we are life, and this is the Truth that Jesus Christ practiced, the Truth Christ presented to us, so those who understood His teaching said. Now is the accepted time, and today is the day of salvation; here and now is the accepted time, and today is the day of salvation; here and now is the accepted time for healing, for health, for prosperity, for wholeness, for the enjoyment of our good; now is the accepted time, because there is no other time. You never lived one moment in the past, you never lived one moment in the future, everything you have accomplished in your life was accomplished in the present and what you will accomplish will be accomplished in the present. You cannot do anything ahead, or in the past. Then, let us make more of the now for it never ends; the past holds nothing from us, and is not dominating us and the future holds nothing from us; all is now. And why did Jesus Christ heal the body, instead of saying kill out its nature? Simply because it was God's will that we should be healthy and maintain it in Truth. So He sent His disciples out to heal the sick, and say the kingdom of heaven is at hand. They were to preface everything with the kingdom of heaven at hand; they were to heal the sick and raise the dead.

Why? Because the kingdom of heaven is always at hand. They were not to go out and teach people to go somewhere to get to heaven, or to go away at all; but to enter the enjoyment of it here and now. It is within you, it is at hand. It is here. Why? God is here, heaven is here and the earth if here, all good is here, and when we say this, we mean all good is at hand.

Malinda Elliott Cramer, (1905), published in *The Christology Connection*, (Mercer), 2015, p. 41.

June 11

TRUST

Leave the future to our Father,
Trust Him still to care for thee;
Living bravely in the present,
As He gives thee light to see.

Refrain:
All thy days are in His keeping,
Be they dark or be they fair,
And He watches, never sleeping,
Holds thee in His tender care.

Take thy life as He may give it,
For He knoweth what is best;
Every day shall show thee duty,
Every night gives sweetest rest.
Refrain

He will teach thee all thou needest,
Guidance give from day to day;
In the sunshine or the shadows,
Look to Him, for He's the way.
Refrain

Florence Scripps Kellogg, published in *Hymns for the People*, 1912, Hymn 104. Tune: "What a Friend We Have in Jesus." No known copyright in effect.

June 12

SOMETHING IS WORKING FOR YOU

Now know I that the Lord will do me good.
Judges 17:13

When we accept unwaveringly the "Nowness" of eternity, we do not look upon today as a cross to bear, but as a bridge to cross. Life is difficult for all of us at times, but as we seek divine guidance, our way becomes known to us. We must talk things over with God. Something behind what we see with our physical eyes is ever working for our eternal good. To this Something we should give our full attention. Unless we are aware of this prevailing good, we live a life without Christ.

Life, like a dome of many-colored glass, Stains the white radiance of eternity.
— Shelley

We choose our own life colors. When we fail to recognize the invisible beyond appearances, we stain the white radiance of eternity. Today, the Eternal Now is our chance to achieve an awareness of an ever-present God, working quietly through us and with our best interest at heart always. If we truly believe this, we will become less distracted by the distortions of what appears to be. We shall know that there is a solution in the making. Our problems will no longer be insurmountable barriers, but stepping stones to a fuller realization of the Omnipresence.
Father, may I ever know that there is a Genius at work in my life. Amen.

F. Bernadette Turner, published in *Aspire*, August 1975, p. 27. Copyrighted material reprinted with permission of Divine Science Federation International.

June 13

TOLERANCE

To judge is to be dishonest, for to judge is to assume a position you do not have. Judgment without self-deception is impossible. Judgment implies that you have been deceived in your brothers. How, then, could you not have been deceived in yourself? Judgment implies a lack of trust, and trust remains the bedrock of the teacher of God's whole thought system. Let this be lost, and all his learning goes. Without judgment are all things equally acceptable, for who could judge otherwise? Without judgment are all men brothers, for who is there who stands apart? Judgment destroys honesty and shatters trust. No teacher of God can judge and hope to learn.

Helen Schucman, *A Course In Miracles*, 1975, Manual For Teachers, p.11. No known copyright in effect.

June 14

GOD MAKES MY DAY GLORIOUS

God is my strength and power: and he maketh my way perfect.
II Samuel 22:33

I begin this new day by praising and thanking God for the lavish, ever-flowing stream of abundance which ceaselessly pours out to me and to my loved ones, and to all human beings who are receptive to it. There is plenty for all, more than enough for everyone. The Infinite never withholds Its good. I give thanks for my good which is flowing to me from every direction.

I affirm with thanksgiving that the pure, radiant life of God is permeating every atom of my physical body, filling every cell, every tissue, nerve, gland, and organ with health and gladness. The joy of God reenergizes and revitalizes my mind and my body.

I affirm with praise and thanksgiving that Infinite Wisdom is guiding me today. I make wise choices, right decisions, and arrive at the correct solution of knotty problems, because I lay aside my prejudices and preconceived human opinions, and let the light of Truth illumine my way. Divine Love sustains me, invigorates me and guides me.

Claudine Whitaker, published in *Creative Thought* for February 6, 1965.
Copyrighted material reprinted with permission of SOM Publishing.

June 15

ALPHABET OF PRINCIPLES

Absolute and Self-Existent Cause --
Becoming manifest in Creation --
Continually expressing through Man --
Dwelling in each Soul --
Emulating the Christ Spirit.
Faith recognizing Truth --
Gains Wisdom and Understanding.
Heaven the Kingdom of God within --
Inspiring and All Powerful --
Judiciously supplying every human need --
Kindly providing for every desire.
Love operating thru Universal Mind --
Master and Man in Conscious Unity.
New Thought regarding Age Old Ideas --
Outcome of common sense --
Persistently seeking illumination --
Quietly determined to know the Law --
Real, Creative, Indestructible, Eternal --
Speaking through every living thing.
Truth the revelator of God --
Utilizing every avenue, surging for expression --
Visible In All and Through All --
Waiting to be recognized --
Xylographed on the Face of Nature --
Yours for the asking --
Zealous to operate at your Constructive Command.

Hazel Foster Holmes, *Religious Science Monthly*, January 1929, p. 2.
Copyrighted material reprinted with permission of SOM Publishing.

June 16

FORGIVE AND YE SHALL BE FORGIVEN

Take heed to yourselves: if thy brother sin, rebuke him; and if he repent, forgive him. And if he sin against you seven times in the day, and seven times turns again to thee saying, I repent; thou shalt forgive him.
Luke 17:3-4

All evil must be forgotten, whether it be in you or your brother. To hold perpetually in remembrance your brother's faults and sins is to create an imperfect, distorted pattern from which you will be fashioned.

Release, and ye shall be released.
Luke 6:37

Thoughts of evil weigh us down and make our only burdens. Man changes so rapidly in body and mind as to be totally incapable of doing today the wrong which he did yesterday. He is a different person and should not be judged by his past.

Nora Smith Holm, *The Runner's Bible*, 1913, pp. 82-83. No known copyright in effect.

June 17

OCEAN OF SPIRIT

We live in an ocean of Spirit. It is formless, limitless, undifferentiated, impersonal, intelligence, power, life and substance. It is differentiated only by "the word," which is often in terms of limitation.

Who thinks except Man? What does he think into except this Spirit Substance?

This substance is so volatile, so vital, so responsive that It is taking shape continuously, not because It has specific plans, of Itself, but because of Its inherent responsiveness. This responsiveness is what we know as life or livingness which takes form according to the determining factor, which is Man.

The God-idea of Man is Christ. And every human being is a representation of Christ, just as every grain of wheat is a representation of the God-idea of wheat, or every rose is a replica of the Principle of rose.

Man, the one determinant, must exercise his birthright. He is also choosing, deciding, measuring, limiting the Universal Substance. His "man-ness" is his "author"-ity, authority.

Spirit does not limit him, Spirit does not determine what his experience is to be, Spirit does not hand out conditions. It cannot, because It is unlimited, impersonal.

Awake to the responsibility of this stage of unfoldment. Think strength, and you will realize strength. Think opulence and you will know supply. Speak your word of good and know that it will be fulfilled. Maintain that word until it comes into form.

Study: Hebrews 2:3-8, Psalm 8:4-9

Ruth B. Smith, published in *Divine Science Monthly*, February 1933, p. 13. Copyrighted material reprinted with permission of Divine Science Federation International.

June 18

MEDITATIONS FOR WEDNESDAY NIGHT CLASSES

TRANSCENDING NEGATIVE EMOTIONS

I trust God's universe. I know there is nothing in my tangible or intangible world that exists without value and purpose. Therefore, I know my every feeling has value. Anytime I feel a low-frequency, depressed or hurtful feeling I stop and in that instant I turn inward to discover the root of that feeling. Simultaneously, I ask for the learning behind that feeling to be revealed, and then I let it go before it mounts into anger, resentment, blame, guilt, or any other negative emotion. I remind myself there is something spiritually profound at work for my growth and peaceful evolution, and I trust the universe to reveal it to me. I give thanks for my ability to thus transcend negative pitfalls and to grow through wisdom.

RESPONSIBLE CHOICE

I have the power through responsible choice to accelerate my own evolution and to make my pathway to wholeness a joyous journey. I follow my feelings to become aware of the conflicting parts of myself. I look honestly, openly, and with courage into the dynamics behind what I feel. I let go of the demands of my personality that conflict with the needs of my soul. I let go of any idea that conditions have any power over me. I take into account the consequences of each and every choice and then choose to act through the wisdom of my soul. This is the conscious road to a life of wholeness.

TRANSCENDING GUILT AND SHAME

Knowing that all of life is the out-picturing of consciousness, I have come to know that when I have felt guilt, I have done something that dishonored the boundaries of another's consciousness and risked personal hurt. I further realize that when I have felt shame, I have allowed another to penetrate the boundaries of my consciousness and I have felt diminished. I now honor the boundaries of each individual consciousness and take full responsibility for my own. I see guilt and shame as products of experience and not the Truth of me. I give thanks that in this expanded awareness, I can now transcend the effect of guilt and shame in my life -- now and forevermore.

Doris Jones, from her collected works. Reprinted with permission of her family.

June 19

MAKING HEAVEN HAPPEN

I'm going to share with you some tools to help make heaven happen in your lives. Now for those of you who already are enjoying the good life, so be it. Good. But, I'm going to ask that you share of all that you have with others that need it. Reach out and take them by the hand and lead them to where they would like to be.

I want you to know that Your God and my God are not the same God. Your heaven and my heaven are not the same heaven. One man's medicine is another man's poison. We are so unique. We are so different. We know that we are One; but out of that One came the many of us and each one of us is unique. Let's choose our heaven for ourselves. For some people heaven is living on a yacht. There are some people who are living in the mountains, overlooking the ocean. There are some living down there at the ocean looking up. That's what heaven is.

My formula is this: Make a Decision. Make a choice. Decide what you really want in life. Until you know, God doesn't know. And after you decide what you want, I want you to become that thing that you want. How do we do that?

If we are looking for prosperity, I want you to think, act and speak prosperity. I want you to hang with prosperous people. I want you to associate with like-minded people. I want you to act as if you already are and that you already have it. Now maybe you think that's easy. It's simple but it's not easy because you have to reprogram all of those old subjective negatives into that which is right and good. Then after you choose what it is that you want, then you take that which you have chosen and work toward that thing.

We have to work as if everything depended on man and pray is if everything depended on God.

Juanita Bryant-Dunn, from *The Voices of Guidance 43rd Anniversary Tribute*, 2010. Transcribed and printed with permission of Guidance Center for Spiritual Living, Los Angeles, California.

June 20

I AM AN IRRESISTIBLE MAGNET

I am an irresistible magnet, with the power to attract unto myself everything that I divinely desire, according to the thoughts, feelings and mental pictures I constantly entertain and radiate. I *am* the center of my Universe. I have the power to create whatever I wish. I attract whatever I radiate. I attract whatever I mentally choose and accept. I begin choosing and mentally accepting the highest and best in life. I now choose to accept health, success, and happiness. I now choose lavish abundance for myself and for all mankind. This is a rich friendly Universe and I dare to accept its riches and hospitality now!

Vetura Papke, published in *Angel in Residence,* (Neuwirth), Copyright SOM Publishing, 1995, p. 91. Reprinted with permission of SOM Publishing.

June 21

BLESSING THE HOME

Fill your home with blessing. Remove every suggestion of discontent. If there is a room that savors of selfishness or impurity or deadness in its mental atmosphere, heal it. You can do this by spending in it each day a half hour of silence in which you meditate upon the omnipresence of heaven, declaring that some special expression of heaven centers there.

The richness of your spirit must enter the place where you reside and permeate it, even thou it be a cellar or hall bedroom. The ease and comfort of a rich consciousness must radiate from your personality. For riches draw riches, and prosperity gravitates to the things and the people that are like it, especially when backed by principle. There are people who look prosperous and who yet are undermining themselves by a false state of mind; and there are people who look prosperous, and they are missing some of the good things that belong to them.

The kingdom of heaven appears when there is perfect harmony and unity between the without and the within.

Annie Rix Militz, *Both Riches and Honor*, 1945, pp. 96-97. Copyrighted material reprinted with permission of Unity, Unity.org.

June 22

TRANSLATION

I am
A translator for God
In all I do each day.

His love I translate into friendliness,
Into a smile, a greeting, a selfless service,
Into warmth and appreciation for those I meet.

His wisdom I translate into wise decision,
Into thought and word acceptable to Him,
Into harmony in every circumstance of life.

His abundance I translate into willing tithes;
I give to Him the tithes of time and talent,
And of service too as well as substance.

I translate His abundance also in joyous use
Of all that I possess, giving thanks always.

His strength I translate into perfect health,
Into energy for work and play and relaxation.

Daily I check my translation with God,
Going back to the Source in prayer communication.
Oh, I am glad that
I am a translator for God!

Elizabeth Searle Lamb, published in *Aspire,* February 1963, p. 12. Copyrighted material reprinted with permission Divine Science Federation International.

June 23

WHATEVER THE PROBLEM

Whatever the problem, God is the answer. He comes forth for us accordingly as we learn to turn to Him in trust; trusting Him rather than the sorry circumstances that seem to enmesh us. Trust Him ceaselessly! We can be released and divinely aided. We can be lifted up into the realm where we know we are secure because we are under divine dominion.

God is the answer. Thank Him. He frees us from human angers, suspicions, unruly emotions and impulses, doubts, contentiousness, the sense of human danger and pain. He fortifies, strengthens, and heals us; He provides for our every need.

Dana Gatlin, *God Is The Answer*, 1939, p. 11. Copyrighted material reprinted with permission of Unity, Unity.org.

June 24

NO GOOD THING SHALL BE WITHHELD

The supply for every want awaits the demand. Then it comes to you, possibly, from a source you least expected. The demand is the knock at the door. Faith is the secret key that unlocks the door, takes hold of the thinking hoped for, and delivers it to you, bringing into evidence the thing not seen. The desire in the heart for all good things is God tapping at the door of your soul-consciousness with His Infinite supply – a supply that is ever useless, unless there is a personal demand for it. "Before they call I will answer," saith the Lord. Oh wonderful mystery of life! Surely it is the paradigm of all the glory and splendor of the world's redemption, administered to each person.

Agnes J. Galer, published in *The TRUTH*, (ed. Grier with F. Holmes and E. Holmes), June 1918, p. 10. No known copyright in effect.

June 25

JESUS' REVERENCE

Jesus' reverence for the scriptures of his people was always apparent in his teaching, they formed the source of his inspired faith in God and man. With his understanding, born of deep study and faithful living, the spirit of Truth was revealed to him, and by virtue of his integrity to the truth he had discovered, fulfilled not only prophesy, but the complete work of a spiritual messiah. All through his career he displayed a sense of proportion, a spiritual efficiency unequalled among men of all time. He was both wise man and prophet, but greater than either, he in every way surpassed every law-giver, seer, sage and prophet, because *He* spoke for all generations, past, present and future.

Ada B. Fay, *The Evolution of the Ten Commandments*, 1937, p. 95. No known copyright in effect.

June 26

AFFIRMATIONS

Every particle of my body glows with the radiant Healing Light of the Christ.

I become transformed by the lifting of my mind into the level of the Spirit of the Christ.

The wisdom of God dwells in me and through me – now and always.

No matter what the outer picture is, my faith is strong and centered in God, my Creator.

There is no problem or inharmony that will not yield to the power of God's great love.

Prayer keeps me tuned to the order, rhythm, and harmony of living.

God is Love. I am that which God is. Therefore I am Love.

I turn to the quiet center within myself so that I can always maintain a balance in my life.

I do not meddle in the affairs of others, but express my love in thoughts and deeds of kindness.

In God there is a perfect solution to every problem.

The realization that God works in and through me gives me faith in myself and in my abilities.

Grace L. Faus, *For So It Is*, 1971, pp. 1-12. Copyrighted material reprinted with permission of Divine Science Federation International.

June 27

WHAT IS TREATMENT?

What is treatment and what will it accomplish? Treatment is a definite and specific science, it is convincing our thought until it no longer doubts that we are free and divine. It will accomplish results equal to the conviction, always.

We treat until the desired experience is brought about, until we have built up on the subjective, creative side, a tendency which is stronger than the previous state of our thought.

We choose the kind of an experience we wish, but we leave all the particulars for its working out up to an Intelligence which sees the whole picture and so can work it out intelligently. We do not suggest things to people. We do not compel people in our treatment. We leave everyone out of our treatment but ourselves, knowing that that which will benefit us must benefit all and hurt none.

We do not deny facts and experiences, but we do say that man is greater than all experience. Facts are facts, but there is a transcendent truth about man and that is what we affirm in our own words until our thought believes it and we demonstrate that greater belief in our divinity in some specific form or experience.

Josephine Holmes Curtis, *Religious Science Monthly*, September 1934, p. 62. Copyrighted material reprinted with permission of SOM Publishing.

June 28

HEALING AS RELEASE FROM FEAR

Healing is a not a miracle....All healing is essentially the release from fear...

A major step in the Atonement plan is to undo error at all levels. Sickness or 'not-right-mindedness' is the result of level confusion, because it always entails the belief that what is amiss on one level can adversely affect another. We have referred to miracles as the means of correcting level confusion, for all mistakes must be corrected at the level on which they occur...the body cannot create-and the belief that it can, a fundamental error, produces all physical symptoms...

Only the mind can create because spirit has already been created, and the body is a learning device for the mind. Learning devices are not lessons in themselves. Their purpose is merely to facilitate learning...the body is merely part of your experience in the physical world....

The value of the Atonement does not lie in the manner in which it is expressed. In fact, if it is used truly, it will inevitably be expressed in whatever way is most helpful to the receiver. This means that a miracle, to attain its full efficacy, must be expressed in a language that the recipient can understand without fear. This does not necessarily mean that this is the highest level of communication of which he is capable. It does mean, however, that it is the highest level of communication of which he is capable now. The whole aim of the miracle is to raise the level of communication, not to lower it by increasing fear.

Helen Schucman, *A Course In Miracles*, 1975, Text, pp. 19-21. No known copyright in effect.

June 29

LISTEN AND SPEAK THE WORD OF GOD

WATCHWORD -- I resolve to listen and speak the word my Father gives unto me.

"He that is of God heareth God's words."

Jesus emphasized the truth of his divine origin and nature, but all that he claimed for himself, he claimed for us, the children of God. He said to those who believe in him, "if you continue in my word then are you my disciples indeed."

All who love the Truth believe on him, the Christ within, and throu the knowledge that we are born of God, we can hear and speak the healing words of God.

These words are Life, Health, Joy, Peace and Power, every so called "word" stands for a message of Truth, hence when we "Speak the Word" for another we mean that we are declaring his true and eternal state of Being as the direct expression of God. According to the realization and acceptance of this word is its healing power made manifest.

Throu lowly and earnest listening we receive from the Father the exact word that is needed in each particular problem and the result, even though the expression of the Law often seems marvelous to others.

Daisy Baum, *Individual Responsibility*, 1918, p. 25. Copyrighted material reprinted with permission of Divine Science Federation International.

June 30

EVERYDAY AFFIRMATIONS

Here are a few common affirmations you may want to adopt for your daily spiritual practice. You can use them often without any disruption of your regular activities. You can say them silently or – if you are alone – say them out loud. In these days of electronic equipment, no one will notice when you talk to yourself as you are walking or driving. Be sure and watch the road.

Thank God I am rich.
My health is excellent.
I have a wonderful memory.
I am a straight "A" student.
I have a wonderful lover who cares for me.
I am healthy, wealthy and wise.
My perfect mind and my perfect body work together for my perfect good.
Life is fun.
I am beautiful.
I am handsome.
I am happy.
I love life and life loves me.
I receive money from many sources including surprises.
I am a money magnet. Money comes to me easily.

The beauty of affirmations is that they are so short you can use them anywhere. You can also stick them on your bathroom mirror, your refrigerator door, or anywhere you frequent.

One key to using affirmations effectively is to use them often. However, if you do not get the results you wish within a few weeks, you might want to consult your teacher or practitioner for more ideas about how to do the spiritual work. Long standing beliefs can be pesky. Please remember that your true aim is to change your thinking and beliefs about whatever goals you choose. Conscious, direct spiritual work is very powerful.

Jane Claypool, posted in her blog, July 29, 2014. Reprinted with permission.

JULY

July 1

FOR HIGH NOON

Because of what I am in being, I stand upright before God. Above me is the sun of righteousness; materiality is under my feet. I cast no shadow that can alarm or deceive me.

The night of sense-consciousness is past and I am awake to the light that can never be extinguished. In its rays matter is transparent to me and I see the soul-world which is molded and peopled by my thought. I know its nature and that it is subject unto me. I am no longer drawn by it but by the attraction of this sun, and I am held upright, for my face is turned toward it, and not toward the ground.

I am poised, and though my feet are upon the ground I have found my wings which have been close-folded so long. I spread them wide and none of the assaults from the soul-world, none of the clamor and strife can overthrow my equilibrium, for they bear me up while the light is on my face.

I see no longer the likeness of my false ideal of man, I see instead the likeness of God. The distorted shadow has faded away and the real man is come into his own. The heavens are opened unto me, I see and I hear that which dwells therein. I know my home and my wings will bear me there.

I hold my hands wide to help those brethren whose wings are not yet unfolded, because they are still weighted with that false consciousness that bows them toward the ground. I desire to help them to stand upright and turn their faces to the same sun, for I know that my home is also their home and that we have one Father....

I am of the Father, I go to the Father. I came down from heaven that I might ascend up to it with my own wings. I read the riddle, there is no mystery, all is light.

Ursula Gestefeld, *The Breath of Life*, 1897, pp. 13-15. No known copyright in effect.

July 2

WHERE IS GOD?

Purpose: To make universality and His immediacy still more vivid to the student and to show that Truth, wherever found, is One.

All flesh shall come to worship before me, saith the Lord. Isaiah 66:23

And they shall not teach every man his neighbor and every man his brother, saying, Know the Lord: for he shall know Me, from the least to the greatest. Hebrews 8:11

Schiller says, "There are three words that I would write in tracings of eternal light upon the hearts of men. And the three words are faith, hope and love; the same that Paul chose for his wonderful discourse."

There is one word that I would write upon the hearts of men – Omnipresence.

Omnipresence! Repeat it to yourself; say it often; get the fullness of its meaning. It can never grow old; it can never become threadbare; it can never wear out. I prefer it to faith, hope and love, because it is greater than these. Omnipresence is beyond hope; it is fulfillment. It is greater than either faith or love, because it includes these and more within itself. Omnipresence, the All-Presence, the Presence that is always present!

This Presence is around us right now, and It is in us; It is around, through, and in all; It fills heaven and earth.

Nona L. Brooks, *Short Lessons in Divine Science*, 1940, p. 17. Copyrighted material reprinted with permission Divine Science Federation International.

July 3

TRAVELER'S PRAYER

I praise thy presence, O God. The joy of thy presence within heals me. The joy of thy companionship within and without makes me glad, through and through.

The air speaks to my ears; it is as Thy whisper. I am filled with joy at the sound of Thy voice.

In the stillness of the night, when the world sleeps, I hear Thy voice again, and I rejoice in Thy steadfastness.

The wildflower smiles at me through the faint warmth of spring. Thy face looks through its face. I laugh at the happiness of Thy approval. When I laugh, I hear the ripple of Thy voice within my own; the sound of it increases my joy.

If I pray upon the mountain peak, Thy words blend with mine. My prayer is established and I exult in heart.

In the stillness I feel Thee moving softly in my soul. Then I keep quiet, that I do not drive Thee into retreat.

When I inhabit the solitudes, Thou art by my side. When I travel the thronged places, Thou art by my side. I am jubilant in Thy company.

The stars light my path by night, the sun by day. Their radiance is the effulgence of Thy countenance, and I sing in the ecstasy of my rapture that Thou art always looking upon me.

At noonday I rest in the shelter of Thy presence. When I walk Thy feet keep step with my feet.

When storms sweep the landscape Thy lightenings show me where to set my foot. The thunders speak thrillingly to me.

Because Thou art my companion the hoarfrosts spread jewels and the dews emblazon rainbows about me.

I go rejoicingly forward, for Thou art my future and my past.

Imelda Octavia Shanklin, *Selected Studies*, 1926, pp.127-128. Copyrighted material reprinted with permission of Unity, Unity.org.

July 4

FREEDOM OF CHRIST

I am free with the freedom of Christ. Through Christ within me I am free from bondage to any person, free from any situation that seems difficult, unhappy or insurmountable. I am free from any condition that has been called incurable or pronounced to correct. I am free from the mirages of lack and failure. No matter how tightly human bonds and human beliefs have held me, I am no longer a prisoner. I declare in faith, "I am free with the freedom of Christ!"

I am unfettered and unbound; I am uplifted and blessed. I am free with the freedom of Christ. I need never run from a situation, avoid responsibility, or struggle to escape appearances, for my release is certain the moment I turn in consciousness to remembrance of the truth that I am a beloved son or daughter of a loving Father. Right where I am now, my freedom exists. Right where I stand now, God stands with me. Right here and right now, my indwelling Christ is the victor and overcomer.

Mary L. Kupferle, *I Am Free*, Unity pamphlet, 1963, pp. 1-2. Copyrighted material reprinted with permission of Unity, Unity.org.

July 5

WILL

WILL and determination are not the same, nor does the ability to repress oneself or others indicate "a strong will."

WILL is the ability to decide; to move directly in line with the decision, to enforce the decision and become possessed of it.

WILL is man's tool with which he determines, seizes upon and struggles toward a selected goal. He longs for Power to enforce his decisions and constantly endeavors to control his own life and others by the means of his decisions.

WILL is God's Power to maintain His own course through eternity. It is His Power to enforce His own decisions. His decisions are always impersonal, untrammeled by individual demands, creative, and successful.

WILL in the mind of God is an idea of decisive action.

WILL in man is the Power to act decisively.

Ella Pomeroy, *Powers of the Soul*, 1948, p. 136. No known copyright in effect.

July 6

GOD IS LIFE

God *is* Life. There is only one life, God-Life. Life is an attribute in Divine Mind.

Life is the animating principle in the creation. It is the creative propelling force. It is the vital, lively essence that animates the whole of creation.

All movement and animation are expressions of the idea of Life in Divine Mind. This Life idea inheres in the omnipresent spiritual Substance, ever ready to come into manifestation according to the thought patterns of man.

God as the principle of orderly good is the life or vitality and activity within the creation.

Divine Life is the vital action of Divine Mind. It is the workable principle; creative activity; the full propelling force. Without life there would be no expression.

All manifest life has its first cause as an idea of life in Divine Mind. The cause is perfect. Any imperfect or evil effects are due to man's mistaken use of the power to think. The character of the manifestation is dependent on the character of the thought and feeling patterns of man. Therefore it behooves us to make a consistent effort to change our thinking, to change our acceptance of unstable appearances to realization of invisible Truth.

Through the ages, man has accepted appearances around him as cause. Ignorance, fears, and lack of reasoning have caused man to build up a mountain of false beliefs that come into form as unhappy formations.

So, we must learn to clear out the false and to build into consciousness acceptance of the divine ideals. Then these ideals will come into form without a struggle, increasing in power as we become established in faith. Spirit fulfills.

Helen Zagat, *Faith and Works*, 1955, pp. 25-27. No known copyright in effect.

July 7

YOU ARE LIFE

Stop thinking of Life as a span of a few short years stretching from the cradle to the grave. God is Life, and you are One with God. Therefore, you, too, are Life, "birthless, and deathless, and changeless." Awaken to the joy of it! Stop contemplating death and live! Feel the thrill of it! Sense the wonder of it! You are one with Eternal Life! The One Life pulsing and throbbing in all Creation! It is all yours and you are One with It! "The mountains shall frisk as lambs and the leaves shall clap their hands for joy." 'Tis life, "Life more Abundant," and you are one with It!

Helen Van Slyke, *Mountain Thoughts*, 1927, p. 5. Reprinted with permission of SOM Publishing.

July 8

GOD'S HELP

No matter what problem of difficulty you are facing today, God's answer is already on its way to you.

In the midst of inharmony or confusion, in the face of fear or grief, remind yourself that God's good, God's answer is already seeking you out.

God's help, which comes to us whenever we need it, may come through a friend, or it may come in the form of a stabilizing thought, a feeling of increased assurance, a renewal of courage, a new surge of life, strength, and joy. We do not always know what the channel for our blessing will be, or its method of reaching us, but we may be sure that the help we need in any given situation will reach us without delay.

God is the giver of all good. His blessings are never withheld but are poured out continually and abundantly upon us and our lives. Our part is to keep ourselves open and receptive to Him, to keep ourselves ready and willing to receive His good.

Mary L. Kupferle, *Help Without Delay*, 1955, p. 3. Copyrighted material reprinted with permission of Unity, Unity.org.

July 9

COURAGE THAT DEFIES FAILURE

"I have the Courage that defies failure."

I am FILLED and thrilled with power, as I keep repeating these words in the SILENCE.

Armies invisible are gathered around me, and I feel I can go forth with strength undreamed of, so strong has grown my consciousness of God.

I know this power is not my own. It is the power that always lived. The power that holds the worlds. The power which, when once permeated, makes the frailest vessels strong.

Of myself I can do nothing, but I remember what Moses said when the voice of God called him through the purifying fires. "Who am I that I should do this deed?"

I feel the voice has called me, yet like Moses of old, I have made the same reply.

But now I remember that Moses, timid, weak and leaning, went forth linked with the great "I AM," and was able to defy failure. Even when pursued by an army, he was able to pass through the waters untouched; able to lead the children of Israel, and make the terrible wilderness endurable, because the Lord of hosts was with him.

Like Moses, I have ever before me the vision of the promised land.

I know I have been placed on this plane with a mission and I shall continue to have faith in my God-given ability, which will lead me through all obstacles to obtain my goal.

Evelyn Whitell, *The Silence*, 1925, pp. 65-66. No known copyright in effect.

July 10

THE REALM OF UNTOLD RICHES WITHIN

The kingdom of God within me is the realm of untold riches.

I release myself from bondage to the rags and tatters of poverty and don the garment of abundance by freeing my thought of fear, of lack, of doubt, of uncertainty.

I am master over conditions and not a slave to them, for I use the power, the intelligence my God has given me.

I place God first, remembering the words of the Master: "Seek ye first the kingdom of God and all these things shall be added."

The Giver of all gifts withholds nothing from them that trust His Love, His Power, His Intelligence.

God gives His Good freely, abundantly, without measure. Why have I a child and heir of God, failed to receive that which my Father has apportioned me? Has God withheld His Good? Has God denied me anything? Is God, the Giver of all Good, responsible for my lack? No! Within myself lies the reason for my failure to receive the gifts of God. Is it fear, indifference, impatience, discouragement, envy, ill will, self-righteousness, insincerity? I earnestly seek to remove the cause for my failure to receive His abundance.

I rely upon Thy inexhaustible storehouse of riches and abundance, O my God, to supply my needs.

Elizabeth Nordman, published in *Divine Science Monthly*, August 1932, p. 37. Copyrighted material reprinted with permission of Divine Science Federation International.

July 11

UNIFICATION WITH GOD

The experience of Oneness with God is known to surpass all other human experience. No other experience is as reliable, potentially present, available or capable of providing wholeness, harmony, and peace. Uniting and remaining united with God as an inner attitude of mind and heart has so much to offer that it is seen as the only true purpose of life. To accomplish this unification while living in the midst of your everyday, practical life, can become a statement of living life to its full capacity.

The journey toward attaining Oneness with God is long and difficult, and setting forth requires complete faith in an indefinable experience which is not guaranteed, except possibly by grace. In spite of the difficulties, religious and philosophical writers continue to aim the practicant towards unification…St. Dimitri of Rostov, a Russian monastic, speaks of "the duty of all Christians – to strive always and in every way to be united with God…because the center and the final purpose of the soul – must be God Himself alone, and nothing else."

Carol Ruth Knox, *The Prayer Of The Heart*, 1992, p. 17. No known copyright in effect.

July 12

PEACE OF GOD

My peace flows deeply –
The rivers of God,
And Glory ascending in the midst,
As fountain sprays of Power.

Thy life moves within the depths,
All mysteries hidden there within the womb of Time.
Ever-moving in majestic Tides,
The Heart-beat of Thy Love.

Universes, stars and systems,
Borne on the crest of Its wave.
Flung forth in the delight of BEING –
The Ecstasy of God.

O Holy Life, O Breath Divine,
Fill this cup upturned to Thee.
Pour the nectar of Thy Love
Out, and over, and through all that lives.

Vida Reed Stone, *Come Now Into Your Freedom*, 1946, p. 79. No known copyright in effect.

July 13

I WILL HELP THEE

With God nothing shall be impossible.
Luke 1:37

If any trouble seems fixed beyond your control, put it into God's hands. If it comes again into your mind, put it back, affirming, *"God will perfect that which concerneth me.* Tremendous power lies back of this truth.

Then shalt thou call and the Lord shall answer; thou shalt cry and He shalt say: Here I am. If thou take away from the midst of thee the yoke, the putting forth of the finger and speaking vanity.
Isaiah 58:9

Nothing can yoke or burden one but one's thoughts – thoughts of hate, of fear, of lust, of greed, of evil in any form. It is better, however, to liken evil thoughts to veils which hide from one's eyes the Truth, the beauty of things which grow in the sunshine of Love. These veils are thick and of ugly color. They distort. Many there are who grope about all their lives because they wear such a number; they run into danger, injure themselves and others, and finally in seeming darkness they lose their way. The truth is that they were all the time in the light, but they knew it not, for they *would* wear the veils. God acts upon the assumption that every one sees clearly, and who would suspect His ever present help when behind so many thicknesses of evil?

Nora Smith Holm, *The Runner's Bible*, 1913, pp. 95, 97. No known copyright in effect.

July 14

A HEALING TREATMENT

God, I feel like I've been hurt. There are people who I believe have taken advantage of me, misused me, and abused me, God. There is pain in my soul today. I don't want to remain in this condition. I have made a decision that I no longer want to be in pain. Help me! Help me to let this go. Help me to be free. I know today that if I don't free others, I cannot be free. God, the joy of my salvation and my wholeness, I know you hear me. I know you always hear me. Give me the strength that I need to let it all go because it's not worth it. Give me the strength to let go so that I can go forward and experience the good that you have prepared for me. I know intellectually that all things work together for my good; but let me know it in the depths of my soul. Help me to see all people as you see them – especially those who have caused me pain. For, like me, they are children of God, unfolding and becoming. I send to them my love, wherever they may be – even if they have made a transition into the invisible side of life. I loose this pain and let it go. Amen.

Mary A. Tumpkin, *Before You Pray – Forgive*, p. 19. Copyright 2005, by Mary Tumpkin Presentations. Reprinted with permission of the estate of Mary A. Tumpkin.

July 15

MY LIFE IS IN ORDER

Let all things be done decently and in order.
I Corinthians 14:40

What I can do tomorrow, I will do today.
What I can be tomorrow, I am today.
I no longer procrastinate. I will not give myself excuses but will step forth and claim my good through a definite action on my part. As I look to God and trust him completely I am shown what I can do to help myself. A true feeling, extending from my heart in the form of a desire to help myself, has a way of reaching God -- a way not known to me -- yet a way that fulfills my desires.

Trusting God each day develops my mind, causing it to listen from within. In this trust I receive instruction and strength to obey the instruction. Today I let nothing prevent me from doing what is before me because I have the great promise, "That the crooked shall be made straight, and the rough places plain." This is a promise of order from Divine Mind, which is always on time, equal to any demand, and fulfills my every need.

Lola Pauline Mays, published in *Creative Thought*, June 1964, p. 32.
Copyrighted material reprinted with permission of SOM Publishing.

July 16

WORSHIP

I stood on the edge of the forest. All around me and before me, as far as the eye could see, were the trees, awe-inspiring, mighty in their majesty… Here breathed a solemn dignity, the hush of the forest, the holy temple of the Lord; here pulsed the stillness and peace of God.

And I thought of man, intent upon affairs, and how often for us also life is too big, too magnificent, too marvelous. We gaze out upon the universe, in the sky a multitude of stars. Science tells us that the nearest of them is 25,000,000 miles away; that every galactic system contains thousands of millions of stars, and that two million of such systems are known. It is inconceivable….

Our imagination fails us before the vast immensity of the picture. Yet man, an infinitesimal fragment upon a tiny earth, pushes and pulls and hurries and hurts his fellow men. Are we not to the Universe as the ants are to the trees? Yet, not entirely. For within man lies the urge, the power, the ability to comprehend. Through the ages, his mind has reached out with increasing clarity, not only to grasp a concept of the immensity, the marvelous mechanism of this material Universe, but to seek his unity with the wondrousness of its Creator, with God, with Life Itself.

Let us pause for that second, now and then: let us pause from our push and pull and hurry. Let us pause in the peace of the forest, pause in reverence before the mighty majesty of the trees, pause in awe before the vast immensity of the stars, pause, and in the silence, in the very center of our being, "be still," for a moment. Let us gladly, joyously, reverently, "Be still, and know that I am God."

Hazel Deane, published in *Science of Mind*, March 1935, p. 24. Copyrighted material reprinted with permission of SOM Publishing.

July 17

NEW THOUGHT IN THE TWENTY-FIRST CENTURY

Religion has provided the inspiration that has awakened humankind to the spiritual dimension of life. But religion has also been extremely divisive. As we view our world's history, we find that religion has been the root cause of many of the conflicts that have plagued our civilization. And now in the twenty-first century, it is religious extremists who are committing acts of violence in the name of God. In this century, some of the most established religions are being shaken to their foundations by inner conflict.

If we are to bring forth the millennium as described in Revelation, we must begin expressing a transcendental spirituality that supersedes the extreme biases of religiosity. This is not to say we should all have the same belief system; to the contrary, it is the diversity of our search that makes our journey joyously and mysteriously adventurous. However, we are living in a time of revolution. Science and technology are leading us into incredible dimensions of new possibilities. Reality is rapidly outstripping science fiction and fantasy. The communications revolution, combined with the globalization of commerce and the speed of travel, has made us a global community whether we like it or not. What happens anywhere happens to us. And if we think we can put the genie back in the bottle, we had better think again; we *are* one world right now.

The old paradigms will not work in a changing universe. The challenges facing our world today cannot be solved in the same consciousness in which they have been created. Life is demanding that we think in higher categories. To survive as a human species, we must learn finally and forevermore that violence begets violence, and the eye-for-an-eye morality, as Gandhi so aptly said, ends in a world of darkness. The urgency of this time calls for a revolution of consciousness. Revolutionary times demand revolutionary thinking.

Rosemary Fillmore Rhea, *That's Just How My Spirit Travels*, pp. 204-205. Copyrighted material reprinted with permission of Unity, Unity.org.

July 18

SOWING AND REAPING

The Law is: as you sow, so shall you reap. However, there are many different kinds of sowing and therefore many kinds of reaping.

In tropical countries, when the weather is hot the air is hot, very hot. The hot air rises…and rises. As the air is ascending it collects particles of dust and other things, which form clouds. When the clouds are full they burst and fall as rain, thus returning to the earth whatever they had taken up in the first place.

What does this mean for us? The quality of vibrations we send out – Love or Hate, Peace or War, Faith or Fear, Prosperity or Poverty; all accumulate, all rise and all descend as experiences in our lives. When they have been stored up in our personal orbit, they come back in forms of experience. Often, we do not recognize that they are ours, and we wonder where these experiences came from. They are ours, or else they could not find us. Jesus Christ taught his followers, "Whatsoever a man sows that shall he reap."

It is good for us to understand this truth as we consciously try to keep clean in our thoughts, words and deeds. The payoff comes as wonderful experiences in this life.

PRAYER: By the Grace of God, I now consciously release from my mind those thoughts that are not of absolute good. Right now I feel myself grateful to God for all the new happiness manifesting in my life. Thank God. Amen.

Judith G. Weekes, *Out Of Troubled Waters,* p. 5. Copyright 1992, Universal Foundation for Better Living (UFBL) Press. Reprinted with permission.

July 19

KNOWING I AM ALIVE

The body without the Spirit is dead.
James 2:26

One thing *I* cannot doubt -- that *I* am at this moment alive. Since the body without the Spirit is dead, then Spirit must be within me right at this point in time as it has been since the hour of my birth.

I now accept that this body is nothing more than a collection of atoms held together by an invisible magnet or Spirit. Spirit then, controls the body.

As I identify my self with Spirit, instead of with its garment of flesh, I see I have the mastery of body and affairs. Keeping my contact strong with Self as one with the great, infinite Presence pervading all space, I feel that, "Hour by hour I am filled with Christ Power," and that whatever I do is destined to meet with full fruition.

Serene, steadfast, I realize that though "change and decay" are all around me, they indicate but the changing of form. Knowing this, I have assurance that I am deathless, undying.

Ruth E. Chew, published in *Creative Thought*, June 1956, p. 37. Copyrighted material reprinted with permission of SOM Publishing.

July 20

BITTERSWEET FAREWELLS

Lord, I will follow Thee; but first let me go bid them farewell, which are at home at my house.
Luke 9:61

There is no end to the Divine nature and therefore no end to the possibility of expressing it. *The Science of Mind*, p. 490.

All through life we are saying goodbye to someone or something. Change is essential to growth, because without it, stagnation takes place and everything is soured and finally disintegrates.

It is often traumatic to say farewell to a relationship, to a loved one, or to a companion. This is when we remember Richard Bach's wise comfort. In his book *Illusions* he says: "Don't be dismayed at good-byes. A farewell is necessary before you can meet again. And meeting again, after moments or lifetimes, is certain for those who are friends."

No one is ever lost. There is one eternal world and we all inhabit it. Should we find ourselves in a different place than our loved ones, it doesn't mean that separation is forever. Change constantly takes place and the threads of our lives are woven together, then away, and then together again to make the beautiful pattern of our world.

There is also another farewell that has to be said. When illumination takes place within us, we say goodbye to certain types of thoughts that people our mind and with which we can no longer stay. It is always a challenge to leave the familiar and comfortable, but when we step into a larger vision of the whole, the bitterness turns to such sweetness that we never regret it for a moment. Farewells are bittersweet, but the bitterness is soon forgotten in the glory of the change.

My thought is creative. I am ready to enter a new life. My farewells are being said, and the beauty and glory of that which is ahead of me bring a peace which passes all intellectual understanding. I have let go of the lesser to enter the larger.

Norah Boyd, published in *Science of Mind*, June 2000, p. 75. Copyrighted material reprinted with permission of SOM Publishing.

July 21

WHEN THERE IS A NEED FOR PATIENCE

I know that time is but my own perception and feeling, and that what seems to me a long time is only a moment in the great all.

I know that with the Lord a thousand years is as one day.

I know that my real being is the same during all this change in perception and feeling that I call time.

I know that this real being of mine is working out its own manifestation, and I can wait.

All is good, there is no evil anywhere. I can see the end of time, for I was before it and I shall be after it.

I am only getting acquainted with my own nature and finding its Principle.

I welcome all I experience. I am willing to let patience have its perfect work....

All that I encounter in time is friendly and I will make none of it an enemy.

Now, this moment, I am able to overcome all that seems hard and unpleasant, for I have dominion over all things as my birthright. "He that endureth to the end shall be saved" from the necessity for endurance. I know that I, in my real being, am free from all that afflicts, and that I suffer only in my sense-consciousness.

I have God-given power to rule this consciousness. I am ruling it with patience and steadfastness.

The way is short and the work is easy, for the Christ is my Helper and Comforter.

The Son of God is with me, and he helps and strengthens the Son of Man. I am that I am, and no thing or experience in time can change my being. I have taken His yoke upon me and the Christ works with and for me. I am housed in God all the while I look upon the mortal. I am able to wait for manifestation of the immortal, for I know that it is. I am, and nothing can make me cease to be.

Time and space are naught for me who am more than they. I speak and they obey.

All is here and now. The work that is proof, is being done. I am.

Ursula Gestefeld, *The Breath of Life*, 1897, pp. 52-54. No known copyright in effect.

July 22

THE WONDER-WORKING POWER OF GOD

Praise is a miracle-worker. Nothing brings good into manifestation more quickly than praise and thanksgiving. Today, I take time to lift my voice in praise to God for the many gifts that He has bestowed unto me.

I praise God for the power of thought. Through this power my thinking is illumined and I bring forth only good and positive ideas in my life. My heart sings a song of praise and thanksgiving to God. I praise Him for His peace that quiets turmoil and strife. I praise Him for the abundance that is mine. Today I am offering my sincere praise to God and in so doing I become attuned to His love.

Praise and thanksgiving are true multipliers. Whatever I praise responds to me favorably. Whatever I praise gives back to me more of the good I put out through praise. As I praise others, I am really praising God expressing in and through them and so God has to express Himself more to me.

I praise and give thanks for the wonder-working power of God!

It is good to give thanks unto the Lord,
and to sing praises unto Thy name, O Most High.
Psalm 92:1

Olga Una Barker, published in *Daily Inspiration*, Copyright 1980, *Daily Inspiration for Better Living*. Reprinted with permission of the Universal Foundation for Better Living (UFBL) Press, November 1980, p. 21.

July 23

DEMONSTRATION IS FOREVER

You have demonstrated improved health, a better job, or a new home. You have received divine guidance leading you to a wise decision. You have used the great Law of Mind and gotten results. Your prayer has been answered. Does that end the matter?

Our use of spiritual science takes on vastly higher significance when we realize that back of every tangible demonstration there is an even greater, intangible, good: the increase in faith which becomes a permanent part of our consciousness as a result of our proven knowledge of the Law.

This intangible gain is inevitable and can never be lost. The job, the house, the visible answer to prayer, may cease to be. Certainly the total physical demonstration of our life experience will be separated from us when we leave our physical bodies. But consciousness is undying, and any increase in faith is ours forever.

Let us not, then, consider demonstration "materialistic," but know that every minute spent praying for good is an investment in our eternal spiritual stature.

Elena Goforth Whitehead, published in *Creative Thought*, January 1965, p. 4. Copyrighted material reprinted with permission of SOM Publishing.

July 24

SPIRITUAL MIND TREATMENT

Spiritual mind treatment is affirmative prayer. It involves a realization by the one praying that the good which is desired already exists in Divine Mind and only needs to be accepted in order to be experienced. In spiritual mind treatment there is a recognition of the unity of an individual with God, and it differs in this regard from forms of prayer which involve petitioning God for something. Those kinds of prayer are based on the belief that we are separate from God.

Spiritual mind treatment is a scientific approach to prayer, because it is based on an understanding of universal laws, especially the Law of Mind. Through the activity of this Law, whatever a person deeply believes automatically tends to manifest in outward form, so when a practitioner sees God, or Perfection, where a problem appears to be, the Law of Mind acts on that perception to bring about a change for the better.

We as practitioners work in our own mind to recognize perfection in regard to a particular problem. Thus, Ernest Holmes defines treatment in *The Science of Mind* as clearing the thought of negation, of doubt and fear, and causing it to perceive the ever-presence of God.

As a practitioner, my job is to use spiritual mind treatment to help my clients experience greater good. We work together to recognize Divine Perfection in what appears to be their problem, and the result is what is called a 'demonstration' or healing.

Vetura Papke, published in *Science of Mind*, April 1988, p. 10. Copyrighted material reprinted with permission of SOM Publishing.

July 25

SOUL FOOD

Every department of man's being requires sustenance, nourishment, or food suited to its needs. There are many kinds of food suited to each one of the three planes of human existence: the flesh plane, the mental or intellectual plane, and the soul plane. The physical body craves that which ministers to the flesh *only*....The intellect craves knowledge, and cannot be satisfied without the means by which it can gain knowledge....

With his discovery that he is a living soul, man needs to understand that *as a soul* he requires different food from what was required by either the flesh or mental plane.

Our thoughts, beliefs and ideas constitute the soul food; and by the great law of Cause and Effect the character will accord with whatever thoughts and ideas the soul feeds upon. The *self idea* is the first important factor to consider; for as a living Soul, according to the wise man of old (Solomon) *"As he thinketh in his heart, so is he."*

Jane Yarnall, published in *Washington News Letter*, (ed. Sabin), July 1902, p. 617. No known copyright in effect.

July 26

GOD FILLS ALL SPACE

There is only one presence and power in the entire universe…God, the Good, Omnipotent. God created all space, the same God of love who made our planet made all planets and stars. The same God created all men in His image and likeness.

There will be no peace until there is love. Through the power of God's love active within all persons, our world is blessed with perfect peace.

Peace begins with me! I let the peace and love of God flow from my heart to enfold and bless the world. Your peace, O loving Father. Your peace! In our world and affairs, in our relations with all nations, let your peace permeate our entire consciousness. In the name of Jesus Christ, let us be unified in peace, and open ourselves to an outpouring of love, light, and comfort upon the entire world.

All of space is filled with the same loving and protecting Spirit of God. Let us trust this loving Spirit within all men. Let us know that it is everywhere present.

Love thee one another.
John 15:12

Christina Knox-Walthall, published in *Daily Inspiration*, Copyright 1985, *Daily Inspiration for Better Living.* Reprinted with permission of the Universal Foundation for Better Living (UFBL) Press, September 1985, p. 5.

July 27

WHEN THERE IS DIFFICULTY LETTING GO OF THE PAST (1)

I am no more what I was. I am new-born.
I am awake to my eternal being in which is all glory and all power.
What I was when I was asleep is gone.
It belongs to the dead past.
In the recognition of my possible divinity I am resurrected from the dead.
I leave in the tomb all that belongs there. I carry nothing of it with me; I desire none of it.
I see that no soul cometh to the Father except by the resurrection and the life.
I am quickened from on high and I rise above the region of graves.
I am not holden of them, neither indeed can I be.
I am new, all things are new, my future is new.
Though my soul-journey is not finished, I know that my face is turned in the right direction and the land of graves is behind my back.
Through the quickening spirit in me I shall conquer as I go, and find my home.
1 have no useless regrets. In my heart of hearts I am thankful for the measure of wisdom which is mine today, and which my past experiences have brought forth to me.

Ursula Gestefeld, *The Breath of Life*, 1897, pp. 43-44. No known copyright in effect.

July 28

WHEN THERE IS DIFFICULTY LETTING GO OF THE PAST (2)

They have borne some fruit; they will bear more.

But in the strength of the Lord, by the help of His Christ, I shall gather this fruit with rejoicing and not sorrow.

By it I am made strong. By it I prove my power of mastery over all unlikeness to God.

I am exercising this power now. By means of it I get farther and farther from the dead past.

I am resurrected continually into more abundant life.

All is good. There is no evil.

All that I have called evil has been good for me, for by it I have learned something.

I have no sorrow, no regrets. I am filled with praise and rejoicing.

I know that I am being weaned from my mortal sense self that I may show forth the divine likeness.

All that this sense calls affliction are but the growing-pains which are sure to be left behind.

Nothing that anyone can say of me can hurt me or turn me aside.

I press forward steadily with no thought of blame for them who judge me according to the dead past.

I know but one Judge and one Deliverer.

All malice, hatred, and enmity are left with that past.

I bow only to love, I feel only love, for every human being.

I begin to know God, for God is Love.

Ursula Gestefeld, *The Breath of Life*, 1897, p. 45. No known copyright in effect.

July 29

DIVINE WISDOM

God is Wisdom. Because we have accepted the truth that God is Mind, Spirit, Living Intelligence, we can more readily comprehend the attribute of Wisdom.

Wisdom is the idea of absolute knowing in Divine Mind. God is all. Therefore God is Wisdom. Wisdom is the movement of Divine Mind, the light of creative Mind activity. This is knowing in the absolute.

Since man stems forth from God as the individualization of the perfect Idea -- Man, Wisdom is available to man. As man becomes receptive, so is he quickened by the movement of Mind. The light of Divine Wisdom quickens, inspires and uplifts him.

Divine Wisdom is the absolute aspect of knowing. Intellect is the human or relative aspect.

Since the creation is in Mind, the movement of Mind gives us a basis for our power to think. The One Mind "sees" its own image. The Christ Mind has within it the original principles of the Creator and the creation. Man partakes of the qualities of the universal Christ Mind when he turns consciously within.

The intellect is mind embodied. It is the human use of mind. It is not perfect. It has accepted experience as real. The intellect can turn within to Truth, or without to the evidence of the senses. In the intellect is the power of choice. So man can choose the type of thought, feeling and action that he shall follow.

Helen Zagat, *Faith and Works*, 1955, pp. 29-30. No known copyright in effect.

July 30

GOD'S WILL MUST BE GODLIKE

We cannot conceive of God willing for us sickness or sorrow, weakness or sin. We have come to know that these inharmonies are the result of man's ignorance. As he is enlightened by Truth they will disappear. God wills for us only life, health, goodness, love and power. He wills that we should be wise in our day's decisions. He wills that we should be loving, kind, uncritical, fearless, trustful, joyful. He wills brotherhood throughout the land; and, also that we should say with Jesus and Paul, "I of myself do nothing, the Father in me doeth the works." If we understand God's will in this way, and try steadfastly to fulfill it, we find ourselves gradually freed from bondage to race hypnotism. Self-centered thought – selfishness – goes. We forgive perfectly. We serve efficiently. From our earnest endeavor comes clear vision. We are led definitely not only to understand the great principles of right living but also to know God's immediate intent for us. We know whether God wishes us to go forth or to be still, to give or to withhold, to cherish or to lose. Such is the life of power.

This is the greatest human achievement, this knowing the God-Will and fulfilling our Divine Purpose.

Nona L. Brooks, *Short Lessons in Divine Science*, 1940, p. 73. Copyrighted material reprinted with permission of Divine Science Federation International.

July 31

MEDITATION ON PEACE OF MIND

We take words with us unto God. Our words today are: I bring every restless thought home to God.

Most of us have experienced times when we cannot concentrate, when our thoughts are restless. They seem to race from people to places to events in confusion and disorder. How do we then gain peace of mind? These words of St. Augustine offer a powerful and helpful answer, "Thou hast made us for Thyself, and the heart of man is restless until it finds its rest in Thee." We can gain peace of mind by bringing any restless thoughts home, where they belong, to God within. In the presence of God, our thoughts become quiet, harmonious and peaceful. Order and peace are restored. We are able to think clearly and to reestablish goals. We find that our emotions are also calmed.

From now on we can say to every wandering thought, "Like a lost sheep, I bring you home to the fold. Today, I bring you home to God, where you really belong." We take every thought captive, to obey Christ. Today I bring every restless thought home to God.

Jane Paulson, meditation at the Golden Pyramid, Unity of Houston, Houston, Texas, about March 1981. No known copyright in effect.

AUGUST

August 1

THE PRAYER OF FAITH

God is my help in every need;
God does my every hunger feed;
God walks beside me, guides my way
Through every moment of the day.

I now am wise, I now am true,
Patient, kind and loving, too.
All things I am, can do, and be,
Through Christ, the Truth that is in me.

God is my health, I can't be sick;
God is my strength, unfailing, quick;
God is my all; I know no fear,
Since God and love and Truth are here.

Hannah More Kohaus, published in *Wee Wisdom*, August 1898. Copyrighted material reprinted with permission of Unity, Unity.org.

August 2

UNDERSTANDING

UNDERSTANDING is more than and different from a knowledge of facts. It does not necessarily go along with or follow obedience; nor can the intellect of itself be counted upon to produce it.

UNDERSTANDING both springs from and produces an inner feeling for right relations. It is the ability to lay hold of right relationships and utilize them; it is the Power to grasp the essentially right relations which should exist between all objects and mental states upon this earth.

UNDERSTANDING prompts man to investigate his world, its nature and purpose, for he is able to enter into, to feel, to sympathize with all persons, conditions and circumstances around him; and he is able to bring both accustomed and unusual details into successful combination in proportion to his perception of intrinsically right relations.

UNDERSTANDING in God is His constant Power to estimate meanings, significances, and values correctly. And He is invariably successful because of His invariable rightness of perception and conception.

UNDERSTANDING in the mind of God is an idea of rightness.

UNDERSTANDING in man is his ability to conceive and perceive right relationships.

Ella Pomeroy, *Powers of the Soul*, 1948, p. 137. No known copyright in effect.

August 3

HIM THAT FILLETH ALL IN ALL

I will pour out of my Spirit upon all flesh.
Ezekiel 37:14

It has always been "upon" you, around you and through you. From it you have drawn, though unconsciously, all the power that you have used in your senses, your intellect, in every way. But your eyes have been closed and you have not seen the greater possibilities. In the midst of plenty -- enough for every need and every aim – you have not had sufficient understanding to open your eyes and take possession. Finally something awakens you – it is often sorrow – and then you see the Truth that is, in which you live, move and have your being, the seat of all Power, "the very present Help," the inexhaustible treasury of Good. Then you hasten to put yourself in harmony with it by right thinking, humility and faith.

Nora Smith Holm, *The Runner's Bible*, 1913, pp. 16-17. No known copyright in effect.

August 4

THE FUNCTION OF A MIRACLE WORKER

You can do much on behalf of your own healing and that of others if, in a situation calling for help, you think of it this way:

I am here only to be truly helpful.
I am here to represent Him Who sent me.
I do not have to worry about what to say or what to do,
because He Who sent me will direct me.
I am content to be wherever He wishes,
knowing He goes there with me.
I will be healed as I let Him teach me to heal.

Helen Schucman, *A Course In Miracles*, 1975, Text, p. 24. No known copyright in effect.

August 5

WHO AM I?

God created each one of us "a special enterprise," and He endowed us with a mind. He gave us Self-consciousness. No other species on the face of this planet has that. You know who you are. You may not know the all of who you are, because no one does. But you do know "I am So-and-So." You do have the power of original thought. You can form a concept. You can carry it out. There is an interesting test you can try for yourself that is very revealing. Ask yourself, "Who am I?" Then watch the first three replies that come into your mind. You will inevitably find that your answers will include, "I am a salesman," or "I am a housewife." But you are not that. That is your field of activity; that is not what you are. This is a simple way of learning just what you think about you.

You have Self-consciousness. You have the kind of mind that recognizes its own identity. You have free will. You have the potentiality and the possibility of developing that mind. You are not a slave. You do not have to live at the beck and call of every peril that seems to lurk in the outer world. You are supposed to live as a child of God, a Son of God, a co-creator with God. That is the essence of Being, which is instilled in every human soul.

You are not here to live a possible sixty or seventy years, and for the most part of it go through hell. You are here to create something in your life that only you can do for yourself….Each one of us offers God a slightly different, unique experience as we begin to find ourselves and proceed to build our lives in accordance with the Divine Plan. That is why there are no two people exactly alike in the world. Not even identical twins are completely identical. No one else can do it in exactly the same way. "You are a special enterprise on the part of God."

Mildred Mann, *How To Find Your Real Self,* 1952, p. 5. No known copyright in effect.

August 6

THE FINAL WORD: AMEN

In the original Hebrew, "Amen" means "so it is, it is done, this is the truth." Thorndike adds that "amen" is "an expression of assent after a prayer; an expression of approval." In Revelation "Amen" is used in place of "the Spirit of Truth," and in Isaiah in place of "God of Truth." Thus "Amen" is a word of mystical and powerful meaning, usually used in a traditional sense without awareness of its deeper meaning.

"Amen" to the ancient Egyptians meant "master" or "ruler." They gave this word great power and incorporated it into the names of their great leaders: Pharaoh Amenhotep, Tutankhamen, etc. Translations of ancient Egyptian prayers use the word "Amen" for the name of the sun god. Obvious connection exists between the use of this word for deity in Egypt and the Hebrew use of the word. The meaning of "so it is" has striking similarity to the name of God revealed to Moses, "I am that I am."

"Amen" is more than a word at the close of prayer. It is a state of consciousness. It is the acceptance of God into your life. "Amen" is a consciousness that I have spoken the word and God will honor it. Anytime you accept something as being true, you are saying "amen" to that thing. The consciousness of "amen" conditions us to keep our prayers positive and to release that power of faith to do its work through our prayer and treatment work.

What you say "amen" to is your master. End your prayer treatment with the emphatic realization that "I have spoken the word. It is the Truth. I accept it. I know it is done. I rest in this consciousness." All this is implied by your "Amen."

Betty Jean House, 1999. Copyrighted material reprinted with permission.

August 7

IMPERSONALITY

There seem to be many beings, separate beings, whereas there is only one. With our minds we see many, but with our insight, with our spiritual Consciousness, we see unity, oneness. God is *infinite* and so includes all in one.

I love that life is unchangeable, immutable, everlasting.

I love to know that I am a trinity – Self, Son, Understanding;

I love to think of the Self as Mighty, Majestic, Unconquerable,

I love to think of man as the Son shining forth the love and joy of Being,

I love to think of Understanding as coming to man like blazing light, like shining gold, like fiery flame.

I love to think of heaven as here, at hand, a land of beauty, aglow with the divine energy of Life!

I love to perceive the nothingness of matter and mind and personality.

I love to behold the unity and the allness of *the One.*

Lillian DeWaters, *Gems*, 1928, pp. 72-73. No known copyright in effect.

August 8

DIVINE IMAGINATION

Affirmation: *Jesus Christ is now raising me to His consciousness of divine imagination, and I see spiritual perfection everywhere.*

Divine imagination is the chisel we wield in molding the paradise of our inner thought kingdom. While in the silence, therefore, the thought forms we permit to be imaged in consciousness have as great an effect on our lives as our spiritual realizations. Intelligent seeing is a form of divine imagination; we should always behold ourselves in a state of keen, intelligent knowing. We should see God, Good, as the source of life, and we should see ourselves majestically springing from that source.

It is through divine imagination that the soul first gets the impulse to expand. In the silence we learn to lift our vision above things as they commonly appear, and this helps to bring all the other faculties of man into captivity to the obedience of Christ. Thus we learn to acquaint ourselves with God and with God's world of reality. Divine imagination, working in consciousness, sees the kingdom of the heavens fashioned after the divine pattern shown on the mount of high spiritual illumination.

Cora Dedrick Fillmore, *Christ Enthroned In Man*, 1937, pp. 53-54.
Copyrighted material reprinted with permission of Unity, Unity.org.

August 9

THE RISE OF MAN

The fall of man was the fall into consciousness of things as substance. The evolution of man is the rise into consciousness of the life of things as substance.

The fall of man was the fall into a material conception of life. His emancipation from the bondage of things material comes through a rise into an entirely new conception of life as spiritual. We do not live in a material world, but in a material conception of the world. To live in a conception of the world as spirit and life, not matter, is to recognize things and their limitations.

All power and wisdom reside in Life itself, which is purely spiritual and mental. There is no life or power or intelligence in matter – matter is in Life, as the thoughts are in the mind. Matter moves in life and by the power of life, just as thought moves in individual mind and by the power of the individual mind.

This old mortal conception of the world shall give way to the immortality conception of life itself as all power and intelligence and substance.

The cause of the material world is Life itself.

The world is built by life, it is rebuilt by life, its every change is the effect of the motions of life itself.

We live in a spiritual world, not a material one. To remember this, is eternal life.

Elizabeth Towne, published in *Washington News Letter*, (ed. Sabin), October 1915, p. 56. No known copyright in effect.

August 10

IN THE SHADOW OF HIS WINGS

As we practice the work of forgiveness we discover more and more that forgiveness and healing are one. We find indeed that all forms of prayer fuse into a high consciousness of God. Thus the break in the pipeline that connects us with God who is love is mended, and the water of life fills us to the brim and overflows into our homes and workshops and churches.

This inrush of God's Holy Spirit heals us naturally. But it does far more than that. Indeed, as we pursue the spiritual life we lose sight of physical benefits in our increasing vision of God Himself. We find after a while that we desire God more for His own sake than for ours. And as this comes to us we begin to understand a little bit of that process by which the world will be filled with the glory of God as the waters cover the sea. More and more we seek the beginning within us of the manifestation of the sons of God who will walk the earth with power, accomplishing the works of Him who sent them. More and more surely we know that the day of the Lord, when nation shall not rise up against nation neither shall they learn war any more, can only be brought about by us, the children of Light.

Agnes Sanford, *The Healing Light*, 1947, p. 68.

August 11

DESTINY AT MY COMMAND

If God's plan (destiny) for us is in the abstract, how do we make it concrete? A scriptural verse comes to mind as being apropos: "You will decide on a matter, and it will be established for you, and light will shine upon your ways." And in the New Testament we have the remark of the centurion to Jesus concerning his servant's need for healing: "Say the word, and let my servant be healed." Decree. Say the word. In other words, "Affirm the Truth."

In Truth, as presented by Unity, this "decreeing," "saying," or "speaking" comes under the heading of affirmation.

What occurs when a strong affirmation of Truth is uttered silently or audibly? A definite change of a positive nature takes place in the mind, the consciousness. The idea back of the word draws thought substance to the idea and builds what Emmet Fox calls a "mental equivalent." As the idea back of the word has drawn the invisible mind substance to form a mental picture, so this mental equivalent acts as a magnet to draw manifest substance to clothe the idea in some tangible form – a home, clothes, food, a job, harmonious human relationships, happiness, success.

In order that our divine destiny may manifest in practical ways, the mind must be clear and calm so that the thinking and feeling processes may handle the events and circumstances of everyday living in the best possible way. Decreeing, speaking the word, with a clear, calm mind is a step in taking command of our destiny, a step toward claiming that which is ours by divine right. If there is a need of bodily healing, we decree the word of life, vitality, strength, in the full knowledge that life is our birthright, that to be healthy is our destiny. Should there be lack in our finances, we decree that God is the one source of all good. By our spoken word we take command of our thinking. Rather than thinking in terms of lack, we decree the infilling of God's substance. To be prosperous and successful is our destiny.

Vera Dawson Tait, *Take Command,* 1981, pp. 157-158. Copyrighted material used with permission by Unity, Unity.org.

August 12

THE CHRIST WITHIN ME IS MY FULFILLMENT

Love is the fulfilling of the law.
Romans 13:10

My Christ Self is one with the Father. It is my individualized expression of the Spirit; as such, It expresses all of the Love of God, all of the life of the One Life, all the Power of the Infinite and all the Presence of Omnipresence. Therefore the Christ within me at this very moment knows the answer to every seeming problem and is Itself the Substance out of which comes the out-picturing of my every desire.

All of my good is right where I am, waiting for me to accept it. I now realize that God is Himself the substance of the fulfillment of my every desire, so I cease searching on the out-side for my good and direct all my attention to seeking the Kingdom of God within. I know that the Father knoweth my needs, and that even now all these things are being added unto me.

The Christ within me is my fulfillment and I am One with Harmony and Joy in every department of my life. And so it is.

Cornelia Addington, published in *Creative Thought*, February 1955, p. 30. Copyrighted material reprinted with permission of SOM Publishing.

August 13

PURSUING WISDOM

Over the years, I have seen many people come and go from the Center of Spiritual Living. They enter the teaching for one reason or another and choose to leave for one reason or another. The details change and patterns of movement remain. Some stay for a long, long time. Others move from the area and go to a new Center. Some die. Some are disappointed. Others get what they want and move on without dreaming new dreams.

Wisdom has many pathways. Everyone must travel his own road and no person, place or thing outside himself has all his answers. The answers have to be unique because we are unique individuals. So I learned to bless them as they came and love them if they stayed. I also learned to bless them if they went. I learned to trust the process. Whatever piece of this wisdom teaching they got, that taste will eventually prod them to find a way for more. Light is powerfully attractive.

Jane Claypool, posted in her blog, February 28, 2013. Reprinted with permission of her family.

August 14

TODAY IS A DAY OF PEACE

And let the peace of God rule in your hearts.
Colossians 3:15

    A heavenly peace flows over me, not because of me, of what I have done or have not done, but because I have turned to God, my Father, who is the Prince of Peace.

    In this moment I am lifted into a divine realization and see the truth about myself, my family, my neighbor, and my country. I realize that God within me, as intelligence, can clear my way as my mind remains in a state of peace. I no longer fight a battle of appearances, because I have accepted victory from within. In this calm trust I am awakened to the truth that all God can do for me must be done through me. This stabilizes my mind and my answer is assured.

    Everyday I seek to realize more fully the meaning of "my peace I give unto you," because in such moments I see that my quest is answered and my prayer is finished. I thank God, my Father, today for inner peace.

Lola Pauline Mays, published in *Creative Thought*, August 1964, p. 16.
Copyrighted material reprinted with permission of SOM Publishing.

August 15

DOMINION

*...in every place, every action or outward occupation,
thou be inwardly free and mighty in thyself...
that thou be lord and governor of thy deeds, not servant.*
Thomas a Kempis

Perfect dominion over our thoughts and emotions, as well as our deeds, is signified in this message. There is no mention of being lord over someone else; the emphasis is placed on *self-control*. The governor of anything is the perfect control of that thing, which allows for a consistent flow of pure energy to be released in all action. We might say that to have perfect dominion is to be in perfect control of our intellectual and emotional output. Qualities that can be developed toward good governorship are flexibility, open-mindedness, diplomacy, and thoughtfulness.

God-Life is everywhere present and all-sufficient, and It is my life now. I am abundantly supplied with all I need spiritually, mentally, and physically. I am relaxed. Nothing irritates or aggravates me for I have self-control. The Lord-God is the Governor of my life and I am happy. Right action is the law of my life. And so it is and shall ever be.

"There is such a thing as demonstrating a control of conditions. We shall be able to prove this in such degree as we are successful in looking away from the conditions which now exist, while accepting better ones." *The Science of Mind,* page 266.

*...His dominion is an everlasting dominion, which shall not pass away and His
kingdom, that which shall not be destroyed.*
Daniel 7:14

Georgia Carmichael Maxwell, *Science of Mind*, December 1955, p. 56.
Copyrighted material reprinted with permission of SOM Publishing.

August 16

REAL LOVE

Real love is selfless and free from fear. It pours itself out upon the object of its affection, without demanding any return. Its joy is in the joy of giving. Love is God in manifestation, and the strongest magnetic force in the universe. Pure unselfish love *draws to itself its own;* it does not need to seek or demand. Scarcely anyone had the faintest conception of real love. Man is selfish, tyrannical or fearful in his affections, thereby losing the thing he loves. Jealousy is the worst enemy of love, for the imagination runs riot, seeing the loved one attracted to another, and invariably these fears objectify if they are not neutralized.

Florence Scovel Shinn, *The Game of Life and How to Play It*, 1925, p. 47. No known copyright in effect.

August 17

GOD NOT CHANGED BY PRAYER

One mistake that has been made by those who have advocated the use of prayer as a means to a successful life, is found in the notion that God, through prayer, might be persuaded to change His mind, or that the unwilling or dull ear of the Almighty can be won by supreme effort on the part of the aspiring soul. Truth exposes the false note of this idea as springing from ignorance of the science of Being, "I am the Lord, I change not" (Malachi 3:6), and as Jesus supplies light in his affirmation, "Thou hearest me always" (John 11:42). With this point cleared up prayer may become spiritually strong and intelligent. No power on earth can change the Absolute God. It is man who needs to change until he understands the perfection of Being. Prayer, then, is for the benefit and blessing of the one who prays.

Harriet Hale Rix, *Christian Mind Healing*, 1914, p. 51. No known copyright in effect.

August 18

OPEN MY EYES

Open my eyes, that I may see
Glimpses of truth Thou hast for me;
Place in my hands the wonderful key
That shall unclasp and set me free.
Refrain

Open my ears, that I may hear
Voices of truth Thou sendest clear;
And while the wave-notes fall on my ear
Ev-'ry-thing false will disappear.
Refrain

Open my mouth, and let me bear
Gladly the warm truth ev-'ry-where;
Open my heart and let me prepare
Love with Thy children thus to share.
Refrain

Refrain:
Silently now I wait for Thee,
Ready, my God, Thy will to see;
Open my eyes, illumine me,
Spirit divine.

Clara H. Scott, (1895), published in *Divine Science Church School Hymnal*, 1925, Hymn 52; *Unity Song Selections*, 1947, Hymn 51; and *Religious Science Hymnal*, 1954, Hymn 66. Copyrighted material reprinted with permission of Divine Science Federation International, Unity, Unity.org and SOM Publishing.

August 19

THE SCIENCE OF BEING

The real meaning of the word religion (re-ligio) is to bind back. And that is just what the student does in his application of the Omnipresence. In the allegory of the Garden of Eden is a portrayal of the Omnipresence; One Presence, Mind or Intelligence creating or coming forth in the invisible out of its own substance. And it was said of each manifestation, "good and very good." Man in "the image and likeness of God" with every good provided for him was commissioned to have "dominion over all things." There was just one thing he was not to do – to "eat of the tree of good and evil," or conceive for himself a world of duality.

Throughout the remainder of the Bible we find man, working his way out of sense delusion and illusion into conscious Oneness with his Source made manifest by the man Jesus....

Ida B. Elliott, published in *Mind Remakes Your World*, (ed. Holmes), 1941, pp. 100-101. Reprinted with permission of INTA.

August 20

I NOW FREE MY SELF

As a man thinketh within himself, so is he.
Proverbs 23:7

I do accept that what I think, believe, dwell upon, does happen. My life from now on is to more than make up for the past, for I keep my mind stayed on good and good alone.

I utterly refuse to let thoughts of what I do not want cheat me, and mine, of the wonderful things I need and want, which God has prepared for each of us. Since I can think as I please, I focus the tremendous power of my every thought on those things which bring joyous satisfaction and lasting good.

Right this minute I mentally see myself as healthy, happy, useful, prosperous and lovable. I practice seeing only well, worthwhile, joyous, successful, likable people all around me, in my family circle, my home, my business world, my every contact.

Like a first-class Trouper I rehearse and rehearse the part I want on the Stage of Life. I assume the character. I loose myself in it.

Through constant right thinking I free myself into all that I want to be and to have. I am at peace.

Ruth E. Chew, published in *Creative Thought*, May 1956, p. 24. Copyrighted material reprinted with permission of SOM Publishing.

August 21

REMEMBER THAT YOU ARE HIS COMPLETION AND HIS LOVE

And now in all your doings be you blessed.
God turns to you for help to save the world.
Teacher of God, His thanks He offers you,
And all the world stands silent in the grace
You bring from Him. You are the Son He loves,
And it is given you to be the means
Through which His Voice is heard around the world,
To close all things of time; to end the sight
Of all things visible; and to undo
All things that change. Through you is ushered in
A world unseen, unheard, yet truly there.
Holy are you, and in your light the world
Reflects your holiness, for you are not
Alone and friendless. I give thanks for you,
And join your efforts on behalf of God,
Knowing they are on my behalf as well,
And for all those who walk to God with me.
Amen.

Helen Schucman, *A Course In Miracles*, 1975, Manual For Teachers, p.69. No known copyright in effect.

August 22

PROSPERITY'S TEN COMMANDMENTS

1. THOU SHALT LOOK TO NO OTHER SOURCE BUT GOD FOR THY SUPPLY.
"Thou shalt have no other gods before me."

2. THOU SHALT MAKE NO MENTAL IMAGES OF LACK.
"Thou shalt not make unto thee a graven image…"

3. THOU SHALT NOT SPEAK THE WORD OF LACK OR LIMITATION.
"Thou shalt not take the name of Jehovah thy God in vain; for Jehovah will not hold him guiltless that taketh His name in vain."

4. THOU SHALL LET GO AND LET GOD DO IT.
"Remember the Sabbath day and keep it holy…"

5. THOU SHALT DEAL HONORABLY WITH GOD AND WITH ALL HUMAN INSTRUMENTS THROUGH WHOM GOD'S GOOD IS MANIFESTED FOR YOU.
"Honor thy father and thy mother, that thy days may be long and the land which Jehovah thy God giveth thee."

6. THOU SHALT NOT TAKE THY WEALTH OUT OF CIRCULATION.
"Thou shalt not kill."

7. THOU SHALT NOT ABASE THY WEALTH TO IDLE OR EVIL USES.
"Thou shalt not commit adultery."

8. THOU SHALT NOT SEEK SOMETHING FOR NOTHING.
"Thou shalt not steal."

9. THOU SHALT NOT BEAR FALSE WITNESS AGAINST THE SOURCE OF THY WEALTH.
"Thou shalt not bear false witness against thy neighbor."

10. THOU SHALT NOT LIMIT THYSELF BY COVETING THAT WHICH IS ANOTHER'S; THOU SHALT CLAIM THY OWN.
"Thou shalt not covet thy neighbor's house, thou shalt not covet thy neighbor's wife…"

Georgiana Tree West, *Prosperity's Ten Commandments*, 1946. Copyrighted material reprinted with permission of Unity, Unity.org.

August 23

GOD MY MIND

Bible: *I stir up your pure mind by way of remembrance. Let this mind be in you that was also in Christ Jesus. That ye may with one mind and one mouth glorify God.*

It is my privilege to keep ever in the pure thought of Truth for God hath given me of his Mind. The Mind that was in Christ Jesus is in me. God is the only Mind. This is my Mind. There is none other.

I glorify God by remembering that this Mind of mine is perfect, giving me today thoughts and words of perfection. My mouth cannot transgress.

The Mind that is All is pure. As partakers of the one only Mind, our thoughts are pure.

One Mind omnipresent is the Mind of all. I acknowledge this as my Mind, my all Intelligence. I could know nothing outside this one Mind, for it is all Knowledge and Understanding.

A statement to be learned: I rely this day upon the one Mind for my Wisdom and clear judgment.

Fannie Brooks James, *Truth and Health*, 1901, p. 140. Copyrighted material reprinted with permission of Divine Science Federation International.

August 24

NON-RESISTANCE

From the day that Jesus propounded his doctrine of non-resistance, to the present time, there has been an increasing interest in that thought. Jesus speaking to the people in his wonderful Sermon on the Mount, came at length to that particular fallacy in the popular belief, "Ye have heard it said, An eye for an eye and a tooth for a tooth." Over against this conception of law and justice he placed a new idea, "That ye resist not evil," exhorting the people to carry this doctrine to the length of loving their enemies, giving good for evil and blessing for cursing. Centuries have passed since that truth was proclaimed, and while it has not been lived strongly during that time, it has, nevertheless, survived, and today Divine Science renews the teachings that resistance has no true place in God's creation, and that harmony is the only law.

The revival of interest in this law of Truth, is especially opportune at a time when, to many earnest souls, there seems to be so much in the world to be overcome, and which apparently cannot be overcome unless it is resisted. Sin and sickness seem to have multiplied despite all the customary efforts to counteract them, and the belief may be quite natural that the great need is for some resisting force to overcome them. Resistance as a means of securing harmony is a fallacy. True harmony cannot spring from inharmony, nor peace from discord. Resistance fails because it is not in accord with harmony, which is the only law.

Daisy Baum, *Studies in Divine Science*, 1909, pp.79-80. Copyrighted material reprinted with permission of Divine Science Federation International.

August 25

I WILL LIFT UP MINE EYES

Life itself is mysterious, containing all that appears; 'tis the source from which all activity of spirit and truth proceed. The secret of each life, as it has been recorded in sacred or secular history, is an expression of Truth. It has its direct appeal, with a living touch to every soul, who is awakened to hear the harmony, ever active, ever present.

David, early in his youth manifested a wonderful expression of power and light. A devoted lover of nature, he saw in all things the Spirit of the Lord; in response nature whispered her secrets, obeying its dictates, his soul rose to the heights, and his whole being sang for joy.

The love-light of the Father's presence, made him always ready and willing to serve, this gave the boy power over every evil thing that disturbs the heart of man.

A love ever present to protect and deliver him, even from his enemies.

Agnes J. Galer, published in *Religious Science Monthly*, February 1929, p. 35. Copyrighted material reprinted with permission of SOM Publishing.

August 26

NO REGRET

Behold I will do a new thing…I will even make a way in the wilderness, and rivers in the desert.
Isaiah 43:19

Does regret bind you to the past? Dear friend, heed these paraphrased words of the Scriptures. "Today is the day the Lord hath made; rejoice and be exceedingly glad."

The past is but a shadow on the screen of time. It will cast long or short shadows according to your emotional-mental projector. The past played its part in bringing you to your present understanding; therefore, it had its place in your unfoldment. Name it "good."

Labor not in the regret of that which was or might have been. To do so is to allow the long shadow of regret to darken you today. Today offers you everything. It is a fresh beginning with new opportunities, new friends, new horizons.

You live and move and have your being in the now of an omnipotent God. You live in Omniaction!

Let this day be dedicated to Him. Let your prayer be: Father, from this day forward I live in the now of your Presence. I bless the past and I release it in the good that is now. Thank you, Father.

Lucile Frederick, published in *Daily Studies in Divine Science*, 2010, p. 262. Copyrighted material reprinted with permission of Divine Science Federation International.

August 27

MAN'S ASCENDING CONSCIOUSNESS

Revelation is the revealing of the inner Spirit to the consciousness of man. There is no place for this revelation to come forth except through man's consciousness.

We do not know what other creatures there may be in the universe, hearing the voice of God. There may be souls around us that are so fine we do not see them, or they us, and who do see and feel. We do not know the full extension of law, but we do know we are in law. We do know that the law of God is sure, and that the law of God is operating within man. God is. God is a Reality. God is All-good, All-presence, All-knowledge, All-power, All-wisdom from which we, each one, may draw according to our consciousness.

What we need, then, is the consciousness of the fact of God, omnipresent with the self. If we wish greater revelation regarding self, we have the man Jesus as an example. None of us has seen Him; none of us knows Him personally, but we have something within us that ever bears record to the truth of this man's life. It is the revelation in our own soul, of the one who grasps the revelation, of the principle of Light, of Spirit, of God, in which the individual, answering back to the universal Spirit of life says, "Yes, that is true."

Anna L. Palmer, *Christ In You*, 1958, pp. 21-22. Copyrighted material reprinted with permission of Divine Science Federation International.

August 28

SPIRITUAL DISCRIMINATION

When we know the Truth about God, it is God in us knowing the Truth about Himself! This relieves us of all personal sense. It is hard for one to know the Truth about himself, because it is himself that he is thinking of, instead of GOD. God's ways are perfect. They are in continual operation. His sight is never dim. God supplies Himself from out of the infinitude of Himself. God is ALL to Himself. Himself is all there is of ourselves!

God is Mind. Mind can never be deprived of Itself. God is Love. Love cannot divorce Itself. The place whereon we stand is the place where God Is. God is His own Safety, His own Security, His own Peace. Everything in Himself is fully held by Him. His whole Universe of Perfection and Completeness is in Him, and He in It. God is His own Illumination, His own Revelation, His own Heaven.

We have always been God, for God is ALL there is. One becomes aware of this fact only as he stops serving other gods. Spiritual Discrimination reveals thinking to have been the very reason for our sleep. Love for the One as the Whole of us shall be our awakening. Here, we are not in the flesh, but in the Spirit; we are not of this world, but of the Kingdom.

Ye are not in the flesh, but in the Spirit,
if so be that the Spirit of God dwell in you.
Romans 8:9

My Kingdom is not of this world.
John 18:36

Lillian DeWaters, *Greater Works*, 1946, pp. 2-3. No known copyright in effect.

August 29

CUT THE TIES

CUT THE TIES THAT BIND YOU TO THE HUMAN! Through the renewing of your mind, turn back to God. *The journey to God is without distance.* Have you not wondered why you get such a great feeling in church? It is because the focus is on the goodness and grace of God. I truly wish that I could do it for you. I know how important it is for you to think only thoughts of God.

CUT THE TIES THAT BIND YOU TO HEREDITY! You are a free-will being. The choice to acknowledge your divine nature must be made by *you*. Perhaps you started to change your way of thinking but fell by the wayside. *You are the master of your life.* You may start and stop anytime you desire. Oftentimes, we blame our family, work environment, or others for preventing us from staking our spiritual claim. "Greater is he that is within you than he that is in the world.

CUT THE TIES THAT BIND YOU TO CIRCUMSTANCES! Jesus told the man by the pool to "get up and go home." He did not say, "Give your hand to me so I can help you into the waters." It was not the waters, but the faith that people had placed in them. If the waters were the Source of healing, the man would have had to get into the waters. *Your miracle cure is within you.* Become open and receptive to it. God is your Source of health. Awaken to the God idea within you. *"God is your health; you can't be sick."*

Johnnie Colemon, *Open Your Mind and Be Healed*, 1997, pp. 63-64.
Reproduced from OPEN YOUR MIND AND BE HEALED by Johnnie Colemon 9780875167091 DeVorss Publications, www.devorss.com.

August 30

I HAVE NO FEAR

Do not be afraid to ally yourself with God. Hand over to Him every thought, every fact and condition that causes you dread and worry, that is too much for you to handle. Do not hesitate – hand them over. Know that God is regulating these worrisome matters and conditions for you now. Know this as a blessed truth. Thrill to it….God is helping you now. God Himself! Almighty God, with His power and love, and wisdom. Who or what in the world can stand against God?....God is here. He is now doing His mighty work. God Himself, omnipotent, infallible, omnipresent! What can there possibly be for you to fear? Charge your mind with this glorious, freeing, electrifying thought; charge and fill your whole being with it.

It is true. It is true for you in proportion as you fill yourself with it and know it and feel it through every atom of your being, in proportion as you know and feel it to the exclusion of everything else. Of every dull, dire, negative factor opposed to God. God's will for you is good; everything that is harmonious and right….He can and will bring good forth if you give Him a chance. But even He cannot bring it forth if you do not make room for Him, if you clutter your mind, which should be receptive to God and God's Truth only, with doubts and ugliness and fears. Say to yourself, "Today I will give God a chance by putting myself and my affairs wholly and unreservedly in His hands."

Dana Gatlin, *God Is The Answer*, 1938, pp. 124-125. Copyrighted material reprinted with permission of Unity, Unity.org.

August 31

CONTACTING MYSELF

I have told you that in your being there is a throne where the I AM dwells. From that throne flows out all the life forces of your being and your existence. As those forces flow through you, I contact MYSELF in My Universe, thus producing a complete harmony both in the within and the without. Learn to kneel often before that throne and drink the power that reigns thereon. Thus shall My Power become your power to use in all your daily activities.

Only as you kneel before My Throne placing your human personality in entire subjection to My Divine Personality, can you be allowed to use My Power. It must be used only under My direction.

Carry this message with you through the day. Speak often to me. All that I have uttered shall be fulfilled and every word you utter shall be potent with My Power.

Eva Bell Werber, *Quiet Talks With the Master*, 1936, p. 17. Reproduced from QUIET TALKS WITH THE MASTER by Eva Bell Werber 9780875161044 DeVorss Publications, www.devorss.com.

SEPTEMBER

September 1

THE PERFECT LOVE RELATIONSHIP WITH MYSELF

I now claim for myself the Perfect Love Relationship with myself.

I now accept my claim and I know that it is already so in my life. I affirm that I have the ultimate love relationship with myself right now. I now know that I love and accept myself, therefore I am love, peace, joy and happiness. I know that I am the Spirit of Love within me, therefore I radiate love. I now state that I think lovingly about myself at all times and that I see the Christ in me at all times. I know that I always nourish myself with thoughts of love and peace, knowing that these gifts that I give myself always return to me multiplied from the people and situations around me. I now give myself an abundance of love energy, knowing that this giving opens up the channel for Divine Love to pour through me, I now accept this limitless Divine Love pouring through me and permeating every cell in my body and every situation in my life. I now affirm that by loving myself, I only attract people who express from their Christ level, those who express love. I now release all judgment, anger, and condemnation I ever expressed toward myself. I now know the Truth, that Love is the only Power and that is what I choose to give myself at all times. Any and all mental patterns that have caused me to belittle or discredit myself are now lifted into the Light, and they are dissolved in God's Clarity. I now affirm that I love who I am and what I am and that I approve of myself. I now know that I love myself, therefore I allow myself to demonstrate all my true desires in my life.

I give thanks for the purity and perfection of this Love Relationship with myself, I now rejoice in it.

I now release this mighty treatment to the Spiritual Law. I release it into God's Infinite Love and Harmony. I let go and let God. And so it is.

Doris Jones, from her collected works, 2015. Reprinted with permission of her family.

September 2

FEAR

Fear is a state of mind, a state of consciousness, which is so subtle in its influence that it wraps itself about us, befogs our reason, clouds our vision, and dulls our hearing, rendering us unable to get the proper perspective of life.

We are told that what we fear comes upon us, but we are not shown that what is known as fear produces a mental pattern or mold, which creative mind fills, producing on the physical plane that which we have so perfectly pictured on the mental, and that, since thoughts manifest, we thus defeat our purpose. We would not set out a copper kettle for the milkman to fill with milk, knowing that the copper would pollute the milk and render it unsafe for use. And yet this is exactly the thing that we do mentally—we put out a mental mold of failure and expect success to manifest.

As long as Fear remains intangible, it is illusive and goes on with its destructive force without our realization of its power. Let us make a mental effort to drag this subtle thing out of its subjective hiding-place and focus the light of our objective reasoning upon it. Let us mentally create an embodiment, picture it as a monster, big and weird, with numerous claws, devouring all the sweetness and vital force within us and depleting our vitality.

Having been brought to a realization of its deadly power, we could then, in our imagination, take a mental club, drive out this grotesque apparition, close the gate of understanding against it, and thus rid ourselves of it for all time.

Augusta E. Rundel, *Science of Mind*, February 1930, p. 45. Copyrighted material reprinted with permission of SOM Publishing.

September 3

LAUGHTER AS A SPIRITUAL GIFT

Notice how much better your day goes with a good belly laugh? Do you have a friend, a relative, a pet, or a TV show that makes you laugh? Do you understand how laughter enriches your life? Laughter is a part of my daily spiritual practice. How about you?

The scientific, as well as anecdotal, evidence is clear that laughter is good for us. It is a great healing agent. It is efficacious emotionally, physically and mentally, so we should cultivate the people, places and things that encourage us to laugh.

Why not take a moment today to write a list of people, and things, that consistently make you laugh? Everything on your list is a blessing and should be cherished and encouraged.

Jane Claypool, posted in her blog, January 28, 2013. Reprinted with permission of her family.

September 4

SERVICE

Service is a joyous thing. It is indeed the building, hour by hour and day by day, of God's kingdom in the stuff of earth.

"Dear Father-God, open my eyes that I may see the many opportunities for giving service. I seek increased awareness, knowing that I have not always realized where my help was needed until the chance was past. Let me be aware of need and aware of my own strength and ability – of Your strength flowing through me, making me equal to the need. Help me to think only of my kinship with all men as Sons of God, so that I may not be held back by timidity or fear. Guide my hands, my feet, my use of car or telephone or mail service. Guide my very prayers for others, that they may truly be a link between the one in need and Your all-encompassing love, strength, joy, wisdom, and abundance. Amen."

This is the prayer that sings in my heart as I give of myself in service. As I give, I also receive, gladly and thankfully; as I bless, I am in return immeasurably blessed; as I pray for others, my own needs are met with overflowing goodness.

Elizabeth Searle Lamb, published in *Aspire*, November 1957, p. 6.
Copyrighted material reprinted with permission of Divine Science Federation International.

September 5

THE WILDERNESS EXPERIENCE

Truth students have sometimes been accused of turning away from all fear and suffering and unpleasantness. But actually we do not turn our backs upon our difficulties; we face them, seek to understand them, and put the emphasis upon overcoming them quickly. In Truth, we consider problems to be opportunities for training, for growing, for advancing. When we can see them as such, they really become blessings to us.

We can confirm this in the Bible, for it is truly the Book of Life. Here we learn of many cases of wilderness experiences. For instance, we have the wonderful story of the life of Moses. His life was always guided by divine wisdom....His last forty years were the years spent in the wilderness. During this wilderness period, Moses developed some of the very first ideas of democracy known to man. He was the first industrial leader, the first to work out a division of labor among his people. He was a statesman and a spiritual leader. He was a lawgiver and administrator. He was the founder of the first great commonwealth. He was an emancipator, bringing freedom to his people. And many of our modern standards of democracy and justice, right relationships, and individual recognition date from this period of the wilderness experience of Moses.

Grace L. Faus, published in *Aspire*, July 1958, pp. 5-6. Copyrighted material reprinted with permission of Divine Science Federation International.

September 6

KINGDOM OF GOD WITHIN

Jesus taught so plainly that the Kingdom he came to establish is at hand, within the power of man to discern as definitely and consciously as he grasps visible objects with the hand. To make the location of the Kingdom certain he added, "The Kingdom of God is *within you.*"

When man really devotes himself to the establishment of this Kingdom within himself, the world will begin to realize the mighty power of Truth to adjust all the problems of life. The only hope for world healing is in the application of this fundamental truth. Since, as Paul declares, "We are all members of one body," that body will express perfection only as every member is in harmony with every other member, allowing an uninterrupted circulation of life. As this figure of the unity of the great body of humanity is apprehended, man's attitude toward his unenlightened brother will be just the same in gentle solicitude and care that he would give to his good right eye or to his good right hand, if they were not functioning in a normal way.

Ida B. Elliott, published in *The Divine Science News*, May 1945, p. 4. No known copyright in effect.

September 7

SILENT UNITY LETTER

My dear, you ask why you do not enter into the understanding you so desire. I will tell you. You are already in it, but think you have some great thing to do to get there. The kingdom of God is within you! The key to that kingdom is acknowledgment, or affirmation....You have only to open your eyes to the sunlight and your lungs to the fresh air provided by the ever-present supplier of all....Let consciousness lay hold of its boundless supply of life, love, wisdom now! It is your birthright....All you need to do is "Be still and know."

Myrtle Fillmore, from a Silent Unity letter written on September 7, 1891. Copyrighted material reprinted with permission of Unity, Unity.org.

September 8

GOD'S LIGHT WITHIN US

In the beginning God said, "Let there be Light." And so it is. I am that Light. You are that Light – the Light of God. I am an expression of God's Light and Life in the world. I am an expression of this Light that was in the beginning, is now and ever shall be. And in that Light is the Life; and I am that Light and that Life in the world.

In that Light is Wisdom, God's Wisdom, to guide and direct me. When I'm not sure which way to go or what to think I realize that there is a light within me that is very wise. If I am very still and I turn to it, it tells me what to do. It guides me and it is very wise and very loving and very powerful. "In that Light is Wisdom to guide and direct me. In that Light is Life that heals and perfects me."

Science tells us that within every atom and cell of our body there is a point of light. It is the same Light that was first created by God. If you vision that light and feel that light then you become a body of Light.

When we are seeking a healing, when we are seeking peace or freedom from something that troubles us, we should say as God said, "Let there be Light here."

In Truth, the Light already is there, so I say, "Let that Light shine." Let it glow. Let it fill your mind and heart and soul and body with Light and Life and Peace and Order. In that Light is Life. It is the Light of peace and freedom. It is the Light that heals and perfects me. In that Light are joy and abundance that prosper me. In that Light which is the Mind of the Infinite God, All Wise, there are creative ideas. If I am still and I listen and I hear, these ideas come into my mind from that One Mind of the Universe; and they are creative and productive and I think them and I act upon them and I am prospered in any way I desire.

Ruth Hammink Carr, transcribed from her lesson at the Divine Science Church of Birmingham, Michigan, September 2, 1990. Printed with permission of her family.

September 9

SPIRITUAL FORGIVENESS

In striving to overcome the lack of true compassion and spiritual forgiveness, we need to reflect Love's healing compassionate ministry to all who need it. Then the privilege may indeed be ours of binding up the broken-hearted.

Perhaps one of the most striking illustrations of the quality of compassion and brotherly love is given in the beautiful lesson portrayed in the heart of the Bishop for Jean Valjean, that immortal character in "Les Miserables." The Bishop took in for the night the outcast who stole his silver candlesticks. In the morning the police brought the outcast back to the Bishop's house. The Bishop took in the situation at a glance and said, "Why, I gave him those candle sticks. They belong to him. Let him go." After the departure of the police, the good Bishop put his hand on Jean's shoulder and said, "Jean Valjean, my brother, you belong to God now." And in that moment Divine Love entered the outcast's heart and he was transformed.

Such is the miracle performed by love. Peter asked his Lord, "How many times shall I forgive?" He was willing to obey the new rules up to a certain point but he thought there ought to be a recognized limit. This is why it seems so difficult to many of us to grasp the principle of Love.

The Master calmly made the astounding statement, "Love your Enemies," for He knew it is salutary to love. Love is a creative force. One cannot become a good critic of music without first loving music; one can never understand men and women unless one begins by loving them. Wherever we see Love we see something divine and wherever love is, there God is also….

By seeing the true man, the Bishop could pronounce the mistake of Jean Valjean forgiven and wiped out so far as his own consciousness was concerned. This much we can do for another. Thus far is the atonement vicarious.

Alberta Smith, published in *Religious Science Monthly*, August 1929, p. 11. Copyrighted material reprinted with permission of SOM Publishing.

September 10

FAITH IN THE PROMISES OF GOD

We are told in the Old Testament that Abraham's faith was a faith in the promises of God. He was promised that his descendants would cover the earth if he listened to His guidance. He did not know where he was going when he left his home on faith….But he heard a call – a call from the little Voice within. He could not see where he was going. There was only a promise – a promise if he would follow that Voice. That's all. He had faith in the promise; and the promise was fulfilled….

Our faith is in the promise of God; that He dwells within us and that we are one with Him; that we are His Children, we are His Sons NOW. Our faith is in the promise that a new being, transformed, the Son of God within us, the Christ Jesus self, can be actualized in daily living. Our faith is in that promise of a God of fulfillment, a God who does have the power to fulfill, in spite of anything.

Faith is believing where you cannot see, where there is no possible way of seeing how it could happen. Faith is in the invisible promise that says, "It shall be done unto you, for I am the Lord, your God. My arm is not shortened. Whatever has been done before, I can do now." Faith is acting on the promises of God, "Look unto Me and I will save you." Faith is acting on that promise that He will not stop short of that fulfillment. "Look unto Me; Call upon Me; I will deliver you; with long life I will satisfy you." Faith is acting on that promise. Faith is acting on a belief in a Presence and Power that works above man's beliefs, at a rate of vibration above time and space, and knows how to bring His Presence and Power and Glory into human experience to fulfill every human need. It is this kind of faith that is needed today.

You are a ray of spiritual power shining ever out from the heart of God!

Ethel Barnhart, from her lesson at The Santa Anita Church, Arcadia, California, (est. 1950), Volume 1, No. 4, pp. 2-3. Reprinted with permission of The Santa Anita Church.

September 11

I AM IN GOD'S HANDS

Let not thine hands be slack.
Zephaniah 3:16

My hands are God's hands. This is true because through these hands flow the only life, the life of God. My hands are the manifestation of the one creative principle which is perfect and is within every hand. I thank you Father for the wonder and beauty in these, your hands. As I look upon these hands a tenderness filled with gratitude comes over me for the service they give. These hands are deft and sure because through them flow a service that is a manifestation of Thee, a service which no other hands can give because they are individual. My hands are free and elastic because they are open to receive good, yet they are strong and firm in their ability to give a perfect service to mankind. As I bless and praise the elasticity and perfection in my hands, I have released to some degree this same perfection in all hands everywhere because they too are made by my Father, the one principle of creation.

Lola Pauline Mays, published in *Creative Thought*, September 1964, p. 27. Copyrighted material reprinted with permission of SOM Publishing.

September 12

TRUTH IS GOD

Truth is an eternal principle. Truth is God, and the very nature of a true thought is deathless. It is the word of God. "My words shall not pass away."

"Every thought sent out in the silence is charged with the character of the mind that sends it," and it goes forth to slay or make alive. If charged with that which is evil and false, its seeming influence is toward death, because of its carnal character. If charged with truth it is the deathless messenger that brings comfort and life, and blesses wherever it strikes. Who can fail to see their duty in this respect? Let every one who loves the truth proclaim it, by sending out the true thought strongly charged with the firm denial of any evil power, and repeat it over and over and over again.

Say it to your friends. Say it to your foes. Say it to your household. Say it to your neighbors. Say it to the community. Say it to the world at large. Say it daily, and hourly, and wherever the thought strikes that denies the reality and power of evil, declaring that the only power in the universe is good; the evil, the crime, and the sordid selfishness begin to die and fade away; characters begin to change; trouble and sorrow in the home, and injustice and oppressions fall away, hope steals in, and things begin to brighten, better days begin to dawn, simply because you have sent the Divine word of truth to erase the false, while you yourself will be doubly blessed by the sweet echo that comes back to you in the assurance that you have blessed others.

It is the majesty of the Principle you understand and proclaim that works the happy change from sorrow to joy, or from sickness to health, or from poverty to plenty. You set it into action by your true word spoken *or thought* in confidence.

Jane Yarnall, *Practical Healing For Mind and Body*, 1891, p. 24. No known copyright in effect.

September 13

IMMUTABLE LAWS

THE LAWS OF NATURE

We know something about the laws of nature and how they work, and we are discovering more. We will always find that any law, insofar as we know about its manner of operation, always adheres to that manner of operation. With every law of nature there is this procedure: impetus, direction, instigation, on the part of the one using the law; and an exact response on the part of the law itself, bringing about a result which exactly corresponds to the direction.

THE LAW OF CAUSE AND EFFECT

May we not say then that it is a law of laws to respond to cause, producing effect. Can we not further postulate a parent law which we call the Law of Cause and Effect.

But, "God is Infinite Spirit, the limitless, conscious Life of the Universe; the One Infinite Person within whom we live. The Law is simply a force." Everywhere we see effect. Effect is the only tangible thing with which we may deal -- whether we call it physical universe, body, physical objects, form or condition. But there could not be effects without something to cause them and in order for effect to come out of cause there must be some way, method or means in which this takes place.

Josephine Holmes Curtis, published in *Science of Mind,* September 1934, p. 62. Copyrighted material reprinted with permission of SOM Publishing.

September 14

IN THE SILENCE

I close my surface senses to all mortal things
        and find security in the silence that waits my coming;
I open my ears to the music of the spheres
        that beats its beauty in vibrant variations;
I open my eyes to the Light within
        that shows the luminous trail ahead;
I open my mind to be moored in the deep waters
        of Infinite Wisdom;
I open my heart to illimitable Love
        that unfolds…grows…glows;
I open myself to free-flowing Life
        that pulsates and surges.

The *real of me* emerges in wondrous ways
        of harmonious power…
        radiant light…disarming love
        that dissolves disease, disaster, dissent
        and opens the door to glories unknown before.

In awe I stand poised in the Great Silence;
        humbly grateful, I accept…
        and let it flow to you…
        and you…
        and you…

Elizabeth R. McClellan, published in *Science of Mind*, August 1980, pp. 54-55. Copyrighted material reprinted with permission of SOM Publishing.

September 15

COMMUNION

I will tell Thee all my thoughts. I will speak face to face with Thee, as friend to friend.

My most secret desires I will declare freely to Thee. I will even search within myself, that I may find and present to Thee whatever the depths of my heart may treasure. This I will do, that my soul may be made all clean.

I will listen for Thy words to me as the flower roots listen for the spring rain.

Thy voice is as the music of a starlit night to my hearing. It is the song of the warm south wind in the fragrant pines. It is the cooing of the babe to his mother's smile.

Thy voice is as the voice of the robin when his long northward flight is ended and he sings from the high bough of the maple tree at the red sunrise.

I will send my mind to Thee, running to meet Thee, to learn what I may do in obedience to Thy thought for me.

Thy speech is to me such joy as never poet knew or harpist felt. My soul is rapt in an ecstasy of devotion at Thy most casual word.

The voice of the beloved in the ears of the lover is not as sweet as Thy whisper to me, when in the stillness of mortality. Thy infinite understanding reaches my finite understanding.

Long have we spoken, the one to the other. From that bright morn in which time was given birth, to this present moment, my words have flown to Thee, Thy words to me.

My thoughts melt into Thy thoughts, and peace possesses me as the air possesses space.

I know Thy heart, and Thou knowest mine; not two hearts, but one.

Imelda Octavia Shanklin, *Selected Studies*, 1926, pp. 5-6. Copyrighted material reprinted with permission of Unity, Unity.org.

September 16

POWER

God is Power. Divine Mind moving on itself generates power. There is only one Power. This is the power in the creation. It propels ideas into manifestation. Without power, there would be no manifestation. Faith, love, wisdom, life, require power and strength to fulfill their offices in the creation.

The human consciousness must accept power in its divine aspect, in order to achieve results on life's pathway. But there must be the realization that there is only one power – God-Power. This power is good and only good. Any manifestation of power used wrongly is the result of man's mistaken use of free will and of the power to think. For instance, both the inventor and the counterfeiter use the one power.

The counterfeiter misuses that power for selfish ends; the inventor lets the power work through him for good purposes.

There is the good use of power, and there is the false use of power resulting in tyranny and dictatorships.

Jesus said: *"All power is given unto me in heaven and in earth."* Matthew 28:18

We understand this to mean that when we unify with the Christ Mind, we can receive the flow of power in thought, and on earth which represents our body and circumstances.

Helen Zagat, *Faith and Works*, 1955, pp. 41-42. No known copyright in effect.

September 17

REALIZATION FOLLOWING MEDITATION

Realization is the outcome of the three exercises: relaxation, concentration, and meditation. Realization is purely spiritual in its working and in its power. We begin with the physical and go through the mental into the intellectual, where we meditate upon whatever we desire to hold in mind, until the spirit of it becomes a part of us and continues to unfold in realization. [This example is based on the word Omnipresence.]

Realization is not temporary; it is an eternal activity. After realization the soul becomes more and more identified with its own divinity. The more we practice realization, or letting the reality of the subject of our meditation take possession of us, the more we know of it and the more quickly we find its value and observe its enlightenment of our whole being. We come to know God, to know ourselves, and to know the relation between ourselves and God. We advance into the realm of conscious knowledge in which we know that our eternal Father, the source of all, is one with us in omnipresent power and wisdom….

In realization we cease thinking about the word upon which we have concentrated, and we come into the center or heart of consciousness, symbolized by the heart. We penetrate this innermost region when we have concentrated and have meditated upon the word Omnipresence until we know its power and have felt the Presence. Let us continue to feel the Presence without thinking about it. At this point begins a continual realization of the presence of our Source, our Father. Here we become conscious of the activity of the Cause manifesting in the son, Christ Jesus, within the very heart of us. We should endeavor to feel the reality of the Presence and to make real in our consciousness the fullness, the joy, and the freedom of the Presence as it unfolds us within and without.

Jennie H. Croft, *Methods of Meditation*, 1928, pp. 5-6, 33-34. Copyrighted material reprinted with permission of Unity, Unity.org.

September 18

THE CREATIVE FORCE

While there is no human science to prove that God is, every human science is founded on that fact. We know that we live and breathe and that we were born into this world through no efforts of our own. We know that we did not plan our entrance into this world, nor did we choose our parentage or environment. Yet all this must have been thought out, planned and executed in its minutest details by a great creative power which must be omnipresent, since its works are everywhere.

As this creative force made us of the substance which was in and of itself, so we must realize that there can be no separation between Spirit and substance or matter. If God is omnipresent, then He is present in matter, and the spiritual and material man are one.

Kathleen M. H. Besly, *The Divine Art of Living*, 1917, p. 23. No known copyright in effect.

September 19

YOU ARE AN OVERCOMER

Through the power of FAITH, Noah built the ark.

Through the power of FAITH, Abraham left the land of his birth.

Through the power of FAITH, Abraham offered Isaac.

Through the power of FAITH, Jochebed hid the baby Moses.

Through the power of FAITH, Jericho's walls came tumbling down.

Through the power of FAITH, David overpowered Goliath.

Through the power of FAITH, the widow of Zerephath fed Elijah.

Through the power of FAITH, Joseph fled to Egypt. And,

Through the power of FAITH, *you are making your overcoming now!*

Johnnie Colemon, *Open Your Mind and Be Healed*, 1997, p. 48. Reproduced from OPEN YOUR MIND AND BE HEALED by Johnnie Colemon 9780875167091 DeVorss Publications, www.devorss.com.

September 20

LOOK NO LONGER

Enter into the secret place within your own soul; there, you will find God's alter established, overshadowed by the wings of wisdom and love, waiting, to carry your Living Message to the heights, to feed the earth's hungry souls. Spirit knows what they have need of.

Look no longer for your Lord and Master in the clouds and shadows of earth's sorrow and crying! Lift up your eyes; see the sunrise over the hilltops. Behold! A new illumination, the rainbow of His Covenant, the law of God fulfilled in each Life, health, peace, joy "unspeakable and full of Glory."

Wherever I go
My soul is aglow
With the love-light divine,
This is my Lord, my guide,
My preserver and keeper,
My sleepless protector.
My Uplift –

Agnes J. Galer, published in *Religious Science Monthly*, February 1929, p. 36. Copyrighted material reprinted with permission of SOM Publishing.

September 21

FAVORITE AFFIRMATIONS

I live today, not yesterday or tomorrow.

In God there is no lack or limitation.

I am reverent toward each day.

I now accept my birthright.

I meet life with courage, for I have faith in God.

God is greater than any problem I ever have to face.

Infinite Wisdom guides and directs my every thought and act.

The spirit within me flows forth in joyous action and all is well.

In the stillness I become consciously aware of the Presence of God.

I know that divine order and health are working in and through me at all times.

Through knowing my Christ within, I easily meet the pressures of the outer world.

I place my loved ones in the care and protection of the Father, knowing all is well with them.

I trust God implicitly to right every wrong and dissolve every misunderstanding in my life.

Life becomes joyous and free when lived in Love.

Grace L. Faus, *For So It Is*, 1971, pp. 13-24. Copyrighted material reprinted with permission of Divine Science Federation International.

September 22

LOOKING AHEAD

What does your future look like? Whatever you're thinking right now, your state of awareness, is shaping your future. Is it what you want it to be? Many of us will be repeating our past. To change our experiences we must change our internal awareness of who we are. A prayer or an affirmation will not change the content of our consciousness. We must engage the power within ourselves to create this change.

Our attitudes and expectations have a lot to do with making this change in our lives. We can acknowledge what happens to us as part of the unfoldment of who we are. Nothing that can happen to us is against us. Despite this fear, we are truly an extension of God and we need to make this discovery and bring it forth. We have lived our lives from the surface level. There is no security in living on the surface of life. Security is found by turning within, communing and staying in touch with our own inner voice, our inner power and our inner creativity. That's the only place where we can make a difference in our future. We must focus on this inner search.

We have a choice to live life as a battle to be fought; fearful and anxious with a lack of trust. This is not the kind of living that will bring us joy. Our own attitude is what gets in the way. Ernest Holmes said, "Have no fear of tomorrow. Refuse to carry the corpse of a mistaken yesterday into our future. There is no future to be afraid of." We are free to look at life in a new way, to see that the source of our life is within us. Our future is infinite with possibilities. We must reclaim our lives from the circumstances around us. Then we begin to regain our freedom to live life as we choose.

Peggy Bassett, from her recorded lesson at Huntington Beach Church of Religious Science, November 1989. Transcribed and printed with permission of Huntington Beach Center for Spiritual Living, Huntington Beach, California.

September 23

DIVINE LOVE

In the spiritual body, the love center is the heart, symbolized by Jesus' disciple John. John loved the Master. During Jesus' journeys with his disciples through Palestine, John was almost continually by the Master's side. Even when Jesus was crucified and all the other disciples fled, John was not far from the Master. While John was in exile on the island of Patmos, he was *in the Spirit of the Lord's day* and was lifted in consciousness until he beheld a vision of the perfect man Jesus Christ in all his glory. Thus love beholds the transforming, uplifting power of the Christ.

Love holds the body together. Love is the attractive force that draws our good to us according to the depth and strength of our realization of love.

Cora Dedrick Fillmore, *Christ Enthroned In Man*, 1937, pp. 39-40.
Copyrighted material reprinted with permission of Unity, Unity.org.

September 24

GOD IS LOVE

"God is Love." These are the greatest words ever written or spoken by man.

To believe them, to understand them, above all to accept them as true and present here and now, to *feel* them as true, is the greatest thing that can ever happen to any man.

But there is a step beyond that. Beyond believing, understanding, accepting, or feeling them to be true. There is the *thing* itself. It is as though we sat around talking about electricity, believing it, arguing about how to use it, interpreting it, making designs and plans about it — and never discovered or used the thing itself. For once, in simplicity and quietness, in gentleness and glory, we ask to feel the *thing* itself, the Love of God, through which healing, grace, enlightenment take place.

God, the creator of the Universe, God the ruler, the power, the source, and force is Love. God IS Love. God is LOVE. Be still and know that God is Love. Very still. With open heart and mind stilled, that Love may speak to you. I am still. God is Love. Thy son heareth.

The spirit can give us only what we can take; it imparts of itself only as we partake of its nature….Every man stands in the shadow of a mighty mind, a pure intelligence, and a divine givingness! *The Science of Mind*, p. 40.

Adela Rogers St. Johns, published in *Science of Mind*, March 1956, p. 52. Copyrighted material reprinted with permission of SOM Publishing.

September 25

THE POWER TO CHOOSE

You have the power to choose what shall find a welcome home in your mind. You do not always have the ability to choose what your ears hear, but you can decide what you will let into your consciousness, what you will feel deeply. We are all so vulnerable to the news media. We are all susceptible to the insidious influences all around us, and we all carry on silent dialogues with ourselves most of the time. What do you say to yourself when you are alone? Do you find yourself asking, "How will I make ends meet with prices going up so alarmingly?" or "What security is there in such a world?"? If you have had such questions, whether they are verbally expressed or not, your responsibility is to BE AWARE of your thoughts, your actions and your reactions to outside stimuli. Instead of saying, "I can't afford that," substitute this thought: "I choose not to buy this today." Instantly, you will lose the feeling of deprivation. You have made a choice. Remember, there is only one Source – God. People, jobs, investments, are simply channels for the delivery of God's good into your life. God is totally unaffected by changing conditions and fluctuating economies. When you find yourself giving way to fear and negative thinking and feeling, immediately replace that thought with a statement such as this:

GOD IS THE ONLY PRESENCE AND THE ONLY POWER IN MY LIFE. ALL IS WELL!

Margaret M. Stevens, *PROSPERITY is God's Idea*, 1978, pp. 24-25.
Reproduced from PROSPERITY IS GOD'S IDEA by Margaret M. Stevens, 09780875162645 DeVorss Publications, www.devorss.com. Reprinted with permission.

September 26

I ARISE

I believe if I serve and wait with loving patience I shall hear the voice that the disciples heard, commanding me to throw my net in on the other side.

I believe that I shall draw to me my heart's desire. The mists of doubt shall break around me and no more upon the ocean of unrest, I shall pull my boat of plenty to the shining shore.

With this vision in front of me I arise full of energy. I take up the work I disliked, the work which I thought was not mine, but I keep my eyes on the ideal, as the laborers kept their eyes on the door through which they desired to enter.

Every hour of selfless service is drawing me nearer the beautiful goal which love's hands have prepared.

I resolve to fret no more for what is not here. I will employ each golden moment with beautiful thoughts which will build themselves into my mind, and make me strong to endure until the door of my heart's desire swings open and the call of love bids me enter.

Evelyn Whitell, *The Silence*, 1925, p. 56. No known copyright in effect.

September 27

TURNING ON THE LIGHT

In order to receive God's light in the body, we must first be able to forget the body so that we can quiet the mind and concentrate the spiritual energies on God. Let us sit comfortably with the head at rest and the hands folded in the lap. Many people find it helpful to meditate with the feet raised, resting upon a footstool or even upon another chair. The spine may be relaxed and comfortable as one sits, but it must not be curved or cramped.

The one who prays will discover the reason for this as he connects more and more closely with the life of God. He will find that he is filled with such fullness of life that his spine must be free so that his chest can expand. He will notice as he relaxes that even his breathing is altered, becoming slow, thin and light, as if to leave room for the Spirit of God within. If we consider the body just enough to make it comfortable so that it can relax, the spirit will direct its care and provide its needs.

Agnes Sanford, *The Healing Light*, 1947, p. 37. No known copyright in effect.

September 28

WHAT IS IT THAT WE HAVE?

"Whatsoever is not of faith is sin," says the Bible. "What then, do you make of faith?" you may ask. The Bible, we believe, is the outgrowth of religion rather than vice versa. Statements are not necessarily true because they are in the Bible, but because they are true, they are included in the inspired parts of the Scriptures. Since modern scholarship realizes that the word, sin, means merely missing the mark, we can readily see how significant the above verse is. It states a reality: If we lack faith in what we do, we fail.

Practically everyone needs to learn that faith does not descend like a dove from Heaven lighting only a chosen few. Neither does it grow overnight anymore than does a rich, velvety lawn. Not a bit of it. But if you are willing to throw yourself enthusiastically into cultivating faith, you can raise a bumper crop. Like a lawn, though, it takes active desire, knowledge, time, perseverance. Know, too, that the moment we look at appearances, that moment we have to let go of whatever faith we had, that hoping to have our good at some future time, is only vain hope, not scientific faith. We must make ourselves think and feel, speak and act as if something delightful has already taken place and in a wonderful way.

This, I think is what Jesus, the Master, meant when he said, "When ye pray believe that ye have received and it shall be given you." Joyous persistency in holding a vision is true faith and brings results.

Ruth E. Chew, published in *Mind Remakes Your World*, (ed. Holmes), 1941, pp. 54-55. Reprinted with permission of INTA.

September 29

GOD AS SPIRIT

When Jesus revealed God as Spirit, living Intelligence, He made it easier for mankind to understand His omnipresence as a creative power instantly ready to respond to the call of faith; a power having within itself the potentiality of limitless supply ever seeking expression in form. All growth in nature illustrates the way potential power expands into myriads for forms under the right conditions. An acorn has all the potentialities of the mighty oak, but its outer shell and inner meat show no evidence of the tree that is to be. However, the tree is there as potential power, power that remains static until the right conditions of moisture, heat, and nourishment are provided. Within man there is mighty power, the power of the Spirit that God has given him, in which lies the potentiality of all the good his heart can ever desire. This power is static until brought forth into expression by conditions furnished by mind; nourished by faith it expresses itself in forms shaped by thoughts.

Georgiana Tree West, *Prosperity's Ten Commandments*, 1946, p. 13.
Copyrighted material reprinted with permission of Unity, Unity.org.

September 30

PATIENCE

Those who are certain of the outcome can afford to wait, and wait without anxiety. Patience is natural to the teacher of God. All he sees is certain outcome, at a time perhaps unknown to him as yet, but not in doubt. The time will be as right as is the answer. And this is true for everything that happens now or in the future. The past as well held no mistakes; nothing that did not serve to benefit the world, as well as him to whom it seemed to happen. Perhaps it was not understood at the time. Even so, the teacher of God is willing to reconsider all his past decisions, if they are causing pain to anyone. Patience is natural to those who trust. Sure of the ultimate interpretation of all things in time, no outcome already seen or yet to come can cause them fear.

Helen Schucman, *A Course In Miracles*, 1975, Manual For Teachers, pp. 13-14. No known copyright in effect.

OCTOBER

October 1

SONG IN MY HEART

There is within me a joyous song…It holds such gladness that to catch even the lilt of its tones refreshes and restores me. As I listen, every part of me sings its melody…there is not a cell in my body but is aroused, awakened, and attuned; not an organ but responds and enters in the harmony of perfect functioning. The joyful rhythm pulses through my veins and arteries, purifies the life stream, tunes my heart to beat in unison with the great heart of God, breathes into and out of my lungs with the cleansing, renewing God breath. I become so illumined by the song…that it creates in me a joy and a harmony that radiate from me to others along the way.

Frances W. Foulks, *Prayers, Blessings and Meditations*, Unity pamphlet, 1958, p. 16. Copyrighted material reprinted with permission of Unity, Unity.org.

October 2

LIVE IN THE NOW

There are two thieves that enjoy controlling our lives – "past hurts" and "future fears." What these thieves do is sap our energy and clog up our ability to do what needs to be done by us. I believe that what needs to be done by us is to make the world a better place in which to live. We are unable to fulfill this responsibility if these two thieves are controlling our thoughts.

The clue to arresting these two thieves is to live only in the now. Making a decision to live only in the now does not close the door on the past or mean that we make no meaningful plans for the future. We are aware of our past and we express gratitude for it as it brought us to the present. We learn the lesson and then move forward to express our gifts from God in the future. The future no longer holds fear for us when we live in the moment.

Understanding and knowing that God energy has been with us in the past and is present in us today, produces a profound hopefulness in us regarding the future. With this in mind, we begin to understand that by taking each day as it comes, we are planting seeds and preparing the soil for a brighter future.

Nancy Purcell, *A Flow Chart of Life*, 2012, p. 55. Reproduced from A FLOW CHART OF LIFE by Nancy Purcell, 9781466966765 Trafford Publishing, www.trafford.com.

October 3

WHO IS GOD?

Why, *you* are God. And you. And you. And I AM God. And everybody, the whole two billions of us on earth – everybody is God. Not one of us is alone – not Jesus the Christ alone – he was the "first *born* of many brethren," all children of one God. God, the I AM of everybody on earth, or whoever was on earth, or ever will be!

Can I put my finger on God in me? Sure. My CONSCIOUSNESS is God – not a little piece of God, but the FULLNESS of God.

And the same is true of you, and you, all round the world. The fullness of the infinite God is YOU – your *consciousness*. Not a little piece of God; but the FULLNESS of God, is you.

Elizabeth Towne, published in *Mind Remakes Your World*, (ed. Holmes), 1941, p. 256. Reprinted with permission of INTA.

October 4

LABOR WITH LOVE

God gave us life, and His work to do in it. Therefore, as co-creators with the Divine, each of us has his or her particular niche to fill. Though many of us shy away from the idea of "work," it is the only way in which each of us fulfills the Divine purpose.

Our crucial functions *are* to work and to love. Work is love made visible. It insures survival by providing for our basic *needs,* and satisfying certain *wants.* Love serves to create the conditions which complement and give reason for working: establishing home and family, and providing for personal and family needs. Work and love go hand in hand as the means of self-validation, of social validation, and of spiritual validation. Therefore, work and love are the reasons for being.

If work is love made visible, what kind of love are we talking about? Of course, there are all kinds: love of spouse for spouse, parent for child, brother for brother, and so on; also selfish love, greedy love, and possessive love. However, the love we're concerned with here is mature love – which has nothing to do with the number of one's years, but with feeling and attitude. It is the love that desires to give rather than to take; giving, not in a sense of sacrifice, but through care, responsibility, respect and knowledge. To carry out these elements requires work.

Attitudes about work and love reveal a great deal about our emotions. Emotional and spiritual balance involve the recognition that work is part of our creative identity, through which we achieve realization of our innate potential. Work is engagement in productive activity....Loving to work and working to love is what makes for personal dynamism, which has nothing to do with personality or temperament. Neither does it mean being a flamboyant go-getter. We are dynamic when we do something in a new and a better way; when we are creative, inventive, useful; when we make the world a better place because we live, love, and work in it.

Doris Dickelman, published in *Science of Mind*, September 1970, pp. 8, 16. Copyrighted material reprinted with permission of SOM Publishing.

October 5

FAITH

I acquaint myself with God and am at peace.

Fear is a mental warfare. We find our peace only when we find God.

If we have not the faith that wins, the faith that demonstrates, it is because we are not well enough acquainted with God and His peace. When we really know God and are convinced of His Omnipotence, we have an unshaken faith.

We cannot help having the faith that is the very substance of the things we hope for, and the evidence of things not yet seen, when we are so well acquainted with God that we KNOW His Reality, His Omnipresence and His Changelessness.

Often people will try so hard to get more faith, and others seem to think that in some mystical way faith will come to them. Some are envious of another's faith, and then conclude that one is either born with faith or without it. I believe that everyone has faith and he puts it into that with which he is best acquainted: evil if he knows more of evil; God the good if he knows more about the Realities of life.

We acquaint ourselves with God by giving our attention to the things of Spirit – in our reading and studying: our meditation and silence, our constant mental attitude, and our conversation.

Study: Job 22:21-30 and Hebrews 11.

Alice R. Ritchie, published in *Divine Science Monthly*, October 1933, p. 19. Copyrighted material reprinted with permission of Divine Science Federation International.

October 6

TRINITY OF MIND

The Christian trinity is called Father, Son and Holy Ghost. The metaphysical trinity may be stated as Mind, Idea, and Manifestation. Mind is the Father, Idea the activity of Mind, and Manifestation the offspring, the form which Idea takes. For example, Mind – or Intelligence – desires to express repose and It creates, through man, a chair. The chair, or manifestation, is a form which the understanding of repose takes. Mind produces a companion for man to express the faithfulness of love, and we have a dog, which symbolizes fidelity. Mind, expressing the continual vivifying action of life, produces rain, which symbolizes the multifarious ideas of God replenishing the earth. "He causeth the rain to fall upon the just and the unjust." Here we have a perfect example of Mind's impersonal attitude toward man. Mind judges no one. It gives of Its all to each one. What each receives is a question of how much he as an individual can avail himself.

Elizabeth Carrick-Cook, published in *Mind Remakes Your World*, (ed. Holmes), 1941, p. 67. Reprinted with permission of INTA.

October 7

THOU SHALT WALK IN THY WAY SAFELY

Whoso keepeth the commandment shall know no evil thing.
Ecclesiastes 8:5

The eternal God is thy dwelling place,
and underneath are the everlasting arms.
Deuteronomy 33:27

No one has the daring to deny that there is a power protecting and caring for him. This much is universally admitted. But more is revealed to the seeker after Truth; he knows that this power is from the Creator, the One, the only Power (Romans 13:1), therefore limitless; and he firmly believes – one must believe, must *know*, that as easily as the river carries the little bark down the stream, so will Spirit carry him on Its bosom throughout all of his experience.

Nora Smith Holm, *The Runner's Bible*, 1913, p. 131. No known copyright in effect.

October 8

THE CHRIST IN ME IS THE CHRIST IN YOU

... I am in my Father and ye in me and I in you.
John 14:20

    As I recognize that the Christ within me is the Christ within you it is as if to say: the Love, Life, Intelligence, Goodness, and Peace of God within me, salutes the Love, Life, Intelligence, Goodness and Peace of God within you. I automatically dissolve in my consciousness and yours any thought of discord, any hint of the less than Good. In Christ we become brothers, branches on the same vine, partaking of the same Substance, one in the Spirit. Because I trust the Christ Self of every man, I trust Life to bring me my highest good. Because I love the Christ in every man, I love all men and that love returns to me enriched a thousand fold. As I unify with the Christ in every man I unify with all of Life and in that sense of Wholeness I find that I am whole and the thoughts with which I once contended have no power to disturb me.
    The Christ in me salutes the Christ in you and we are One. And so it is.

Cornelia Addington, published in *Creative Thought*, March 1955, p. 15.
Copyrighted material reprinted with permission of SOM Publishing.

October 9

THE FINISHER

Are we finishers of ourselves, or, have we had a Finisher? Without the Finisher ye can do nothing. Without the Spirit of Christ in us, our efforts, no matter how strenuous or how supreme, are built upon *self* as power and understanding and will end up in disappointment and failure. When we stand upon our own ideas and opinions, what does it amount to? They change from day to day. When we stand upon the systems and opinions of others, of what permanent value are these? Theories come and go; rise and fall.

Then, upon WHAT shall we stand? Stand on the "Rock that is Christ!" I Corinthians 10:4 "The same yesterday, today and forever!"

While it is true that Jesus Christ is our Way, our Door, our Finisher, there is an individual work for us to do. If we do not *accept* Him as the Way, the Finisher, the work that He did for us is not benefiting us; that is, we are not experiencing the good that is prepared for us. The finished kingdom is here, yet all are not appropriating it or experiencing it….

Our part in life is to lift our vision, behold and accept the path that is already made for us and walk in that path. We are to take and to enjoy the great good already prepared, and to cease trying to cut new paths and create new ways. *Let us "work out" or express that which we already possess,* that which we already ARE.

Lillian DeWaters, *The Christ Within*, 1926, pp. 21-23. No known copyright in effect.

October 10

THE CHRIST WITHIN

I, if I be lifted up,
      Will draw all men to me;
'Tis I, the Christ Within,
      That speaketh now to thee.

Yea, I, the Christ Within,
      Proclaim anew my birth, --
Look unto me and be ye saved
      Ye uttermost ends of the earth.

Saved from all that hinders
      The onward march of the soul, --
The petty limitations
      That keep thee from the goal.

Destructive thoughts and wrong endeavor
      Have earned their measure of the pain, --
I look to thee, Oh Christ Within,
      And I am whole again.

Helen Van Slyke, *Mountain Thoughts*, 1927, p. 12. Copyrighted material reprinted with permission of SOM Publishing.

October 11

SPIRITUAL SUBSTANCE

God is substance. Spiritual Substance is spiritual energy, emanating from God-Mind in creative activity. Spiritual Substance is the idea of all-ness in Divine Mind. It is the real out of which all things in the creation are formed.

We have accepted the truth that God is Mind and that Divine Mind is all; but for many people there remains a vague doubt or puzzlement as to how the eternal verity can be transformed into the minutiae of our daily needs in our little human lives.

At this point, let us be clear as to the real meaning of substance. We must make the distinction between the use of the word in the popular, worldly sense, and the metaphysical meaning. We are not using the word, substance, to designate a material manifestation, such as "an object made of a hard, shiny substance." Spiritual Substance is invisible to the five senses of man.

Spiritual Substance is invisible Mind-Energy, or Mind-Essence. It is the reality within the creation, either the invisible or the visible creation. Substance is that out of which all things are formed. It is the reality back of and within every visible form or expression in the creation. It is ever in process of movement. It is responsive to the pressure of man's thoughts and feeling. That is why it is important for man to train his essential thinking patterns, and his emotions.

Spiritual Substance is really Omnipresence. It is the "body of God," or the permeating essence. In this Substance inhere all the basic, creative ideas in Divine Mind. All that is needed is within the invisible, shimmering, radiant Substance. It is swift and unfailing in its response to man's call of faith.

Helen Zagat, *Faith and Works*, 1955, pp. 44-45. No known copyright in effect.

October 12

OMNIPRESENT LIFE

Emerson says there is but one mind, and that we are all different expressions of it.

The Mental Science student means the same thing when he says there is but one Life, of which we are but individual manifestations.

If there is but one Life, then life is omnipresent -- it fills all space. There is nothing outside of it. Indeed, there is no outside. There is but one Life. This Life is the universal Principle of Being that men call God.

There is a Life Principle, and it is unlimited; it is one. It holds the visible universe in place, though it is invisible. It is a self-existent principle. It underlies universal law. It is the one Law -- the Law of Attraction -- and beside it there is no other law. It is also the very essence of love; and the recognition of it as love is expressed by us in love for each other.

All the races of men have felt the presence and the power of this Law of Attraction, whose ultimate expression is love, or life, in a myriad of different forms.

The undeviating Law has never been violated, and never will be. And this is our hope. It is unchanging, diseaseless, deathless; and a knowledge of it conforms us to it in a way that renders us diseaseless and deathless.

For the law does permeate all visible forms. It is one with all substance. And no doubt that an expanded and spiritual interpretation of the word "God" has been the foundation for the expression that "God and man are one."

For, in spite of the personal, and, therefore, limited interpretation of the word God, there have been in all ages of the world a few thinkers who were not so entirely confined to its narrow meaning, but they were able to see it in an enlarged, spiritual sense; in a sense that proved it to be the moving impulse of all visible life. And these men have said, "God and man are one."

Helen Wilmans, *Home Course in Mental Science*, 1921, p. 11. No known copyright in effect.

October 13

DO YOU WORK FOR A LIVING?

It is a mistake to work for a living. To work this way is to be a slave under dominion to the laws of slavery. Never work for a living. How can you gain a life? *Life is!* You cannot pay for it. You have no price to give in exchange for life, for your breath and your being. You are not here to work by strenuous effort to make life. You are here under the blessing of God to live a life of wholesome, loving kindness, of success and good will towards each other and the bringing out of your own nature, the *divine self*.

God lives you every moment. If you are conscious that God is your very life and being you will not work to express it in terms of mortal consciousness, in dollars and cents and salary. You will no longer serve the old world conception of prosperity. What you do you will do with your might in the service of Principle, like Brother Lawrence – he did not work for a living, he worked to *express God* by living in so attractive a way as to draw other men to the Divine Life. The kitchen of that monastery where he cooked was more magnetic than any other part of the whole concern. He was rich towards God and man, not like an ox driven by the duties demanded of him. He was a man serving a great Principle and he lived in security.

Harriet Hale Rix, *The Rich Mentality*, 1916, pp. 9-10. No known copyright in effect.

October 14

RECORD OF MYSELF

In most convincing and satisfying ways have I been caused to realize and enjoy the freedom of Truth. I certainly have everything, in realization, to be thankful for. The Truth has enabled me to turn mountains of "Difficulties" into the sea of oblivion. My first promise, after the realization of the omnipresence of the Supreme One, was essentially this, that if I could be healed through a knowledge of Truth, which to know makes free, I would endeavor to serve the Truth, with singleness of purpose, to the best of my ability. I was conscious that the One to whom this promise was made was witness of all things. This thought was somewhat startling when the full import of the promise was realized.

The Truth realized, of being whole now, was so much more than the hope of becoming whole, that it destroyed all dispositions to any "low here, or low there;" for the kingdom of heaven was found to be within, and everywhere apparent. The actualization of the presence of one living and true God, was the rending of the veil of separateness, and made visible to me the Truth of the living things of substance; and as "Through faith we understand that the worlds were framed, by the word of God," it was self-evident that through faith our bodies were formed by the word of God.

Malinda Elliott Cramer, (1894-1895), published in *The Christology Connection*, (Mercer), 2015, pp. 81-82.

October 15

LORD'S PRAYER INTERPRETATION

Our Father, Spirit and Presence, You are Perfection itself. In essence, You have created me perfect, and I am grateful. Understanding this truth about myself, my life unfolds perfectly, in Divine Order. Through and by Your grace, my experiences on earth reflect the pattern of life You have ordained for me in the realm of perfection in heaven, and I am happy.

I realize that I am receiving all the good to which my mind and heart are open and receptive. Consciously I expand my capacity to receive, and an abundance of Substance flows through my life. Therefore, I manifest health, wealth and harmony. I thank You, Oh Father, for the vibrations of love sent through me to bless the world. When I release this love I, too, am blessed by love.

In all things I give as I receive, freely and bountifully. I thank You that I am protected from negative forces by Your powerful rays of light at all times. All glory and praise to You, Oh Wonderful loving Father-God. Amen.

Judith G. Weekes, *Out Of Troubled Waters,* p. 18. Copyright 1992, Universal Foundation for Better Living (UFBL) Press. Reprinted with permission.

October 16

WHO'S DRIVING?

We have been given the wisdom to drive our own lives, to step confidently forward into that which is for our highest good. If disappointments crop up or if there are unpleasant things to be met, we can learn to handle them when we know the truth of our relationship to God.

Religionists have been known to scoff at the words of the poem "Invictus" by William E. Henley, thinking that they make man too important.

I am the master of my fate;
I am the captain of my soul.

But because man is important in God's plan, these words reveal a truth of the inheritance delegated to each of us by our loving Father. Our "fate" is our everyday human experience. The "soul" is the mind where we think and feel. God doesn't *make* us think and feel that which is good, but He has instructed us and left us free to act. However, whatever we think and feel will come forth as our "fate," or will be the experience of our lives, for good or ill. Thus are we each to be master of our fate and captain of our soul (master of our thinking and feeling).

In Job we read, "You will decide on a matter, and it will be established for you." Whatever we speak forth (silently or audibly) as the result of our thinking and feeling will be established in our human experience. Herein lies our responsibility for our "fate."

Another verse found in Scripture bears out the truth of this idea of mastery. "For as he thinketh in his heart, so *is* he." As our thinking is joined to feeling (heart), so are we. Thus we can see that each one of us must be captain of our soul, or be in full control of our thinking and feeling if we would bring forth the abundant life of which Jesus spoke.

Vera Dawson Tait, *Take Command,* 1981, pp. 31-32. Copyrighted material used with permission by Unity, Unity.org.

October 17

LIFE HEALING (1)

God works for us from within outward, and we cannot always calculate how His beneficence will be manifested, except that it is dependent on full self-surrender to Him and absolute trust. During an intense spasm of physical pain a certain woman was trying to keep her attention on God. Prayer had helped her to endure previous attacks, and she had to a certain extent lost her fear that in the midst of one of them she might die. She was straining to remember that God was her life, her physical perfection, her invincible strength, but the contortions of her whole organism seemed to become more violent. Suddenly she ceased all personal trying; "You gave me my life," she thought, "and put it in this body, Father, and if You want to take it away I am not afraid. It is Your life -- do what You will with it. I know whatever You do will be good."

She felt first a soothing sense of peace in her full surrender. Then gradually she felt the terrific physical disturbances amazingly unknotting and smoothing themselves out. Her organism seemed to relax and adjust itself as if under the ministrations of a great, loving, infinitely skillful hand. It must have been that insidious and perhaps unsuspected fears were touched and erased away. "I must not ever forget this," thought the grateful woman. "Oh Father, teach me how to trust You more and more!"

Dana Gatlin, *God Is The Answer*, 1982, pp. 115-116. Copyrighted material reprinted with permission of Unity, Unity.org.

October 18

LIFE HEALING (2)

Later she carried the lesson of this experience into other phases of her life. God would work in every department of her life if she would let Him. She must yield herself to His power and let Him erase whatever obstructions there might be: discouragements, bitterness, anxieties, and petty concern for self. She had to learn human forgiveness and the true meaning of trust and love. Her health improved steadily. A partial paralysis was cleared away as if certain parts of her organism had been freed at the same time that her mind was liberated from constricting fears. She tried not to entertain any thought that had previously caused antagonism or dread. Her health improved, her opportunities increased and her ability to meet them; her environment became happier, her attitude toward her associates, toward her work, and toward life was more friendly and optimistic, and one day she realized that her whole nature had changed.

In all her dealings, enterprises, situations, and in every smallest task she learned to include God by dropping the mere personal attitude. It was first a formulated prayer that helped her, then it grew into the very fiber of the being, whence it came forth spontaneously: "I am a creation of the Most High and am now open to His fullest blessing!"

And veritably in her manifest world she walked with blessings; the most assured and dependable blessings in this changing world, for they came from the Most High. "I am lifted up to the Christ consciousness. I am one with all love (good) everywhere. I am at peace with the world. I am free. I am free."

Dana Gatlin, *God Is The Answer*, 1982, pp. 116-117. Copyrighted material reprinted with permission of Unity, Unity.org.

October 19

SEVEN STEPS IN DEMONSTRATION

There are a number of approaches, or techniques as they are sometimes called, used in making demonstrations. Various methods have been tried and proved successful, but the one that will be most successful for you is the one you can use with the greatest ease. The following is one of the simplest and most effective.

The first step is to DESIRE. Get a strong enthusiasm for that which you want in your life, a real longing for something which is not there now.

The second step is to make a DECISION. Know definitely what it is that you want, what it is that you want to do or have, and be willing to pay for it in spiritual values.

The third step is to ASK. Once you are sure of your need, and enthusiastic about it, proceed to ask for it in simple, concise language. Remember, God is not moved by oratory, but by simplicity and directness.

The fourth step is to BELIEVE. Have faith not only in what you want, but also in the fact that you will get it. Be consciously, as well as subconsciously aware of this. Impress your subconscious mind with faith, so that there is perfect cooperation between the subconscious and the conscious.

The fifth step is to WORK AT IT. Spend a few minutes daily in seeing yourself in the finished picture. Never outline details, but rather see yourself enjoying the particular thing…

The sixth step is to feel GRATITUDE. Always remember to say, "Thank you, God," and begin to *feel* the gratitude in your heart. The most powerful prayer we can ever make is those three words, provided we really feel it.

The seventh step is to feel EXPECTANCY. Train yourself to live in a state of happy expectancy. If in the beginning you feel anything but happy, act it until it becomes part of you, as it must and will.

Mildred Mann, *Become What You Believe, Volume I*, 1970, p. 55. No known copyright in effect.

October 20

MY DEMONSTRATION IS SURE

He shall give thee the desires of thine heart.
Psalm 37:4

There is no delay or obstruction in the manifestation of my desired good. All that God is, is available to me right here and right now. Within me is the Divine Intelligence that knows how to convert the invisible into the visible.

I place my creative Word in the ever-flowing river of Mind Action, as I would place a canoe in a swiftly moving stream. The river of Subconscious Mind carries my Word steadily, inevitably, to the Sea of my larger experience of Good. My Word is dynamic and powerful, for my faith in the Great Law is unwavering. My desire is clear and definite: it is not vague or confused. I desire nothing that interferes with another's good, for I know that the One Mind loves all. There is ample Good for all. I keep my thinking steady, my heart full of peace and love. My demonstration is sure. It comes at a perfect time, in a perfect way. I give thanks for the wondrous Law of Mind.

Claudine Whitaker, published in *Creative Thought* for February 21, 1960. Copyrighted material reprinted with permission of SOM Publishing.

October 21

THOU SHALT LET GO AND LET GOD DO IT

We find many instances in the New Testament showing how Jesus conformed to the idea in this commandment in making His great demonstrations. He would go apart to pray, and after such a period of infilling He would move through a period of intense activity of teaching and healing; then He would go apart to rest awhile. His resting period would in turn be followed by another cycle of work. In these periods of activity we have many instances of His acknowledging His heavenly Father in prayer before performing some miracle of healing that we would call a demonstration. From Jesus we get the perfect model of the way to make a demonstration: pray, work, rest, then repeat the cycle.

Georgiana Tree West, *Prosperity's Ten Commandments*, 1946, p. 51.
Copyrighted material reprinted with permission of Unity, Unity.org.

October 22

GIVE WITHOUT FEAR

Some form of the word *give* is used over six hundred times in the Scriptures. Of all its dictionary definitions, "to surrender" is probably the most descriptive spiritually. Giving ourselves materially, emotionally, and prayerfully is surrendering to the Will of God. This is divine ascendency. All these times our better self takes dominion.

When we give without fear, we are not concerned about limiting ourselves, because we know with an inward knowing that God's supply is inexhaustible. It is through this understanding that we are enabled to give freely. Giving is loving. The love that evolved from a Christ-like consciousness is reflected in one's life and has a salutary effect upon the lives of others. James Russell Lowell wrote, "She doeth little kindnesses that most leave undone." It is these little kindnesses which are characteristic of the fearless giver. They are not measured. They are gifts from the heart. They are God-motivated. "Truly, the only joy I keep is what I give away."

F. Bernadette Turner, published in *Aspire*, March 1976, p. 27. Copyrighted material reprinted with permission of Divine Science Federation International.

October 23

REST AND RELAXATION

It has been written that the night of the body is the day of the soul, for the subconscious mind is always active and creative, although the body is inert in sleep. How important it is to put away the cares, all the concerns of the day, and prepare for a good night's rest.

To do this, you first reaffirm your unity with that Spirit that knows and desires only good for you. You give thanks for the blessings bestowed upon you, especially the gift of life itself. Once again, you recognize how truly wonderful *you* are, when you realize there is some Power greater than you that keeps your heart beating, your lungs functioning as they should, and digests your food. At the same time, the cells of your body are being constantly renewed.

In this knowledge, you can speak your words, affirming that Infinite Intelligence within you knows only perfection and knows what to do concerning any problem in your life. You let go and let God. As you release these thoughts, you know there is a law of mind that can only react to your belief. You can retire, knowing you have started an action for good in your life and that of your loved ones. You awaken refreshed, confident, vital, and equal to any situation the new day might have to offer.

Clara M. Wright, *Prayer in Action*, 1973, pp. 25-26. Copyrighted material reprinted with permission of SOM Publishing.

October 24

ONE SUBSTANCE

Some years ago intuition made one of its bold leaps and declared, "All is mind, all is spirit." Intellect immediately began its work on this proposition, and presented several theories more or less plausible. The following is about the line of reasoning pursued where intuition took the lead -- "All is mind, all is spirit; then there is no matter, hence, there is no form; what we see is illusion, the production of imagination, unsubstantial, unreal, created by mortal mind, etc., etc."

However, this conclusion was not satisfactory to either intuition or intellect, as is shown by their pushing further on; and, working more in unison; intellect, illumined by intuition, comes to a wonderful perception. It says to intuition, "What you proclaim is truth; all is Spirit since God is Spirit; and God is Omnipresence; but this fact does not do away with the visible universe, but makes it evident to us that all form must be the invisible substance, spirit, and visible."

God formed the universe out of his own substance. That which is born of Spirit is Spirit; like begets like; therefore all form, all that is visible as well as all that is invisible, is Spirit; for, since Omnipresence is a fact, there can be but one substance, and that substance must be the substance that is omnipresent, the God-substance.

Nona L. Brooks, (1899), published in *The Christology Connection*, 2015, (Mercer), p. 118.

October 25

PROGRESS

Let there be many windows to your soul,
That all the glory of the universe
May beautify it. Not the narrow pane
Of one poor creed can catch the radiant rays
That shine from countless sources. Tear away
The blinds of superstition; let the light
Pour through fair windows broad as Truth itself
And high as God. ...
      Tune your ear
To all the worldless music of the stars,
And to the voice of Nature, and your heart
Shall turn to truth and goodness, as the plant
Turns to the sun. A thousand unseen hands
Reach down to help you to their peace-crowned heights,
And all the forces of the firmament
Shall fortify your strength. Be not afraid
To thrust aside half-truths and grasp the whole.

Ella Wheeler Wilcox, published in *Effectual Prayer*, (Foulks), 1945, p. 61.
Copyrighted material reprinted with permission of Unity, Unity.org.

October 26

TWENTY-THIRD PSALM INTERPRETED

My Shepherd!
No more want or lack,
Peace and rest,
In the right path.
Through the valley and shadow,
No more fear, Comfort and confidence,
Abide with me,
Protection from adversity,
Ready for Service,
My oil, my light, never fails,
My cup always filled with a supply
Ready to give to others,
Joy is mine,
I dwell in God's holy temple,
Always and ever,
I will praise and glorify
My Shepherd all the days of my life.

Agnes J. Galer, published in *Washington News Letter*, (ed. Sabin), October 1917, p. 23. No known copyright in effect.

October 27

THE POTENTIAL OF YOUR WORD POWER

So shall my word be that goeth forth out of my mouth:
It shall not return to me void, but shall accomplish that which I please,
and it shall prosper in the things whereto I sent it.
Isaiah 55:11

We are all following certain paths, avenues, freeways to everything we experience. We are also creatures of habit and have a tendency to take the same way to work, to the store, to church, etc.

The same thing is true to attain healing. Whether it be a physical illness, emotional experience, monetary lack or whatever the challenge is we need to meet – to arrive at the place we want to be – we must do something.

To come here we had to take a definite and specific way. True, we might have taken other routes, but to arrive at the place we have arrived at, there has to be acceptance on our part of a direction.

Most of us want to change our lives for the better. We want to be healed of something, get rid of something, or acquire something. Religious Science teaches us a way. It is a map, a guide on the highway of life.

Vetura Papke, *Angel in Residence*, (Neuwirth), 1995, p. 100. Copyrighted material reprinted with permission of SOM Publishing.

October 28

FEAR AND DOUBT

Even though I cannot see the way, I do not let fear conquer me, nor do I succumb to doubts. I give myself to Spirit that Spirit may have its mighty way in me.

I have faith in God. I have faith in the perfect action of the divine creative law. And so I do what my hands find to do, with quiet courage. This is true praise of God. I trust the unfailing activity of Divine Wisdom. I rest in the peace of Divine Love. This is my praise, O God. Lead and I follow unwaveringly. This praise enlivens all aspects of my life, and radiates into my world. I rejoice in the Presence ever within me.

Helen Zagat, *Prayers of Praise*, 1959, p. 13. No known copyright in effect.

October 29

WHAT IS FAITH?

Faith is *"the perceiving power of the mind linked with the power to shape substance....the power to do the seemingly impossible"* (Charles Fillmore). Faith is "absolute certainty." Faith is "trust without reservation."
Faith is the substance of things hoped for, the evidence of things not seen.
Hebrews 11:1, KJV

It is the confident assurance that something we want is going to happen. It is the certainty that what we hope for is waiting for us, even though we cannot see it up ahead.
Hebrews 11:1, Living Bible

Faith is the power to *focus* on God the Good....
Faith is to an *idea* what *soil* is to a *seed*. Faith is an idea in Divine Mind embodying hope, trust, belief, and expectancy.

FAITH SEES: Faith perceives the possibility of the result long before there is any visible sign. Faith is the ability in you to see the condition healed regardless of what is being manifested. Faith is your spiritual eye. It looks within and perceives the good in the midst of the appearance.

FAITH KNOWS: Faith is more than idle hoping or believing. Faith knows the truth that God's outpouring of Himself is irrepressible, infinite, and absolute. When you are consciously aware of this, your faith grows courageously and trusts God to get the best out of the worst....
"When in doubt, faith is out!"

Johnnie Colemon, *Open Your Mind and Be Healed*, 1997, pp. 30-31.
Reproduced from OPEN YOUR MIND AND BE HEALED by Johnnie Colemon 9780875167091 DeVorss Publications, www.devorss.com. Reprinted with permission.

October 30

TRUTH

You shall know the Truth and it shall make you free. When you know God and God's will for man, you will know the Truth; and when you are open and receptive to the word of God, and willing to do the will of God, you are working toward perfect freedom. When you accept Truth, you will be free in Spirit, soul and body. Every bond will be broken, and all things whatsoever will be revealed to you. You will no longer walk in darkness, nor be afraid, sick, or in need, for you will know God as your Light, your health, supply, and protection, as your everything. So let the Truth reign in all your activities and be free indeed.

Pearl C. Wood, *Thinking With God: Daily Thoughts*, March 1940, p. 8.
Reprinted with permission of Triangular Church.

October 31

FAITH

If the Sun and Moon should doubt, they'd immediately go out!
William Blake

In this bit of whimsy we are given the reason for faith -- life. God gives us life, we must accept it. No one lacks faith, for faith is an inherent part of our nature. We need only exercise the faith we have in order to gain greater achievement. Emerson said, "We cannot contract the infinite, we must expand the finite." The person who seems to lack faith is thinking of himself, not God; he thinks about his problem, not the solving of it. In order to expand the finite we must put our faith in the Infinite! Some of the qualities of faith are vigilance, obedience, perseverance, confidence, and devotion. The disciplined thinker expands and develops the kind of faith that moves mountains -- disease, unhappiness, and lack.

Today I keep my thought steadily directed toward the good. I let go of my problems, and let God. I know that my faith keeps me whole, for it is God in action. There is no morose-ness, self-pity, or sadness in me. I laugh and sing, dance and live. I always remember who I am and what I am -- God expressing life. I have faith, faith in God, and obey the Law of Mind in Action, and my life is full. It is so, now.

"God gives in the abstract, we receive in the concrete. The gift of heaven is forever made. The receiving of this gift is an eternal process of forever expanding the finite." *The Science of Mind,* page 405.

...thy faith hath made thee whole; go in peace. Luke 8:48

Georgia Carmichael Maxwell, published in *Science of Mind*, December 1955, p. 70. Copyrighted material reprinted with permission of SOM Publishing.

NOVEMBER

November 1

THE SEEKERS OF THE LIGHT ARE ONE

Have you realized that there are people in every nation of the earth who love all humanity, people who are seeking to bring, peace, understanding and brotherhood into the world in which we live? These people are instruments of God wherever they are.

Sometimes as we think of world affairs the outlook seems dark. We see only the working of evil forces and the preparation of instruments of destruction. After all, God, who created this world and called it good, is still in charge. Let us align ourselves with this tremendous power of God.

We are children of God. And cooperation in expressing Him is essential to our secure, satisfying future on this planet….

In every nation on the earth the seekers of the light are one. It makes no difference what creed or dogma they follow nor what they call their faith. The prayers of all people, seeking the light, unite as part of the great good of the world.

May Rowland, published in *Diamonds of Truth: Unity's 75th Anniversary*, 1964, p. 14. Copyrighted material reprinted with permission of Unity, Unity.org.

November 2

RESOLVE: I WILL THINK ONLY CONSTRUCTIVE THOUGHTS TODAY

This is a wise resolve and if practiced day by day will bring desired results. It is the only way to Truth. Just as a child in school must work the problems given him, so must we solve the problems that come into our lives. We do this through constructive thinking and its normal sequence, constructive living. There is no other way. There is no promotion in the school of life until we have done the work given us here, each day.

Constructive thinking? It means thinking true to Principle; it means thinking health instead of disease; it means the thought of faith, not fear; of love, not dislike or hate; of power, not weakness.

If, when things seem dark, we go to ourselves and turn our thought to the One who is ever present, and rest it there, we shall be helped. If necessary, we should affirm over and over, God's presence here is peace. There will come to us a blessed release from the disturbance and we shall receive the assurance that all is well.

There will come also, clear seeing and the knowledge of what to do.
Then we shall go forth with power and joy.
Study: Isaiah 61:1-3

Nona L. Brooks, published in *Divine Science Monthly*, November 1933, p. 13. Copyrighted material reprinted with permission of Divine Science Federation International.

November 3

LET GO

If we find ourselves in a situation that is inharmonious, if we are disturbed and upset by what someone else has said or done to hurt us or cause us to suffer unjustly, we need first of all to let go, to let go deliberatively of all belief in the power of anyone to hurt us or make us unhappy, to let go of any belief in injustice or suffering. And in letting go we open the way for an inrush of God's healing, transforming love. We let God take over in us, in the situation, in everyone concerned; and in letting go and letting God we find peace and joy of Spirit.

We're meant for joyous, happy, healthy living. We were created in God's image and after His likeness. Let us remember this. Let us let God take over in us, infill us, inspire us, renew us. Let us let His creative Spirit transform us into new and living souls.

Martha Smock, *Meet It With Faith*, 1967, p. 11. Copyrighted material reprinted with permission of Unity, Unity.org.

November 4

DECLARATION OF LIFE PRINCIPLES

We believe in the Motherhood and the Fatherhood of God, the Holy Trinity of the Father, Mother and Child.

We believe that God created the world, and He is still here with us, watching us care for it.

We believe in the sacredness of the human body, this transient dwelling place of the soul, and so we deem it the duty of every man and woman to keep his or her body beautiful through right thinking and right living.

We believe that the best way to prepare for a future life is to be kind, live one day at a time, and do the very best that you can do each day.

We believe that there is no devil but fear.

We believe that no one can harm us but ourselves.

We believe that we are Sons and Daughters of God and it does not yet appear what we shall be.

We believe in the purifying process of sorrow and that death is but a manifestation of eternal life.

We believe in sunshine, fresh air, mental freedom, pure friendship, and a world of beautiful thoughts.

Edna M. Lister, from her lesson delivered in Cleveland, Ohio, Saturday, March 12, 1938. Reprinted with permission.

November 5

ALL THAT *IS* GOD CREATED

All that *is* God created. If sin has any pretense of existence, God is responsible therefore; but there is no reality in sin, for God can no more behold it, or acknowledge it, than the sun can coexist with darkness.

To build the individual spiritual sense, conscious of only health, holiness, and heaven, on the foundations of an eternal Mind which is conscious of sickness, sin, and death, is a moral impossibility; for *"other foundation can no man lay than that is already laid."* I Corinthians 3:11

The nearer we approximate to such a Mind, even if it were (or could be) God, the more real those mind-pictures would become to us; until the hope of ever eluding their dread presence must yield to despair, and the haunting sense of evil forever accompany our being.

Mortals may climb the smooth glaciers, leap the dark fissures, scale the treacherous ice, and stand on the summit of Mont Blanc; but they can never turn back what Deity knoweth, nor escape from identification with what dwelleth in the eternal Mind.

Mary Baker Eddy, *Unity of Good*, 1887, p. 64. No known copyright in effect.

November 6

I AM STRONGER THAN MY FEARS

I am stronger than my fears,
I am wiser than my years,
I am gladder than my tears;
    For I am God's image.

I am better than my deeds,
I am holier than my creeds,
I am Wealthier than my needs;
    For I am God's image.

God, whose image thus I bear
And whose likeness I shall share,
All God's glory will declare
    Through the "I": God's image.

Hannah More Kohaus, published in *The Best of Daily Word*, 1986, p. 65. Copyrighted material reprinted with permission of Unity, Unity.org.

November 7

NO OTHER WAY

Could we but see the patterns of our days,
We should discern how devious were the ways
By which we came to this, the present time,
This place in life; and we should see the climb
Our soul has made up through the years.
We should forget the hurts, the wanderings, the fears,
The wastelands of our life, and know
That we could come no other way or grow
Into our good without these steps our feet
Found hard to take, our faith found hard to meet.
The road of life winds on, and we like travelers go
From turn to turn until we come to know
The truth that life is endless and that we
Forever are inhabitants of all eternity.

Martha Smock, published in Unity's *The Best of Daily Word*, 1986, p. 68. Copyrighted material reprinted with permission of Unity, Unity.org.

November 8

CHRIST CONSCIOUSNESS

When the Christ Consciousness is risen within us, we feel the universality of life written everywhere on everything; there is but one starting point for all thought -- God. There is but one ending place for all human faith -- God.

We are filled with a keener sense of the oneness of life, and we are thrilled again and again by the nearness and greatness of God in the world which He projected from Himself.

The Father which we sought in self-consciousness has become real and tangible, and the sense of everlasting unity is in our hearts.

With this great God-self alive within us, we never fear that God will ever pass away from any part of His Creation. We know too well, then, the truth that "as it was in the beginning, is now, and ever shall be, world without end," earth is destined to become a heaven in the lives of men as fast as they develop to the place of understanding, and find the real holy ground within the center of their own being.

God, or the Universal Cosmic Consciousness, has always been revealed to men through the risen Christ consciousness within the self. The men of old who walked with Him were those who had lifted their personal mind to the level of the Universal Mind, so that from the shores of the Infinite Wisdom great thought waves of Love, Truth and Peace beat in on them and filled them, and their lives became a center of illumination for all.

Julia Seton Sears, *The Secret of Health and Healing: Freedom Talks*, 1906. No known copyright in effect.

November 9

FINDING THE CHRIST IN OURSELVES

Throughout all His teachings Jesus tried to show those who listened to Him how He was related to the Father, and to teach them that they were related to the same Father in exactly the same way….

He did all his mighty works, not because He was given some greater or different power from that which God has given us – not because He was in some different way a *Son* of God and we only *children* of God – but just because this same Divine Spark, which the Father has implanted in every child born, had been fanned into a bright flame…

We would detract nothing from Jesus. He is still our Savior, in that he went through suffering unutterable…that He might lead us to God….

We love Jesus…and to prove our love, we would follow His teachings and His life closely…trying to get at the real meaning of all that He said, and letting the Father work through us as He did through Him, our perfect Elder Brother and Savior.

H. Emilie Cady, published in *Diamonds of Truth: Unity's 75th Anniversary*, 1964, p. 6. Copyrighted material reprinted with permission of Unity, Unity.org.

November 10

FORGIVENESS

All things, past, present, and future, that are out of harmony with the divine law are forgiven me by the One who gave His life to set me free.

There is no transgression, no sin of omission, no sin of commission that Thou, O Son of man, O Son of God, hast not wiped out for me, in Thy "Father, forgive them" spoken from the cross.

Ignorance in transgression, willfulness of desire, and all their effects have become as nothing as I enter upon the "crossing out" with Thee, my Savior.

Scars and wounds and hurts are made whole; both those which I have received and those which I have inflicted have been healed by Thy blood shed vicariously for the healing of the nations.

All unforgiveness in me and toward me, all intolerance and injustice, even that present in the lives that I remember no more, are completely blotted out through Thy forgiving love, O Christ of God.

I accept Thine atonement, O Lamb of God, Messiah of the world. Through Thy redeeming love I am washed clean, rising above all human appearances, all material bondage.

Now am I resurrected from the dead in mind, body, and affairs, and enter into the newness that has become mine through Thee. I am a son of the living God, the Word of God made flesh, Savior of my world.

Frances W. Foulks, *Effectual Prayer*, 1945, pp. 122-123. Copyrighted material reprinted with permission of Unity, Unity.org.

November 11

WHAT IS SUPPLY?

Limitation in experience indicates a limited outlook or belief; lack indicates a lack of faith and there is no other reason why any man is lacking in supply. It is not a matter of the station of life to which we were born, the experience through which we have passed, or the pressure of lack which may endure in the world about us today. All of these facts are true and they are effective and do prevail in our experience – but they are effects; they are false gods which we have worshiped and feared. All effects will and must change, as we change the cause or belief behind them.

In changing our belief we are not deserting intelligence or trying to believe anything that is not true.

When we try to grow, to improve or expand along any line, we prepare for that development, by study, by practice until finally we have mastered the principles underlying the desired achievement. We prepare in every way for the new and expected experience which is not ours now, but toward which we aspire. We do not sit in resignation, concluding that our present status is unchangeable….

If we wish prosperity, abundance, we must prepare for it, rather than preparing for continued limitation. We must train and discipline our thought to see behind each and every effect, to cause – to see the cause which produced and is sustaining that particular belief, and to see beyond that cause to First Cause or God, the limitless and perfect principle of life which can and will render unto any man the good he can conceive, and accomplish it in a perfectly logical and orderly way – projecting into the man's experience, through the avenues of thought and belief, the good for which he has prepared.

Josephine Holmes Curtis, *How To Get The Most Out Of Life*, 1937, pp. 79-81. Copyrighted material reprinted with permission of SOM Publishing.

November 12

TODAY I FORGIVE MYSELF

Today I forgive myself for all of the mistakes I have made in the past. I even forgive myself for all of the mistakes I may make in the future. I release all feelings of guilt or shame about sometimes missing the mark as I strive to be all that God intends for me to be. Now I understand that every experience is an opportunity for me to learn and grow; I see that unless I had gone where I've been, I would not be all that I am today. So, I thank you God for this revelation. I leave my past behind me and press forward to claim the healthy, happy and prosperous life that awaits me.

Mary A. Tumpkin, *Before You Pray – Forgive*, p. 12. Copyright 2005 by Mary Tumpkin Presentations. Reprinted with permission of the estate of Mary A. Tumpkin.

November 13

MY HAND IN GOD'S

Each morning when I wake I say,
"I place my hand in God's today";
I know God will walk by my side
My every wandering step to guide.

God leads me with the tenderest care
When paths are dark and I despair –
No need for me to understand
If I but hold fast to God's hand.

My hand in God's! No surer way
To walk in safety through each day.
By God's great bounty I am fed;
Warmed by God's love and comforted.

When at day's end I seek my rest
And realize how much I'm blessed,
My thanks pour out to God; and then
I place my hand in God's again.

Florence Scripps Kellogg, (ca. 1910) published in *The Best of Daily Word*, 1986, p. 96. Copyrighted material reprinted with permission of Unity, Unity.org.

November 14

COMPLETE IN THEE

There is no frustration, no loneliness, no longing in my heart that Thou, O Father, dost not satisfy and fill to overflowing through Thy great love.

There is no sadness, no depression, no limitation in my life.

I am complete in Thee, satisfied in Thee.

I seek Thee with my whole heart; because I so earnestly seek Thee, I find Thy comfort, Thy strength, Thy peace here with me now.

Because of my completeness in Thy love I freely relinquish all the things that are unimportant in my life's experience. They are forgotten, forgiven, and released.

I release everything of the past that no longer contributes to my happiness. I release any apprehension for the future. I live in the joy of the present.

I hold fast only to that which is of the very highest and best, enduring and enriching.

Every condition, every individual adds to my joy because I have first found Thee.

I radiate to every person I meet the joy that comes from my completeness in Thee.

There is peace in my soul and there is harmony in my affairs because I know Thy love.

I place my life in Thy hands without care or anxiety about the future, for I know that all is well.

Thy love satisfies my longing soul and fills my life with Thy good.

May Rowland, *Dare To Believe!*, 1961, pp. 150-151. Copyrighted material reprinted with permission of Unity, Unity.org.

November 15

WHY WE BELIEVE

BECAUSE we live, we hope and we express.
BECAUSE we feel the vital fires of life.
BECAUSE faith is potential, innate, universal.
BECAUSE religion is a natural impulse.
BECAUSE idealism is the pivot on which life revolves.
BECAUSE spirituality is the stabilizing force of humanity.
BECAUSE through meditation we reach the source of Reality.
BECAUSE contemplation reveals the essence of Being.
BECAUSE of roses, moonbeams and desires.
BECAUSE of dreams, poetry and stars.
BECAUSE of the laughter of children, the singing of birds.
BECAUSE of sun-kissed mountains, babbling brooks and laughing winds.
BECAUSE the odor of flowers is the incense of Heaven.
BECAUSE of God's lullaby, crooned by waves and swaying trees.
BECAUSE the blue sky is the dome of the Real Cathedral.
BECAUSE imagination is fanned by angel's wings.
BECAUSE of friendship, loyalty, sympathy and toleration.
BECAUSE of justice, affability, fidelity and philanthropy.
BECAUSE of the availability of our reliable servant-Law.
BECAUSE thought, the director of healing, demonstrates perfect results.
BECAUSE Truth is free to all, undivided, impartial.
BECAUSE of inspiration, caught by the soul of genius.
BECAUSE of the delicately balanced scheme of things.
BECAUSE we sense the Architect, silently functioning within.
BECAUSE climbing the ladder of ideas, Divinity appears. And
BECAUSE Love, unanalyzable, is the motivating, energizing Cause.

Hazel Foster Holmes, published in *Religious Science Monthly*, February 1929, p. 2. Copyrighted material reprinted with permission of SOM Publishing.

November 16

THE PREMISE OF DIVINE SCIENCE

Divine Science is based on a belief in the Omnipresence, Omniscience, Omnipotence and Omniaction of God – One Presence, Knowledge, Power and Action. In other words: God is *all*, both invisible and visible. One Mind, Intelligence and Substance. One Spirit, Life and Law. This Mind is the source of all wisdom, love, knowledge, understanding and power. Its *action* is the expression of these inherencies which man calls the "Law of the Lord." This Law is also called the "Will of God" or, "God in action."

Man is the expression of God and is forever one with his Source. But, believing in two powers, he thought himself separated from the true Source and came into the bondage of his false beliefs. Hence the basic statement: "I accept the Omnipresence *without any reserve.*"

Ida B. Elliott, published in *Mind Remakes Your World*, (ed. Holmes) 1941, p. 97. Reprinted with permission of INTA.

November 17

I REJOICE IN THE TRUTH

As I was with Moses, so I will be with thee:
I will not fail thee, nor forsake thee.
Joshua 1:5

There is no power in conditions. There is no power in personality. Even my own misguided thinking can no longer hurt me as I see it as false. I turn to the Infinite Wisdom within for clarification. The Truth is revealed to me and this Truth is my healing. God speaks to me, in my own mind, as he did to Moses and the prophets of old. Sometimes His Guidance comes through something I read or the spoken word of others. I no longer resist criticism. It may be God speaking to me through one of His other children. Nothing can stand in the way of Truth. It cuts through my mistaken thinking as a strong light pierces the darkness. I am willing to have the Truth revealed to me though it shatter my ego. "Thy rod and thy staff they comfort me." I accept correction. I rejoice in discipline. I am glad to give up all negative thinking. God alone has Power over me. This Power is Love. It will not fail me or forsake me. I am continually grateful that this is so.

Cornelia Addington, published in *Creative Thought*, January 1959, p. 31.
Copyrighted material reprinted with permission of SOM Publishing.

November 18

ONE NATURE, NOT TWO

The Law of Demonstration is worked from God by means of His action, into visible expression. Because there is but One Substance in the reality of our Being, we are all of one nature, we have the same inherent possibilities, and each one can truthfully say: "I have One Nature, not two," which is a permanent state of harmony, for harmony is the eternal state of oneness. It is self-evident that we must start in Holy Spirit, the One All, in our thoughts to draw correct conclusions. Then it is that we find that God has no substance to make his children out of but that which He is; that we in essence are wholly good, and entirely Divine, that there is no law to God save that of His own nature.

Malinda Elliott Cramer, (1899), published in *The Christology Connection*, (Mercer), 2015, p. 126.

November 19

I LIVE IN AWARENESS

Rejoice in the Lord always: and again I say, Rejoice.
Philippians 4:4

Infinite Mind has created me to be an organ of Its expression. I express the Divine Nature by living in awareness that it is my nature, too. All that it is, I am.

I rejoice in the limitless Abundance of God and know that my True Self is limitless Abundance, also. I can never lack for I can never be without my Self, and there is no limit to the wealth which I can externalize from my Self. There is no lack or fear of lack in my thinking; therefore there is no lack in my experience. Abundance expresses joyfully, richly, in all my affairs.

I rejoice in the pure, harmonious Life of God now coursing through my veins. There is no sickness or fear of sickness in my thinking. The radiant Health of God expresses in my body. Love, Peace, Joy, Wisdom, Truth, Beauty, Power -- these God is, and therefore these I am. I rejoice that I am a spiritual, thinking being, created to express the nature of God.

Claudine Whitaker, published in *Creative Thought* for Saturday, February 13, 1960. Copyrighted material reprinted with permission of SOM Publishing.

November 20

OUR DIVINITY

We are only now beginning to understand what is meant by the divinity of man. At last we are recognizing a divine plan, a divine power, a divine seed of perfection in every living being – the Christ in us, the power of God, the Father.

Jesus was able to realize this principle, to express it, and to become it in such a way that He was able to do, absolutely, the Father's will. He gave up the human side of life to express the divine; thus He attained the degree of recognition of that developed consciousness – He became "Jesus the Christ."…Jesus attained the consciousness that permitted Him to perform the work of God on earth in and through a human body, and He became "the Christ."…

Being the Christ, knowing His divinity, Jesus was able to do all manner of wondrous things. And He said, "He that believeth on me, the works that I do shall he also do; and greater works than these shall he do." And He meant all of us!

Grace L. Faus, published in *Aspire*, October 1958, p. 4. Copyrighted material reprinted with permission of Divine Science Federation International.

November 21

BE YE THANKFUL

As we look at the world today…we see it no longer functioning wholly in sense consciousness, but beginning to unfold into the spiritual completeness that it is destined to express. …We know the truth about our world….We give thanks for God's perfect world now coming forth into manifestation.

To praise and give thanks is to magnify that which is praised. This is the law of God, and man uses it again and again when he expresses the spirit of praise and thanksgiving in his heart. When we praise children we give thanks for them and all that is within them. We praise them for the wonderful things that they are going to be and do.

Sue Sikking, *Be Ye Thankful*, 1957, pp. 3-4. Copyrighted material reprinted with permission of Unity, Unity.org.

November 22

HELL

Hell, like heaven, is a state of consciousness, and not a place of torture. We make our own hell. The Holy Spirit is omnipresent, but if we so elect, we may shut ourselves from the consciousness of that presence. This state may be compared to that of a person who shuts his eyes and refuses to see the sunlight that may be all about him.

We deliberately place ourselves in hell when we permit our thoughts to dwell on the negative and unhappy side. When we think of disease and yield to illness it is because, at one time or another, we have yielded to sin. If sin were eliminated from human life there would be neither sickness nor death.

When we eliminate the personal God, we necessarily eliminate the material heaven and hell. It is our duty to create our own heaven and to live in it. If that is done we need have nothing to fear from hell.

Kathleen M. H. Besly, *The Divine Art of Living*, 1917, pp. 24-25.

November 23

DEMONSTRATION

In knowing Truth we know God, and when we reason according to this knowledge of God we consult true Principle, which is in reality asking of God.

Now, there is a condition upon which you receive what you ask for, which is that you abide in truth. Jesus said, "If ye abide in me, and my words abide in you, ye shall ask what ye will and it shall be done unto you."

To abide in Christ is to abide in Truth, and your receiving what you ask for depends upon the accuracy of your reasoning, and your willingness to abide in that line of reasoning, or stand by it, be true to it.

You can readily understand that there must be a great difference between the mind that accepts the whole truth without a doubt of its working power, and the one who doubts and questions every step of the way, and only believes what is proved by sense evidence. It is the one who awakens the interior perception or intuition, who knows and understands how Principle works, and whose faith in what it will do is based upon knowledge. Perfect understanding makes perfect faith, therefore perfect works will follow understanding.

If there is very little understanding there will be very little faith, consequently imperfect demonstrations will be the result.

Jane Yarnall, *Practical Healing For Mind and Body*, 1891, p. 281-282. No known copyright in effect.

November 24

MY JOY MAKES ME POROUS TO MY GOOD

With joy shall ye draw water out of the wells of salvation.
Isaiah 12:3

The power indwelling me is intelligent and knows exactly what to do and how to do whatever I set into action through my thought or my feeling. It is a crime not to be happy while demonstrating this marvelous, unfailing Law. The end is inevitable if I faint not while well-doing.

I rehearse being glad, happy, joyous, jubilant and rejoicing while demonstrating health, strength, energy, wealth, plenty, peace, harmony, satisfaction. I see my SELF *alive with joy,* aglow, shining, scintillating, I identify my outer self with this Inner, Glorious Being which I truly am, though I have been ignorant of it. I make my Joy spontaneous, natural, boundless, continuous -- and contagious. Those I contact catch my joy, priming their own limitless wells.

Joy released energizes, vitalizes, empowers mind, body and affairs, makes me "Porous to Spirit" for Joy is unrestricted Spirit. I draw out of the wells of salvation every good and perfect gift.

Ruth E. Chew, published in *Creative Thought*, September 1956, p. 12.
Copyrighted material reprinted with permission of SOM Publishing.

November 25

AUTUMN - WINTER DROPS OF GOLD

* Never be an enemy to anybody for as such you would be unjust. Be trustful of even those who seem to be at enmity with you. Be loving to all. Make it your principle of life. Also keep this affirmation: *"God is the speech of my tongue, the thought of my heart, and the strength of my right hand."*

* Be sure that the cause you espouse is a righteous one for you are very faithful to whatever cause you espouse. This is your rightful principle of faith: *"All they that know Thy name will put their trust in Thee; for Thou, Lord, hast not forsaken them that seek thee."*

* You must hasten to be posted in some science so that you can speak publicly the great thoughts that are nigh your speech. This should be your constant affirmation: *"My tongue shall speak of righteousness and of thy praise all the day long."*

* Money is nothing to you. Therefore you can have all you like by getting right thought. Great possessions naturally flow to you if you do not hold a foolish thought strongly. This verse will give you your successful idea: *"All my help from Thee I bring."*

* You must learn not to be influenced by the mental conditions of other people. You must know what is right and abide by it. Keep this promise in mind: *"There shall no evil happen to the just."*

* You are by nature just and honest in all your dealings. You are fine in your intuitions. Be not afraid to trust your own judgment unbiased by anybody. This must be your life text: *"Righteousness keepeth him that is upright in his way."*

Emma Curtis Hopkins, (1891), *Drops of Gold*, 1970, pp. 65, 72, 80-81, 88-89. No known copyright in effect.

November 26

BLESS, PRAISE, GIVE THANKS

There is no greater prospering power than the word of blessing, of genuine praise, and of thanks from the heart, directed especially toward those people and those things and events which have seemed to curse us.

As this word must not merely be from the lips, it will require skill, discernment, inspiration, and a prophetic sense to find out what one can praise in one's enemies; to see what one can be thankful for in misfortune or can bless in time of treachery. The very exercise itself will enrich one, as it did the sons of the wise father in the fable.

An Aesopian fable tells us of an old farmer who had four lazy sons, and who in dying told them he had nothing to leave them but a field but that in the field was buried a treasure. So when he died they vigorously dug up that field. But they found no treasure. However, the next crop that grew in the field yielded four times as much as the ordinary crop; and then the sons knew that the treasure in the field was what they put in it – their own energy and faith.

Practice skill and discernment in finding the good in the people who have injured you and in the failures that have burdened you. Let the Spirit inspire your thanksgiving and open your prophetic sense so that you may see the blessing that is coming out of it all. The exercise is enriching both spiritually and materially.

Annie Rix Militz, *Both Riches and Honor*, 1945, pp. 98-99. Copyrighted material reprinted with permission of Unity, Unity.org.

November 27

NEW THOUGHT – A WAY OF LIFE

You have to be a seeker, because there's something in your life that's going on, that there's not a fulfillment there, there's not a sense of joy or happiness. And you may not use those words, but there's something within you that says that there's more to life than what I am doing. There's just a better way to live my life. There is a way to get what I want. There's just a better way of life.

And, you begin seeking and you… start looking at all these things; because you may be going to church and having a religious experience, but it doesn't do anything for you, it's not fulfillment. You find this religion that says: No, wait a minute you know, this is where God is. God is where you are, and when you pray to God, you pray to the God that is within you, that is around you. You don't have to wait for a God way up "there" to kind of get the message through your local computer network or something; you don't have to network with God. It is here!

And you have it because you have been given this powerful, Creative Mind. It is yours to use. And you can use it any way you want. You can bring in abuse, and failure and sadness and poverty, or you can bring in happiness and joy, because that's already within you. These people are seekers, and when you seek, you *do* find what you're looking for. These people are seeking it, and they find it.

So the principle is: You don't have to go outside yourself, it's right there. And we have what you call prayer, and we have spiritual mind treatment, but you are *changing how you are thinking*.

Betty Jean House, from a recorded interview with Diane L. Bullock, mervision@aol.com, Denver, Colorado, September 18, 2000. Copyrighted material used with permission.

November 28

SOUL

We read in the Hebrew Scriptures, "The soul that sinneth, it shall die."

What is Soul? Is it a reality within the mortal body? Who can prove that? Anatomy has not decried nor described Soul. It was never touched by the scalpel nor cut with the dissecting knife. The five physical senses do not recognize it. Who, then, dares define Soul as something within man?

As well might you declare some old castle to be peopled with demons or angels, though never a light or form was discerned therein, and not a spectre had ever been seen going in or coming out.

The common hypotheses about souls are even more vague than ordinary material conjectures, and have less basis; because material theories are built on the evidence of the material senses.

Soul must be God; since we learn Soul only as we learn God, by spiritualization. As the five senses take no cognizance of Soul, so they take no cognizance of God. Whatever cannot be taken in by mortal mind -- by human reflection, reason, or belief -- must be the unfathomable Mind, which "eye hath not seen, nor ear heard." Soul stands in this relation to every hypothesis as to its human character.

Mary Baker Eddy, *Unity of Good*, 1887, pp. 28-29. No known copyright in effect.

November 29

FOR THE EVENING

I have received my daily bread from on high and now I close the door of the outer sense while I digest and assimilate it.

I close this door in perfect confidence, sure of the divine protection which never slumbers nor sleeps.

I know Love is God and is Omnipotent and Omnipresent.

I turn from the objective world to the subjective knowing that I shall find my way, without harm or hindrance, to the green pastures and still waters of His beloved. No psychic influence can turn me aside from this resting-place, for the Lord is my shepherd and him only do I serve.

I am free from all fear. I am free from all sense of injury. I have no enemies. No one has wronged me. I have in my heart no desire for retaliation. I feel only love for every human being.

I go to my rest in the desire to rise from it renewed and invigorated that I may still minister to my brethren. I have laid aside the garments that belong to the outer world and I enter the soul-world clad in its own raiment, by which those who need me shall know me. I turn out the light of the material world.

I see the greater light which guides my footsteps. Its radiance shows me what I still lack and where to find the supply. In this light of God I take my journey for this night and wing my way to my real home, knowing that I shall find it and bring back from it what the kingdoms of this world can never give me.

For I go forth with only love in my heart, and this key will unlock all the treasures of wisdom and power and health and peace. The curtains are drawn; the world fades away. On the wings of love I am rising to the heavenly spheres. I hear their far-off music.

Ursula Gestefeld, *The Breath of Life*, 1897, pp. 10-12. No known copyright in effect.

November 30

GUIDELINES TO PERSONAL PROSPERITY

In matters of Truth, we are all like small children in school who are learning to read. And just as such learning requires books with big print and exaggerated space between the lines, our study of Truth may demand that the essentials be presented with great simplicity and special clarity. Here, then, are ten basic points which are intended to impact clearly on our consciousness and to register solidly in the undercurrent of our thought…

Point 1:. We must look *only* to God for our success….

Point 2: We must make no pictures of limitation or lack….

Point 3: We must not speak the *language* of limitation….

Point 4: We must let go of all personal will and let God work in our affairs….

Point 5: There is an honor with which we should deal with God and what He sends us….

Point 6: We must keep our money circulating intelligently….

Point 7: Spending or passing on your money with a good sense of valuation will always bring back results to you.

Point 8: We should never strive to get something for nothing….

Point 9: Never talk down success by saying that you are limited or that you have been spending too much or by belittling your success to others.

Point 10: Do not compare yourself with someone else or permit yourself in any way to envy your neighbor's success, for his individual use of Law is different than yours….

Elizabeth Carrick-Cook, published in *Science of Mind*, February 1981, pp. 18-21. Copyrighted material reprinted with permission of SOM Publishing.

DECEMBER

December 1

THIS PRESENT MOMENT

As we open our minds and hearts to the message of eternal life, we turn to our Scriptures for confirmation. In the book of Isaiah, the prophet speaks to the magnitude of God's plan for all creation. Read these words with the eyes of your heart:

Do you not know? Have you not heard? The Lord is the everlasting God, the Creator of the ends of the earth. He will not grow tired or weary, And His understanding no one can fathom. He gives strength to the weary and increases the power of the weak. Even youths grow tired and weary and young Men stumble and fall; but those who hope in the Lord will renew their strength. They will soar on wings as eagles. They will run and not grow weary. They will walk and not be faint. Isaiah 40:28-31

Somehow as I read these words I hear and feel the power of Spirit that transcends the ages and feeds me in this moment as I view my life and my purpose. I have a word before me on my computer that reads:

THIS PRESENT MOMENT IS A BRIGHT AND EXCITING PLACE FOR ME TO BE.

I am confident that life is a moving process drawn by an eternal plan of God's good for everyone. We are created in the Spirit of the living God in a universe of life that sings, renews, rebuilds, restores, heals and in every wonderful way contributes to creation. We are meant to soar like the eagles and be renewed in a strength that runs and is not weary! We are meant to live fully in this moment in this present time and place!

We are spiritually the very essence of the Christ Presence so clearly lived by Jesus. Over and over again we walk together on life's paths for we have a destiny that knows no time or space. Let us keep close in prayer and love and let the moment wrap around us as we accept life's fullness.

Dorothy M. Pierson, excerpt from *Keeping Close In Prayer*, 2011.
Copyrighted material reprinted with permission of Unity, Unity.org

December 2

THE FULLNESS OF JOY

Joy is experienced on many different planes in our life and all of it is divine. First, there is the joy of physical activity, and of physical accomplishment. This is the joy we feel when we make things with our hands…. Physical joy also includes such rhythmic motion as walking, dancing, swimming, playing basketball, and playing musical instruments. All of these give us the joy of active creativity. Then there is that delicate feeling of intellectual joy – the gaining of knowledge, the lifting of thought to understand more of the world in which we live. There is great joy in understanding the wonders of the stars, the wonders of chemistry, the wonders of life. Such knowledge brings to us the sense of attainment, of accomplishment – when we understand and use it.

There is the pure joy of listening to our favorite music, or looking at beautiful paintings, or gazing at the sea or the stars. There is the particular joy of being parents and creating a home; the joy of friendships, and of groups, meeting together with common purpose, such as a church group. Then we know the joy of work. We have taken the toil out of labor, because we have recognized it as an expression of the joyous activity of God. With it comes a deep inner sense of fulfilling one's talent or place in life.

Finally, there is that real, original source of joy – the joy of God in the soul of man, the spirit of the individual recognizing the truth of being. We do not *create* spiritual joy; we *recognize* and *accept* it as the gift of God. And God's joy is a permanent abiding quality that is forever undisturbed and unhurt by whatever goes on in the outer.

Grace L. Faus, published in *Aspire*, December 1958, pp. 7-8. Copyrighted material reprinted with permission of Divine Science Federation International.

December 3

THE STORY OF MAN'S SPIRIT

Like the story of the Cross, the story of man's spirit ends in a garden: in a place of birth and fruitfulness, of beautiful and natural things. Divine Fecundity [Fertility] is its secret: existence, not for its own sake, but for the sake of more abundant life. It ends with the coming forth of divine humanity, never again to leave us: living in us, and with us, a pilgrim, a worker, a guest at our table, a sharer at all hazards of life. The mystics witness to this story: waking very early they have run on before us, urged by the greatness of their love. We, incapable as yet of this sublime encounter, looking in their magic mirror, listening to their stammered tidings, may see far off the consummation of the race.

According to the measure of their strength and of their passion, these, the true lovers of the Absolute, have conformed here and now to the utmost tests of divine son-ship, the final demands of life. They have not shrunk from the sufferings of the cross. They have faced the darkness of the tomb. Beauty and agony alike have called them: alike have awakened a heroic response. For them the winter is over: the time of the singing birds is come. From the deeps of the dewy garden, Life – new, unquenchable, and ever lovely – comes to meet them with the dawn.

Evelyn Underhill, *Mysticism*, 1955, pp. 450-451. No known copyright in effect.

December 4

THOU SHALT NOT SEEK SOMETHING FOR NOTHING

One of the most difficult things in life to understand is the apparently unjust distribution of riches. Self-respecting, upright people, with keen minds, who are endeavoring to live constructive, creative lives are oftentimes poor as the proverbial church mouse. Such people frequently become embittered wondering why persons who are unsound ethically, have undeveloped minds, and lead useless and sometimes vicious lives are literally rolling in manifest wealth.

The answer is that wealth is the out-picturing of the state of mind. The earnestly striving person whose efforts are not richly compensated may have a poverty consciousness. This is by far the most common reason for inadequate returns for conscientious endeavor. The mind that is filled with fear of lack or acceptance of lack or rebellion against circumstances is for the time being definitely failing to collect the just compensation due to this outer realm of cause and effect. Since nothing is ever lost, he will at some point of his existence reap the benefit of every effort he makes when he has freed his mind from the poverty complex.

On the other hand, an apparently useless person, who seems to be giving nothing to life, may have a money consciousness. He may be utterly convinced that the world is his oyster and thoughtlessly proceed to grab and use selfishly everything in sight. With no thought of lack in his mind he will continue wealthy, although his wrong use of wealth must eventually bring him misery and disappointment. Such situations call for compassion rather than envy or rebellion, for we are seeing only in part. We are seeing the beginning of a violation of the law of giving and receiving that can only result in disaster at some future time for the one who faces life so unintelligently.

Georgiana Tree West, *Prosperity's Ten Commandments*, 1946, pp. 101-102.
Copyrighted material reprinted with permission of Unity, Unity.org

December 5

I WILL HELP THEE

*Call upon me in the day of trouble: I will deliver thee,
and thou shalt glorify me.*
Psalms 50:15

Thou shalt know that I the Lord am thy Savior and Redeemer.
Isaiah 60:16

*Before the day was I am he; and there is none that
can deliver out of my hand.*
Isaiah 43:13

Remember that the state of peace and happiness is the natural state of the children of God. Therefore, to ask for help from trouble into happiness is your privilege. Never forget to give God the glory – to praise Him. He does not need it, but you need to give it and others need to hear it.

Nora Smith Holm, *The Runner's Bible*, 1913, p. 94. No known copyright in effect.

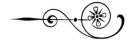

December 6

A CHANGE IN ATTITUDE

I don't know the exact day I was healed. I just know there was no more pain. My thoughts had changed, my feelings had changed, my attitude had changed. I was a new person, feeling good from the top of my head to the soles of my feet. I prayed the prayer that Jesus prayed: "The Father and I are one." I accepted it as the truth about me and everyone else.

I have had many healings since then, because I know exactly what to do. I call on the Master Physician within me. The Master Physician who created me can remake me and revitalize me.

Those years of training challenged me and caused me to make adjustments. I believed I was fulfilling God's plan for me. I held on to God's promise: "I will never leave you or forsake you." However, many nights I couldn't sleep, and I asked, "God, have You forgotten Your promise?" The answer would come: "I stand on My promise. I am with you. You can call on Me whenever you feel that you need a friend. You are My beloved child, and I am expressing Myself as you, through you. So be strong, and be of good cheer, because I'm here with you. Just ask and you will know My presence."

My reason for being on Earth is to help people understand how to live a better life. My prayer is that I do those "greater works" that Jesus spoke of -- and God knows I am willing.

Johnnie Colemon, published in *Daily Word*, November 2001. Copyrighted material reprinted with permission of Unity, Unity.org.

December 7

LET YOUR HEART LISTEN

You are My beloved child. Out of My own self have I created you. My life is your life; My breath is your breath; My Spirit is your spirit. There is nothing to fear, for I am with you, mighty in the midst of you.

I am the life that heals you. I am the love that lifts your heart and sets you free. I am the wisdom of your mind. I am the light of your path. I am the peace of your soul.

I am with you, dear child, through every hour of the day and the night, standing with you, upholding you, supporting you, revealing Myself to you and through you.

I am the love that will not let you go. I seek you out when you do not know how to reach Me. I speak in your heart to comfort you. I am the life of your body, and My life is perfect and eternal. Trust Me. I am your health.

I am with you in all the experiences of your life. I am the power in you to understand; I am the power in you to forgive; I am the power in you to become.

Beloved, I am with you. Live in Me. Rejoice in Me. You are My beloved child.

Martha Smock, published in *Daily Word*, December 1958. Copyrighted material reprinted with permission of Unity, Unity.org.

December 8

HOW I FOUND HEALTH

I have made what seems to me a discovery. I was very sick; I had all the ills of mind and body that I could bear. Medicine and doctors ceased to give me relief and I was in despair, until I found practical Christianity. I affirmed my beliefs and I was healed....

I went to all the life centers in my body and spoke words of Truth to them -- words of strength and power. I asked their forgiveness for the foolish, ignorant course that I had pursued in the past, when I had condemned them and called them weak, inefficient, and diseased.

I did not become discouraged at their being slow to wake up, but kept right on, both silently and aloud, declaring words of Truth until the organs responded.

And neither did I forget to tell them they were free, unlimited Spirit. I told them that they were no longer in bondage to the carnal mind; that they were not corruptible flesh, but centers of life and energy omnipresent.

Then I asked the Father to forgive me for taking His life into my body and using it so wastefully. I promised Him that I would never, never again retard the free flow of that life through my mind and my body by any false word or thought; that I would always bless it and encourage it with true thoughts and words in its wise work of building up my body temple; that I would use all diligence and wisdom in telling it just what I wanted it to do.

I want everybody to know about this beautiful, true law and to use it. It is not a new discovery but, when you use it and get the fruits of health and harmony, it will seem new to you, and you will feel that it is your own discovery.

Myrtle Fillmore, published in *Unity*, 1897. Copyrighted material reprinted with permission of Unity, Unity.org.

December 9

TRUST THE SPIRIT WITHIN

Trust the Spirit within to give you the right ideas to solve anything in your life that needs solving. Trust the Spirit within to illumine your mind. Trust the Spirit within to heal your body. Trust the Spirit within to release you from limiting relationships or habits. Trust the Spirit within to free you from agitation or irritation in regard to the attitudes of others. Trust the Spirit within to quiet your impatience and bring new peacefulness to your soul. Trust the Spirit within to show you how to handle your business, to give you guidance in making decisions, to fill you with a feeling of well-being....

Trust the Spirit within -- within yourself, within others, within any situation or circumstance confronting you. Trust to the Spirit within your business ventures, within everything around you, within the weather, the plane in which you fly, the car in which you drive, or the environment in which you live. If you think that your faith is not adequate or your belief not strong enough, start to build that faith and belief with these very words, saying them boldly and firmly: *I trust the Spirit within.*

Practice trusting God, practice trusting His presence in you, practice trusting God's presence in others. Practice and continue practicing. Repeat the words: *I trust the Spirit within,* then let go. Discipline yourself to affirm this at the very moment you become upset or disturbed about something. Use the wonderful tools of your mind and heart positively and constructively and stay with the affirmative attitude of trusting the Spirit within until you begin to feel an inner response. It will come....

Mary L. Kupferle, *God Will See You Through*, 1983, pp. 136, 138-139.
Copyrighted material reprinted with permission of Unity, Unity.org.

December 10

DIVINE GUIDANCE

He hath showed thee, O man, what is good; and what doth the Lord require of thee, but to do justly, and to love mercy, and to walk humbly with thy God?
Micah 6:8

    Divine guidance is our need and we find it in this brief statement of what the Father demands: justice, mercy, and humility. We are quick to see the desirability of that justice from others which gives us our due; are we equally generous and fair in extending it to others in all the little day-to-day conditions and experiences? If we take advantage of anyone by even a slightly short weight when we sell; by charging for a full hour's time when we have given only fifty minutes of work; by putting less than our best workmanship into whatever we do for another; or by letting ourselves be swayed from the path of absolute rectitude, we are breaking God's law just as surely as we would be if we had committed some flagrant violation of a statute.

    Do we so love mercy that we extend it to others even if, to do so, we must go out of our way and face inconvenience? Have we that true humility which God demands of those who profess to follow His laws?

    Let us ponder these three qualities today and make a new commitment truly to observe them from now on. These are specific points which we now set out to seek; they are foundation stones of spiritual unfoldment. May the structure of our inner growth rest firmly on them.

    Father, I am grateful for Thy guidance today as I earnestly try to put into practice the qualities of justice, mercy, and humility.

Annie S. Greenwood, published in *Aspire*, March 1954, p. 21. Copyrighted material reprinted with permission of Divine Science Federation International.

December 11

WHOLENESS FOR YOU

The ministry of Jesus Christ was founded on healing; healing of mind, body and soul – as well as healing of nations. Who will say that in His mighty service of healing Jesus Christ was working against God's will? Not one. God's will is wholeness.

Holiness is the outworking of God's will in the mind and soul; wholeness is the acceptance of His will in the body; abundance of all good is the outworking of His Will in one's affairs and environment.

The personal ministry of Jesus was short. It lasted but a few years after His baptism. Yet His words and deeds so quickened the minds of His followers that those whom He taught passed His teachings to others; those whom He healed kept His healing ministry alive; those who felt the power of His love talked and sang and wrote of it until now the whole world knows about Jesus Christ.

Every person is a cell in the universal Christ body, so close are we to Him. The work of Christ will not be completed until every cell, every soul and body, is radiant with love that portrays the fullness and glory of divine life. His work will continue until everybody is perfect and whole. Let your life shine with the fullness of His love for you, His joy in you. Do not delay His perfect healing work by a single retarding doubt.

Clara A. Palmer, *You Can Be Healed*, 1937, pp. 184-185. Copyrighted material reprinted with permission of Unity, Unity.org.

December 12

I HEAR THE SONG OF CHRISTMAS

Can you hear the song of Christmas? Listen closely, for it is not an outer song. It is a secret song within your heart.

The song of Christmas is a song of life. Life is singing to you. Life is singing within the very cells of your being. Life is singing a song of renewal. Life is singing a song of health.

The song of Christmas is a song of newness. The melody of this song is beautiful indeed, for it reminds you that even the happy Christmases of the past cannot compare with the present moment, so fraught with power, so filled with God's Spirit. The song of newness reminds you that nothing is ever lost, no love is ever in vain, that God in His love transforms all that has gone before into something new and wonderful today.

The song of Christmas is a song of joy. This song of joy transcends all grief or sadness, it lifts the lonely heart, it awakens new hope. It quickens a new spirit and a new faith.

Listen to the song of joy. It is there in your heart. Peace to your heart it sings. Joy to your heart it brings.

Martha Smock, published in *The Song of Christmas*, Unity pamphlet, 1975, p. 22. Copyrighted material reprinted with permission of Unity, Unity.org.

December 13

THE MEANING OF FREE WILL

And ye shall know the truth, and the truth shall make you free.
John 8:32

...Outside of the automatic and necessary functions of Universal Mind, man is free to do as he will...the Cosmic Engine is started;
but man guides it in his own life.
The Science of Mind, page 395.

Free will means we can accept or reject *anything*—but it does not mean we are without inner guidelines for determining when certain courses of action are better than others. For Truth is always available for us to call upon.

Raymond Charles Barker says, "God provides food for all of us, but doesn't throw it at us." This means that Truth, though forever available, has to be recognized. Our ability to recognize Truth -- and act upon it or not -- is part of what our free will encompasses.

While we can accept Truth or reject it, we can never escape the consequences of what we accept or reject. Every thought, believed in as true for us, becomes an experience of some kind, and that experience counsels us as to the wisdom or foolishness of the choice we have made.

Rejection of Truth means stepping outside the flow of harmonious existence. It means a life of haphazard experience, slowed spiritual growth, stagnation, and a hit-and-miss pathway through life. Acceptance of Truth means steady progress in appropriate thought-management. It means we understand that Creative law awaits our direction, and that we can come into authority over the experiences in our daily life.

We make wonderful tomorrows by Truth-oriented thinking today. The way ahead is clear and we are filled with the certainty of a rich, healthy, peaceful, and abundant life when we embrace the fullness that Truth can bring.

I have authority over my life because I accept Truth -- the truth that Spirit provides guidance and that every thought of mine, believed in, is acted upon by Creative Law and brought to fruition. I am free to experience all the good I can envision.

Norah Boyd, published in *Science of Mind*, April 1994, p. 60. Copyrighted material reprinted with permission of SOM Publishing.

December 14

BE STILL

Be Still! Not as any stillness you have ever known before. The stillness which lies at the bottom of the ocean, eternally quiet, yet eternally vibrant and alive with infinite activity. Only by attaining this super-stillness can the full realization of former talks be attained. You must learn to keep this stillness, to retreat into it at any moment, whenever any confusion arises in your physical or mental world. Thus shall all difficulties solve themselves by My Power working through you. Learn to BE STILL instantly and watch God's Power work! In this potent stillness all demonstrations are made.

Eva Bell Werber. *Quiet Talks With the Master*, 1936, pp. 16-17. Reproduced from QUIET TALKS WITH THE MASTER by Eva Bell Werber 9780875161044 DeVorss Publications, www.devorss.com.

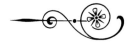

December 15

THE MYSTIC EXPERIENCE

The word mystic has long been a contemptuous and sometimes condescendingly pitying term for the poor misguided souls who were thought "half-cracked." And unfortunately, through the centuries, the description has not been unwarranted in many instances, although the idea was misunderstood.

Too many people at too many times have gotten completely lost in a religious fanaticism and damaged their bodies consciously – and their souls unconsciously – in the belief that this would endear them to God. They believed – and many still do – in the kind of a God that wants us to suffer, wants us to maim ourselves, drive ourselves berserk, in order to worship Him.

But the mystic – the REAL mystic – does not believe that. Once he has made a conscious contact with God, he knows that the Divine Plan for him and every other human being is to express the Perfection of Being to his utmost ability. He knows that God is real, for he experiences that reality within himself. He learns that he is supposed to become a co-creator with God, and to have dominion over his life and affairs. He develops Spiritual Power by harnessing his emotions. He begins to realize that nothing can ever upset his life again, for he has found the Source of all his strength and has learned how to use it. He combines within himself the precision of the scientist and the beauty of the artist – and he expresses them.

The real mystic worships God, not in self-abasement and abject fear, but as a son and heir, in love and confidence, and with the desire to be a true representative of his Father. He walks with God consciously, and points the way for the rest of us to follow. And he begins to understand something of what the greatest of all mystics meant when he said, "God is Spirit, and they that worship Him must worship Him in spirit and in truth." John 4:24

Mildred Mann, *Become What You Believe, Volume II*, 1970, p. 12. No known copyright in effect.

December 16

THE EVER-PRESENT NOW

I'm a child upon the High-way
      And my back is toward the Past;
I'm alive in the glowing Present,
      And no shadow is o'er me cast.

For at High-noon there is no shadow,
      Or if one there seems to be --
I'm between the Sun and the shadow
      and the Sun sees only me.

I'm not looking toward the Future
      For I'm traveling with the Sun,
And I know that what seems Tomorrow
      Will be Today when today is done.

And I know if a Word must be spoken
      The idea in Mind was born,
And that Now is the living Present
      My lips shall give it form.

Substance is ever-present;
      Each day the manna fell;
Gold was found in the fish's mouth --
      God is -- and all is well.

The Love that would find expression
      Is a magnet in itself
Drawing ever the object
      Upon which to lavish Love's wealth.

And so I live in the Present,
      And the Light is on my brow,
For I travel always with the Sun
      In the ever-present Now.

Helen Van Slyke, *Religious Science Monthly*, January 1928, p. 13.
Copyrighted material reprinted with permission of SOM Publishing.

December 17

PEACE PILGRIM'S BEATITUDES

BLESSED are they that give without expecting even thanks in return, for they shall be abundantly rewarded.

BLESSED are they who translate every good thing they know into action – ever higher truths shall be revealed to them.

BLESSED are they who do God's will without asking to see results, for great shall be their recompense.

BLESSED are they who love and trust their fellow human beings, for they shall reach the good in people and receive a loving response.

BLESSED are they who have seen reality, for they know not the garment of clay but that which activates the garment of clay is real and indestructible.

BLESSED are they who see the change we call death as a liberation from the limitations of this earth-life, for they shall rejoice with their loved ones who make the glorious transition.

BLESSED are they who after dedicating their lives and thereby receiving a blessing have the courage and faith to surmount the difficulties of the path ahead, for they shall receive a second blessing.

BLESSED are they who advance toward the spiritual path without the selfish motive of seeking inner peace, for they shall find it.

BLESSED are those who instead of trying to batter down the gates of the kingdom of heaven approach them humbly and lovingly and purified, for they shall pass right through.

Peace Pilgrim, *Steps Toward Inner Peace*, 1983, pp. 27-28. No known copyright in effect.

December 18

MY DESIRE IS TO ACCOMPLISH THE WILL OF GOD

I am sure we have all had a deep desire for something in our life which we didn't get. The important question then is how to handle this disappointment. To accomplish any desire is to know that there is no disappointment with God; everything works for good for those who love God.

Disappointment must be met with utmost honesty and we must strive to be free of deception. There is always something else toward which we can turn. A sign of real maturity is to admit the disappointment, then to turn our desire toward accomplishment. Desire is the first step in accomplishing everything in life. All creation starts with desire, deep within the soul. The highest desire is to let the will of God be done.

God's will for me and all His children is all-good and perfect. My affirmation today is, "Not my will, Father, but Thine be done." I choose to yield my personal will to the universal will of God and reap the rewards of happiness, peace of mind, and complete satisfaction. I desire to accomplish the will of God which is the expression of my true inner self, the Christ. Through the Christ in me I shall accomplish all that I desire to do right now.

What things so ever ye desire, when ye pray, believe that ye receive them.
Mark 11:24

Olga Una Barker, published in *Daily Inspiration*, Copyright 1980, *Daily Inspiration for Better Living.* Reprinted with permission of the Universal Foundation for Better Living (UFBL) Press, November 1980, p. 25.

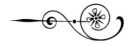

December 19

ALMIGHTY GOD IS WITH ME

Thou knowest, my God, the test before me requires indomitable courage, bravery, faith. I look to Thee for all I need. Thou gavest me Thy Spirit. I *use* what Thou has given me.

I am brave, I am strong, I am fearless, for the Almighty One is with me, and in Him I trust. Fearless, free, rejoicing I go forth knowing that victory and triumph shall reward my faith.

My faith is in Thee, my God, in Thy Power, in Thy Intelligence. My faith must not falter, nor waver; it must be steadfast, firm.

In this crisis I have an opportunity to prove to myself what my God means to me; how much of the Truth I comprehend; what degree of faith I possess. This is a test, an examination.

He who has courage goes forth with a song in his heart, with head erect; confident, serene, assured of success. And God rejoices to see His Spirit manifested through one of His children; His gift of faith brought into visibility, and His presence recognized as the living Presence, immanent and almighty, of Strength and Wisdom, sufficient to meet my need. And God rejoices to hear His child declare: "My God is with me, therefore all is well."

Elizabeth Nordman, published in *Divine Science Monthly*, August 1932, p. 36. Copyrighted material reprinted with permission of Divine Science Federation International.

December 20

I WILL COME AND HEAL

I let my mind and heart feel a deep awareness of God's healing presence; truly, I feel upheld and sustained by His love. I affirm divine order in all things.

When we think in terms of divine order, we let go of anxiety and fear and we never feel that we are alone. We see the power of God at work. We have faith that there is a way out, and we realize that there is a divine fulfillment for every need.

With faith in God's power to heal, fear and insecurity have no place in my heart. I take refuge in God's all-enfolding love, and I am confident and unafraid.

Let us pray: I bless my life. I bless any situation or any circumstance that has caused me concern. I go forth this day filled with confidence in God's guidance, and I rest my concerns in His care. All my steps are guided and directed by His presence and power. All things are working together for good through the wisdom and power of Spirit.

I will come and heal him. Go thy way:
and as thou hast believed,
so be it done unto thee.
Matthew 8:7,13

Christina Knox-Walthall, published in *Daily Inspiration*, Copyright 1985, *Daily Inspiration for Better Living.* Reprinted with permission of the Universal Foundation for Better Living (UFBL) Press, September 1985, p. 4.

December 21

LOVE IS THE ESSENCE

Love is the essence of the Christmas Spirit. The one who loves most will have the most successful Christmas, and his Christmas joy will go with him throughout the year. What a good thing it is to have our thought centered, at least once a year, upon the supreme gift – Love! What a good thing it is to forget ourselves in the thought of others, to share our good with others.

Today the Spirit of Love is abroad in the universe; it is given full sway for these twenty-four hours. But it is working here all of the time. Our province is to know this and to believe in it with deep conviction. In our practice of right thinking, the most valuable factor of all is love. When thought is backed by love, it is all-powerful. Love banishes from the mind hatred, jealousy, ambition, false desires, and wrong attitudes. True love always gives true direction to thought. Love cleanses the mental realm and leaves a clear road for all that is highest and best. When thought is charged with this irresistible force, it is invincible.

Let us, then, give special attention in the year to come to the development within us of an abiding spirit of love. This is the eternal Christmas spirit, the spirit in which "every day will be Christmas."

Nona L. Brooks, published in *Christmas Light*, 1971, p. 25. Copyrighted material reprinted with permission of Divine Science Federation International.

December 22

FOR UNTO US A CHILD IS BORN

For unto us a child is born, unto us a son is given: and the government shall be upon his shoulder: and his name shall be called Wonderful, Counselor, The mighty God, The everlasting Father, The Prince of Peace. Of the increase of his government and peace there shall be no end, upon the throne of David, and upon his kingdom, to order it, and to establish it with judgment and with justice from henceforth even for ever. The zeal of the Lord of hosts will perform this.
Isaiah 9:6-7

We hear a great deal about getting one's self into harmony with certain forces that are supposed to be moving though this universe. We are told that there is a secret "flame" in our atmospheric ether which we can extract after a little practice and it will have an astonishing effect upon us. We are told of elixirs that float and crackle all about us, which only a few on this round ball have ever caught any of, but they have been filled with extraordinary powers.

According to Jesus Christ, whose powers really all start from the soul principle in each of us, and it is what we ourselves have generated that we finally inhale as "flame," "elixir vitae," or "forces."…

The first lesson of Jesus was, "Stop gazing among the ways of men hoping to find a cure of their scourges. Turn your eyes backward and see into that kingdom of heaven that hath its everlasting abode within you. There your eyes will catch fire, light, miracle shining rays, and wherever you look after that, something new and strange will happen."

Emma Curtis Hopkins, *For Unto Us A Child Is Born*, 1894, pp. 3-4. No known copyright in effect.

December 23

WHERE I AM KING

My mind is absolutely my own. What enters it and lodges in it and colors it is under my jurisdiction. Watch your thoughts. Catch yourself up when you find yourself thinking unwholesome or unworthy ones. Say to yourself many times each day, "Today I accept the peace, love, and joy of God."

I think it came to me as one of the profoundest realizations of my life that my mind is absolutely my own. What enters it and lodges in it and colors it is under my jurisdiction. My thoughts are really under my control, and likewise my moods and emotions, although I had previously thought that these were in the nature of powerful waves that washed up over a man from external conditions to bend him to their will....

Your mind is your own. It is your own place. You have the absolute say-so as regards what shall enter and dwell there. This fact should be a source of renewed strength and joy to you. You are the absolute arbiter....Any good gardener is on the lookout for weeds, wants to pull them up, and is perfectly able to pull them up. He gives his loving attention to the plants that will blossom into beauty. So with you. If you then encounter difficulties that seem too great for human control, you always have recourse to God. You can turn to Him, ask His help, and put the tangled garden of your mind in His care. He will surely help you get it back in order.

Dana Gatlin, *Where I Am King*, 1935, pp. 3-6. Copyrighted material reprinted with permission of Unity, Unity.org.

December 24

CHRISTMAS THOUGHTS

Whenever the Christmas season
  Lends luster and peace to the year,
And the ling-long-ling of the bells that ring
  Tell only of joy and cheer,
I hear in the sweet, wild music
  These words, and I hold them true:
"The Christ who was born on Christmas morn
  Did only what you can do."

      Each soul that has breath and being
        Is touched with Heaven's own fire,
      Each living man is part of the plan
        To lift the world up higher.
      No matter how narrow your limits,
        Go forth and make them broad!
      You are every one the daughter or son --
        Crown Prince or Princess of God.

Have you sinned? It is only an error --
  Your spirit is pure and white.
It is truth's own ray and will find its way
  Back into the path of right.
Have you failed? It is only in seeming --
  The triumph will come at length.
You are born to succeed, you will have what you need,
  If you will but believe in your strength.

No matter how poor your record --
　　Christ lives in the heart of you,
And the shadow will roll up and off from your soul,
　　If you will but own this true.
For "Christ" means the spirit of goodness,
　　And all men are good at the core,
Look searchingly in thro' the coating of sin,
　　And lo! there is Truth to adore.

Believe in yourself and your motives,
　Believe in your strength and your worth,
Believe you were sent from God's fair firmament
　To aid and ennoble the Earth.
Believe in the Savior within you --
　Know Christ and your spirit are one,
Stand forth deified by your own noble pride,
　And whatever you ask shall be done.

Ella Wheeler Wilcox, published in *The Life*, (Kansas City, Missouri), January 1902. No known copyright in effect.

December 25

O WONDROUS NIGHT

My weary feet had wandered far
In search of Thee,
Until one night I saw a Star
That beckoned me.

It led me to a stable, where,
Upon the hay,
Oxen, sheep and suckling lambs, there
In stillness lay.

And then I saw a Baby small
On Mary's knee;
Strange kings with gifts were kneeling all
Adoringly.

No throne, no kingly star to wear,
Yet my heart knew
I'd found Thee, Lord, in stable bare,
And I knelt too.

Florence Scripps Kellogg, *My Joyous Spirit Sings*, 1950, p. 12. No known copyright in effect.

December 26

MIND RADIATES

God is mind, and every thought of divine mind is perfect like itself. Man must know himself as God created him, a pure and perfect idea of the first great cause, then will all of his expressions be likewise, good and very good. But as long as he remains ignorant of this truth he will continue to express a mixed condition of sin and peace, health and disease, life and death.

Man is not a creator in the sense that he originates anything, his work is to take the invisible creations of God and to make them visible, for man is the creator of the outer world of form, while God is the creator of the inner world of principle.

This invisible creation is called by Jesus Christ, "The Kingdom of Heaven," and it fills all space, so that it is accessible to man through his own divinity, and by scientific thinking he may externalize it as heaven on earth. Mind, thought, words and deeds, define the process from center to circumference of creation, and when man realizes that he builds his world with his words, he will begin to discipline his mind and pay strict attention to the quality of his thoughts and words, bringing them into conformity with the constructive power of love and wisdom; thus his body and his world will begin to manifest the true, the good and the beautiful.

It is as truly the nature of mind to radiate thought as it is for a lighted lamp to radiate light, yet if the lamp chimney be blackened with soot, the medium has become imperfect and thus the radiations of light will be rendered feeble. Man is God's lamp, His greatest avenue of expression, and must needs keep his conscious mind clear and clean as a perfect vehicle of expression.

Harriet Hale Rix, *Christian Mind Healing*, 1914, p. 30. No known copyright in effect.

December 27

SONG IN MY HEART

There is within me a joyous song…It holds such gladness that to catch even the lilt of its tones refreshes and restores me. As I listen, every part of me sings its melody…there is not a cell in my body but is aroused, awakened and attuned, not an organ but responds and enters in the harmony of perfect functioning. The joyful rhythm pulses through my veins and arteries, purifies the life stream, tunes my heart to beat in unison with the great heart of God, breathes into and out of my lungs with the cleansing, renewing God breath. I become so illumined by the song…that it creates in me a joy and a harmony that radiate from me to others along the way.

Frances W. Foulks, *Prayers, Blessings and Meditations*, Unity booklet, 1958, p. 16. Copyrighted material reprinted with permission of Unity, Unity.org.

December 28

GOD OMNIPOTENT

I know in whom I believe, God Omnipotent.

We cannot possibly be lacking in faith when we know in whom we believe. It is because we do not know God aright that we suffer from doubts and fears. Knowledge of God and His law inspire faith in His Omnipresence.

The first essential in the happy adventure of living an affirmative life is to know what God is and to get ourselves firmly established in this knowledge so that we can at all times stand true to Principle.

I will be still and know the God in whom I believe.
I know the Perfection of my Source.
I know the Fullness of my Supply.
I know the Limitlessness of my Power.
I know the Certainty of my Life.
I know the Beauty of my World.
I know the Harmony of my Home.
I know the Safety of my Family.
I know the Success of my Business.
I know the Source of every Good.
I know in whom I believe, God Omnipotent, Changeless, Eternal, Infinite.

Study: II Timothy, 1:1-13, Psalm 46

Alice R. Ritchie, published in *Divine Science Monthly*, October 1933, p. 28. Copyrighted material reprinted with permission of Divine Science Federation International.

December 29

MY CUP RUNNETH OVER

In the matter of the temporal prosperity that results from worldly methods, it is considered a good principle to gauge one's spending by one's income; and that is good sense when one's prosperity is on a material basis.

But the spiritual law is stated thus: "With what measure ye mete, it shall be measured unto you." "Give, and it shall be given unto you." In other words, learn to spend – not recklessly or in a meaningless way; but with the wisdom of one who is being educated to disseminate riches like seed, thus breaking down fear and sense of limitation and cultivating faith and consciousness of all-capacity in himself....

When one intends to make a gift of money in a certain amount and then lessens it, he is lessening his own receiving capacity. A homely illustration of this law is the good milk cow that keeps up her capacity to receive as long as what she has to give is all taken from her; but if her milker in a foolish moment should think to save her by not stripping her of her milk, she would give him less the next time, even though he milked her dry.

Practice distributing freely because of trust in your unlimited source of supply.

Annie Rix Militz, *Both Riches and Honor*, 1945, pp. 105-106. Copyrighted material reprinted with permission of Unity, Unity.org.

December 30

WE CAN CHANGE

*Put on the new man, which is renewed in knowledge after the
image of Him that created him.*
Colossians 3:10

There is a belief among some persons that when changes are made in our society, man will change. Jesus taught that when man changes, society will change. Today is a new day! We can change.

It is well to return again and again to the teachings of Jesus and be renewed in mind, body, and affairs. Jesus found it necessary to turn often to the Father within. He realized that of his human self he could do nothing, but that as he opened his consciousness to the omniscience of God, he found solutions to the so-called problems of mankind. Today, nearly two thousand years later, we benefit from this great teacher's dedication to his Father-God.

We need to "go apart" in prayer and meditation, as Jesus did, to find refreshment of soul. We do this by turning often to the Source and giving over our concerns, surrendering ourselves to the Father's love and wisdom.

Father, in the quietness of prayer I surrender my self and my concerns. As I partake of food to sustain my physical body, now I partake of spiritual food to feed my soul. I will put on the "new man" in Christ. Thank you, Father.

Lucile Frederick, published in *Daily Studies in Divine Science*, 2010, p. 321. Copyrighted material reprinted with permission of Divine Science Federation International.

December 31

NEW-YEAR EVE MEDITATION

The book of the passing year is spread out before me as I sit alone tonight. Whatever wrong of another toward me that has been written on its pages I forgive and wipe out. Any wrong of mine, intentional or unintentional, I myself forgive, and I open myself to receive forgiveness from anyone whom I may have offended. I let all hurts, all self-pity, all selfishness, all fear, all hate, all sickness and poverty thoughts become as water that has passed away.

The book of my life is cleansed from cover to cover through the forgiving love of Jesus Christ. It is therefore without spot or blemish. I ask, my Father, that before I enter into the new year the Spirit of the Christ may so fill my heart and soul that all the pages of the book throughout the year to come may be filled only with that which I delight to keep in the chamber of my memory and see fulfilled in my life. Let all the spiritual joys of the year that is passing be increased, let all the rich thoughts multiply, all the good sent, from me and toward me grow. Let faith, beauty of soul, compassion, and love become in me as they were in the Nazarene. Let me grow in wisdom and stature and in favor with God and man.

At this closing of the old year I consecrate the incoming year to Thee, and myself to Thy service. Use me, Father, in Thy vineyard; use me: mind, soul, and body. Use all the material goods I possess for the setting up of Thy kingdom on earth through the upliftment of Thy children. Let me be a peacemaker, a healer of discords, of poverty and fear thoughts, let me open the eyes of the blind to Thy beauty, the ears of the deaf to Thy message. Let me point the lame and the halt to the path wherein they can run and not be weary, walk and faint not.

Let me express only the Christ every moment of every day the whole year through, and let the Christ in me call forth the Christ of everyone who enters my life or crosses my path in the time to come.

Frances W. Foulks, *Effectual Prayer*, 1945, pp. 116-118. Copyrighted material reprinted with permission of Unity, Unity.org.

TRIBUTE

A book paying honor and homage to more than one hundred important Women of New Thought hardly would be complete without recognition of some of the visionary women who found their ministries in making certain that we would not forget some of our most beloved early leaders.

Were it not for Ruth Townsend regarding the history and works of Malinda Elliott Cramer, and Marge Flotron as relates to Emma Curtis Hopkins, these two early icons of our movement might not have their proper place in New Thought's philosophical and theological legacy as we know it today.

Between 1973 and 1988 Ruth's Revelation Research of San Diego, California uncovered vital materials concerning Malinda Cramer. Ruth headed a group of diligent researchers: Dorothy Bond, Kim Dines, Lynn Delgadillo, Gayle Jarboe, Ralph Jarboe, Shirley Truitt and Barbara Young. Together they gathered the first complete set of *Harmony* magazines (October 1888 through April 1906) known since the time of the great San Francisco earthquake of April 18, 1906. Had it not been for Ruth and her colleagues Malinda Elliott Cramer might have remained a footnote in American religious thought. They revealed and discussed their findings about Malinda at the October 1988 Divine Science General Conference in Colorado Springs, Colorado – just months before her passing in May 1989.

During much the same period of time Marge Flotron performed similar research, preservation and promotion of the writings of Emma Curtis Hopkins. She devoted more than twenty years of her life to the reintroduction of the "priceless works" of Mrs. Hopkins to the broad New Thought audience through her Ministry of Truth International in Chicago, Illinois. Ministry of Truth was a teaching ministry in contrast to a congregational ministry. Marge traveled widely, using Mrs. Hopkins' metaphysical lessons as the basis for her many seminars and workshops. Marge also was closely associated with INTA throughout her ministry and was a speaker at several INTA Congresses.

More will be revealed. Other historians will follow to discover even greater treasures than these. Nonetheless we pause to pay tribute to two pioneering women who passionately wanted to know more – and succeeded in very significant ways. Marge and Ruth helped reveal the rich literary legacy of Emma Curtis Hopkins and Malinda Elliott Cramer. We are most grateful to them for bringing forth this Timeless Truth.

Marge Flotron   Ruth Fangman Townsend
1922-2004   1929-1989

Photo of Marge courtesy of Desert Church of the Learning Light
Photo of Ruth courtesy of Divine Science Federation Archives

Ruth Townsend leads a discussion with her Revelation Research colleagues,
Divine Science Conference, Colorado Springs, Colorado, October 4, 1988.
Photo courtesy of Divine Science Federation Archives

HISTORIAN'S DILEMMA

Top Photo: Nona L. Brooks, center. Alice R. Ritchie to the right of Nona. No clear identity for the other three.

Center: Only Nona is identifiable on the far right.

Bottom: Anna L. Palmer is second from the left, Nona third, Alice fourth and Daisy Baum sixth. No clear identity for the others.

    The three photographs above come from an album belonging to Alice R. Ritchie when she was a young ministerial student. The photos were all taken in the backyard of Nona L. Brooks' home at 645 Lafayette Street, Denver, Colorado. Judging from the fashions of the day and the fact that Fannie Brooks James is not pictured, the timing of the photos is estimated at 1915. It appears that they all were taken on the same occasion, perhaps an early spring afternoon. The photos picture the women with whom Nona was closest during the early years of Denver's ascendency in Divine Science. We just don't have all the names for all the faces.

There is strong evidence to support the notion that at least Ada B. Fay and Agnes M. Lawson – and perhaps Ruth B. Smith and even Kathleen M. H. Besly -- are pictured within the groups seen above. While no individual photos of these four women could be located in doing the research for this book, the historic timing of their activity in Divine Science suggests their presence in Denver together during this period. We'll never know for sure without more photos and information being revealed. My intuition tells me that they're looking out at us from this page with some amusement and with immeasurable peace and joy. They know they've finally been revealed again, at least in part.

The album of photos from which these images come was a gift to Divine Science Federation International in 2013 from Mary Tanton, granddaughter of Alice R. Ritchie and a cherished friend of the author.

CONTRIBUTOR INDEX

Cornelia Addington
Photo courtesy of Science of Mind Archives and Library Foundation

1912-2005: Cornelia was a well-known New Thought author and speaker ordained in Religious Science. Together with husband Jack Ensign Addington she was ordained in Divine Science in 1963 by Irwin Edwin Gregg. The Addingtons thereafter became the ministerial team at the First Divine Science Church of San Diego, California. Cornelia was a frequent contributor to *Aspire, Creative Thought* and is co-benefactor of INTA's Addington Archives.
August 12, October 8, November 17

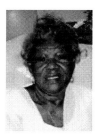

Olga Una Barker
Photo courtesy of Universal Foundation for Better Living

1928-2015: Una became a Unity student in 1964. After meeting Johnnie Colemon she became a UFBL teacher and was ordained in Chicago in July 1978. Una established her ministry in Georgetown, Guyana. She became the first female minister of religion in Guyana and her Lodge Center of Truth was the first UFBL church in South America.
February 27, May 21, July 22, December 18

Ethel A. Barnhart
Photo courtesy of the Science of Mind Archives and Library Foundation

1897-1967: Ethel was the founding minister of the Santa Anita Church of Religious Science, serving from 1947 to 1967. Sometime after 1960, the church became independent. Ethel was the strong leader of a strong church, now simply known as The Santa Anita Church. She was succeeded by Margaret Stevens.

March 26, September 10

Peggy Bassett
Photo courtesy of Science of Mind Archives & Library Foundation

1922-1995: Peggy became a Religious Science minister at age fifty following a successful career in real estate. She built her Huntington Beach church from forty members in the early 1970s to more than five thousand. In 1988 Peggy was the first woman elected President of the United Church of Religious Science.

January 16, May 6, September 22

Daisy Baum
Photo courtesy of Divine Science Federation Archives

1856-1923: Daisy received her Primary Certificate from Fannie Brooks James in 1905, was subsequently ordained and became one of the most active early authors of Divine Science. Daisy was a frequent contributor to *Divine Science Monthly*.

March 24, May 18, June 29, August 24

Clara Beranger
Photo courtesy of Unity Library & Archives

1886-1956: Clara was a screenwriter, and actor in more than forty films of the silent era. She was a member of the original faculty of the USC School of Cinematic Arts. She also was a New Thought devotee and published *Peace Begins at Home* through Unity in 1955.

January 19, May 30

Kathleen M. H. Besly

1858-1946: Kathleen was ordained a minister in Divine Science in Chicago. She was a speaker at the third INTA Congress in 1916 in Chicago. She may have been at the First Church of Divine Science in Chicago from 1919. She is best remembered for her 1917 book, *The Divine Art of Living*.

April 20, September 18, November 22

Norah Braden Boyd

Photo courtesy of Science of Mind Archives & Library Foundation

1915-2012: For many years prior to her retirement in 2005, Norah was the minister of the Bournemouth Church of Religious Science on the south coast of England. She was a frequent contributor to *Science of Mind* in the 1980s and 1990s.

January 23, July 20, December 13

Nona L. Brooks
Photo courtesy of Divine Science Federation Archives

1861-1945: Nona was ordained by Malinda Elliott Cramer in December 1898. She co-founded the Colorado College of Divine Science with Fannie Brooks James and Alethea Brooks Small in October 1898 as well as the First Church of Divine Science in Denver in January 1899. She was Vice President of INTA, 1921-1922. She was a contributing author for *Mind Remakes Your World*, edited by Ernest Holmes in 1941. Nona is the acknowledged leader of Divine Science from 1906 to 1945.

March 22, April 15, July 2, July 30, October 24, November 2, December 21

Helen Brungardt

1931-1998: Helen was a Rosicrucian for ten years before becoming a Religious Science practitioner and a Unity teacher. She was later ordained by Dr. Roy Eugene Davis of the Center for Spiritual Awareness and became minister and president of Symphony of Life Church, Corrales, New Mexico.

February 12, May 4

Juanita Bryant-Dunn

1916-2009: Juanita is known as the "Teacher of Teachers," having taught some of the best known Religious Science figures in her long, storied and devoted career as minister, teacher and spiritual counselor. Juanita was a senior minister at Guidance Church of Religious Science. She also taught at Agape International Spiritual Center, Founder's Church of Religious Science, and City of Angels Church of Religious Science. Peggy Bassett was one of Juanita's teachers in ministerial school.

January 6, June 19

H. Emilie Cady

1848-1941: H. Emilie was a homeopathic physician and author of New Thought spiritual writings. Her 1896 book *Lessons in Truth* remains one of the core texts of Unity Church teachings. Her book is arguably the most widely read book in the New Thought movement.

January 18, February 21, March 2, March 13, March 27, April 16, November 9

Ruth Hammink Carr
Photo courtesy of C. William Mercer

1909-2008: Ruth was a student of Unity teachings from childhood. Her mother kept a scrapbook of articles from *Unity* that she and Ruth read together. She followed her own minister, Dr. Frank Glabach, from Unity into Divine Science in the days of Dr. Irwin Edwin Gregg, Frank's teacher. Ruth was assistant minister at the Divine Science Church of Birmingham, Michigan where she was ordained. She actively served her community into her one hundredth year. Ruth is Dr. Will's great aunt.

September 8

Elizabeth Carrick-Cook
Photo courtesy of Science of Mind Archives & Library Foundation

1896-1953: Elizabeth often used just "Carrick-Cook" as her byline. She earned ministerial degrees from Divine Science and the Christian Philosophical Institute in California. Elizabeth led Absolute Science Center in San Francisco with her husband, Jay Williams Cook. Elizabeth served as Chairman of the 1930 and 1940 INTA Congresses in San Francisco. She was a contributing author for *Mind Remakes Your World*, edited by Ernest Holmes in 1941.

March 30, October 6, November 30

Ruth E. Chew

1879-1965: Ruth was a Truth student from 1909. She was educated at Smith College and became a teacher of positive thinking in Helena, Montana where she founded the Unity Metaphysical Center about 1930. She was a national lecturer for INTA and a frequent contributor to *Religious Science Monthly* and *Science of Mind*. She was a contributing author for *Mind Remakes Your World*, edited by Ernest Holmes in 1941.

July 19, August 20, September 28, November 24

Jane Claypool

Photo courtesy of Science of Mind Archives & Library Foundation

1933-2014: Jane founded CSL Carlsbad, California in 1989. She trained over thirty-five ministers in the field and wrote much of the training curriculum for RSI during this period. In 2002 she received the Raymond Charles Barker Award for her spiritual writing.

June 30, August 13, September 3

Johnnie Colemon
Photo courtesy of Universal Foundation for Better Living

1920-2014: Johnnie was ordained by Unity in 1956. She returned to Chicago, building Christ Universal Temple to a following of some 15,000 people. Johnnie founded the Universal Foundation for Better Living (UFBL) in 1974, an organization she led until her retirement in 2007. She was a highly regarded New Thought leader, a frequent speaker at INTA Congresses and Chairman of the 1975 INTA Congress in Chicago, Illinois.

February 18, August 29, September 19, October 29, December 6

Malinda Elliott Cramer
Photo courtesy of Divine Science Federation Archives

1844-1906: Malinda was the founder of Divine Science, the oldest New Thought denomination. She formed her Home College of Divine Science in May 1888, began her *Harmony* magazine in October 1888 and founded the International Divine Science Association (forerunner of INTA) in 1892. Her Home College burned to the ground in the aftermath of the great San Francisco earthquake of April 18, 1906. Malinda passed four months later.

January 9, January 27, February 5, April 10, June 10, October 14, November 18

Jennie H. Croft
Photo courtesy of Unity Archives and Library

1851-1937: Jennie organized the first Unity Sunday School and was ordained with the first group of Unity ministers in 1906. She was an active supporter of cultural efforts in art, literature and science in Kansas City. She worked in the Unity Library, wrote for Unity publications, and taught classes for ministers.
January 22, September 17

Josephine Holmes Curtis
Photo courtesy of Science of Mind Archives & Library Foundation

1905-1978: Josephine was Ernest Holmes' niece and was on his staff for nearly thirty years. She served as Ernest's personal assistant, later becoming editor of Science of Mind magazine. Josephine also produced two series of twelve lessons in Religious Science that appeared in SOM publications.
March 21, June 27, September 13, November 11

Hazel Deane
Photo courtesy of Science of Mind Archives & Library Foundation

1889-1974: Hazel was a contributor to *Science of Mind* in the 1930s and knew Ernest and Hazel Holmes very well. She maintained close relations with both Religious Science and Divine Science leaders through the years. Hazel is perhaps best remembered for her biography of Nona L. Brooks, *Powerful Is The Light*. Here she is pictured with Ernest and Hazel Holmes in 1947.

July 16

Lillian DeWaters

1883-1964: Lillian was the author of more than forty metaphysical books. Her publications were printed in several languages and circulated worldwide. She lectured widely and provided private instruction at her home and at the Hotel Astor, New York City. Lillian was well known for her work as a spiritual healer. She was a contributing author for *Mind Remakes Your World*, edited by Ernest Holmes in 1941.

March 19, August 7, August 28, October 9

Doris Dickelman
Photo courtesy of Science of Mind Archives and Library Foundation

1902-1988: Doris received her Doctorate of Divinity from the Institute of Religious Science, Los Angeles, California. She was introduced to New Thought through Divine Science. Doris was a faculty member of the Religious Science Institute and was affiliated with the church in Beverly Hills, California.

January 12, October 4

Mary Baker Eddy
Photo courtesy of the Mary Baker Eddy Collection

1821-1910: Mrs. Eddy founded the First Church of Christ Scientist and authored of *Truth and Health*, the seminal volume of the Christian Science movement. Mrs. Eddy was without doubt the chief progenitor of the American New Thought movement after Phineas Parkhurst Quimby. Her differences with people like Emma Curtis Hopkins and Ursula Gestefeld actually resulted in the expansion of New Thought despite her desire to limit the nature of spiritual growth and expansion of "Christian Science" beyond her own foundational teachings.

January 8, February 7, April 13, November 5, November 28

Ida B. Elliott
Photo courtesy of Divine Science Federation Archives

1862-1957: Ida was Malinda Elliott Cramer's niece, ordained by Nona L. Brooks in 1907. She established her own ministry in Oakland, California. Ida wrote several books including *Living by the Law* and *The Great Realities*. She was a contributing author for *Mind Remakes Your World*, edited by Ernest Holmes in 1941.

August 19, September 6, November 16

Grace L. Faus
Photo courtesy of Divine Science Federation Archives

1897-1988: Ordained in Divine Science by Harvey Hardman, Grace was the minister in the Washington D.C. church beginning in 1932. In September 1945 she founded the Divine Science Church of the Healing Christ in Washington D. C., where she served as Senior Minister until her retirement in 1969. She later preached in Denver and thereafter taught many summer classes at her home in Bailey, Colorado.

March 6, April 3, June 26, September 5, September 21, November 20, December 2

Ada B. Fay

1883-1943: Ada joined the Denver church in 1899, became Superintendent of the Adult Sunday School in 1902, was ordained in 1916 and received her Doctorate of Divine Science in 1919. She is best known for *The Divine Science Bible Textbook* and *The Evolution of the Ten Commandments*.

May 7, June 25

Cora Dedrick Fillmore
Photo courtesy of Unity Library & Archives

1876-1955: Cora began her work with Unity in 1911 and was ordained in 1918. She served as personal secretary to Charles Fillmore for many years. Cora became Charles' second wife in 1933 and collaborator on his later works.

January 11, May 27, August 8, September 23

Myrtle Fillmore
Photo courtesy of Unity Library & Archives

1845-1931: Myrtle was co-founder of the Unity movement with her husband, Charles. Known for her healing letters and poetry, she also was the editor of *Wee Wisdom* for many years as well as being keenly involved in the establishment and work of Silent Unity, the movement's prayer ministry.

January 20, March 1, March 31, April 25, September 7, December 8

Frances W. Foulks

1874-1936: Frances was a New York City businesswoman who enrolled in Unity's Intensive Training School in 1921, becoming a close colleague in local healing with Myrtle Fillmore. She edited Mrs. Fillmore's healing letters for publication in 1936 shortly before her own transition.

June 5, October 1, November 10, December 27, December 31

Lucile Frederick
Photo courtesy of Divine Science Federation Archives

1902-1994: Ordained by Irwin Edwin Gregg, and awarded her Doctorate of Divine Science in 1958, Lucile served for more than forty years as a practitioner. She became the Director of the Divine Science Educational Center in Denver, serving more than 20 years. She updated and taught numerous of the core courses for ministerial study during that time, including Spiritual Psychology.

August 26, December 30

Agnes J. Galer
Photo courtesy of Divine Science Federation Archives

1860-1939: After being ordained by Nona L. Brooks about 1907, Agnes established a Divine Science church and school in Seattle, Washington. She is remembered as the minister who ordained Ernest S. Holmes in Divine Science about July 1918. Thereafter, she was a contributor to *The TRUTH* and early editions of *Religious Science Monthly*.

February 19, June 24, August 25, September 20, October 26

Dana Gatlin
Photo courtesy of Unity Library & Archives

1884-1940: Born in Kansas, Dana earned her bachelor's degree from the University of Kansas and her master's degree from Columbia University in New York City. A professional journalist, she also wrote numerous articles for Unity and in 1939 edited *The Story of Unity's 50 Golden Years.*
    June 23, August 30, October 17, October 18, December 23

Ursula Gestefeld

1845-1921: Ursula was a devotee of Mary Baker Eddy from 1884 to 1888 when she wrote her own book on Christian Science and was summarily expelled from Eddy's movement. This encouraged Ursula to launch her own career as a healer and teacher. She wrote several other works of her own thereafter, including a diatribe against Eddy, interestingly called *Jesuitism in Christian Science*.
    January 2, July 1, July 21, July 27, July 28, November 29

Annie S. Greenwood
Photo courtesy of Divine Science Federation Archives

1875-1963: Annie was a New Thought teacher and personal counselor as well as a lecturer and author. She wrote many articles for Divine Science and Unity publications. Her writings also appeared in a wide variety of other metaphysical publications for more than thirty years.

February 2, June 1, December 10

Jennifer Holder

1972-2015: Jennifer was ordained by Unity in 2006. She became Senior Minister at Unity of Gaithersburg, Maryland in March 2012 having earlier served as Associate Minister at Unity Church of the Triangle in Raleigh, North Carolina. She also served on the Board of Unity School of Christianity. Jennifer and her husband Ogun Holder co-hosted the Unity FM program "Family Matters."

January 24, May 8

Nora Smith Holm

1864-1917: Nora's only known contribution to the New Thought movement was her inspired work, *The Runner's Bible*, which she wrote in 1913 as a tool (according to legend) for her daughter's use as she left home to go to school. It was designed to provide her daughter with quick reference to important Biblical passages accompanied by her brief commentaries for those "on the run."

June 16, July 13, August 3, October 7, December 5

Hazel Foster Holmes

Photo courtesy of Science of Mind Archives and Library Foundation

1887-1957: Hazel was the wife of Ernest Holmes and wrote for *Religious Science Monthly* for many years under the name H. Foster Holmes. An attractive redhead and well-connected Los Angeles socialite who married Ernest in 1927, it is said that Hazel had almost as much to do with the early success of Religious Science as did Ernest.

June 15, November 15

Emma Curtis Hopkins

1849-1925: Emma was a student of Mary Baker Eddy and briefly the editor of Mrs. Eddy's *Christian Science Journal* until she wrote material which angered Mrs. Eddy and was summarily dismissed in September 1885. Emma established her own work in Chicago in January 1886, where she became known as the "Teacher of Teachers" for her ordination of Kate Bingham, Mary D. Fisk, Helen Wilmans, the Fillmores and the Yarnalls, among others. Many other early New Thought leaders attended some of her classes or studied with her personally in her later years. She worked with Harley Bradley (H.B.) Jeffery on her seminal work, *High Mysticism*, was voted Honorary President of INTA in 1918, and worked with Ernest S. Holmes as one of her last students in 1924.

January 1, March 18, April 23, May 29, November 25, December 22

Betty Jean House

1928-2005: Betty Jean was a Religious Science practitioner for fifty-five years. She served as International-National Director of Practitioners 1979-1984. She was co-chair of the 1989 INTA Congress with Dr. Roger Teel. Betty Jean received Practitioner Emeritus status in 1997, and the Meritorious Service Award in 2004.

February 26, April 2, August 6, November 27

Fannie Brooks James

1854-1914: With Nona L. Brooks and Alethea Brooks Small, Fannie founded the Colorado College of Divine Science in 1898 as well as the First Church of Divine Science in Denver in 1899. In 1896 she authored *Divine Science, New Light Upon Old Truths* and in 1901, *Truth and Health* -- the primary textbook in Divine Science for more than forty years. She was a speaker at the 1907 INTA Congress in St. Louis.

        January 7, February 13, March 23, May 1, August 23

Doris Jones

1917-2008: Doris was introduced to Science of Mind in the 1940s by Ernest Holmes. She became a practitioner is 1977. In the 1980s she opened the San Francisco Community One Church of Religious Science with Rev. Lloyd Tupper. For many years after 1987, when she retired, Doris provided practitioner training for five different churches in the area.

        April 7, June 18, September 1

Florence Scripps Kellogg

1870-1958: Florence "Floy" Kellogg was a socialite who lived in La Jolla, California. The eldest daughter of William A. Scripps, she married Frederick William Kellogg in 1890. An early New Thought devotee, she is best known for her poem, "My Hand In God's," frequently quoted in Unity publications. She also published her own books of poetry as late as 1950.

June 11, November 13, December 25

Carol Ruth Knox

1938-1987: Carol was the charismatic minister at Unity of Walnut Creek, California for seventeen years, building her congregation from a handful to more than four hundred fifty. She passed suddenly at age forty-eight as the result of injuries sustained in a home invasion. The fact that more than 1,200 people attended her memorial service pays tribute to her ministry.

April 24, May 5, July 11

Christina Knox-Walthall
Photo courtesy of Universal Foundation for Better Living

1917-2005: A member of Christ Universal Temple (UFBL), Christina became a practitioner and assistant minister working with Johnnie Colemon. She was a frequent contributor to *Daily Inspiration for Better Living*.

February 3, April 27, July 26, December 20

Hannah More Kohaus

1844-1914: Hanna is best known for her "Prayer of Faith," adopted by Unity's Myrtle Fillmore and found in virtually all New Thought denominational material.

April 29, August 1, November 6

Mary L. Kupferle

1916-2003: Mary came to Unity in 1935 and became a prolific Unity author, contributing more than two hundred fifty articles, poems and pamphlets. Her book *God Never Fails* is still considered a basic Unity text.

March 11, April 6, July 4, July 8, December 9

Elizabeth Searle Lamb

1917-2005: A major voice in the world of English-language haiku in her later years, Elizabeth earlier wrote many spiritual articles which appeared in *Divine Science Monthly* and *Aspire* magazines.

May 14, June 22, September 4

Agnes M. Lawson

1865-1946: Agnes was ordained by Nona L. Brooks in 1905. She relocated to Portland, Oregon where she established a Divine Science Church. In 1918 Agnes moved to Seattle to work with Henry Victor Morgan. She is best known for *Hints to Bible Study*. She co-authored *Truth and Life* with Albert C. Grier in 1921.

January 4, June 9

Marguerite Lewis

Photo courtesy of New Thought Spiritual Center of Eastern Long Island

1921-2008: Marguerite "Maggie" Lewis was a Broadway actress turned Unity student of more than thirty-two years, culminating in her ministry at New Thought Spiritual Center of Eastern Long Island in Southampton, New York.

February 25, June 3

Edna M. Lister

1884-1971: Edna studied at the Unity School of Christianity and was the founder of the Society of the Universal Living Christ (originally the Society of Christ Healing) in Cleveland, Ohio in 1911. She later headed congregations in Buffalo and Tacoma. She was president of INTA in 1933-1934.

January 29, November 4

Mildred Mann

Photo courtesy of Emmet Fox Resource Center

1904-1971: An ardent student of Emmet Fox, Mildred was active in the New Thought Movement and taught metaphysics in New York City. She founded the Society of Religious Pragmatism, which was later reorganized as the Society of Pragmatic Mysticism in Vermont. Photo provided without proof of authenticity.

March 17, August 5, October 19, December 15

Georgia C. Maxwell

1904-1988: Georgia Carmichael Maxwell was the sister of Hoagy Carmichael and performed with him in her youth. She became a Religious Science practitioner in 1948. Affiliated with Religious Science in Beverly Hills, California, Georgia wrote for *Science of Mind* and edited Ernest Holmes' *Seminar Lectures.*

August 15, October 31

Cora B. Mayo

Photo courtesy of Science of Mind Archives & Library Foundation

1894-1976: Cora was an early president of the Board of Practitioners at Mile Hi Church in Lakewood, Colorado. Later she also served on the Board of Practitioners of the United Church of Religious Science. During her career Cora served as assistant minister at several Religious Science churches in the Denver area.

February 23

Lola Pauline Mays

1911-1993: Lola was ordained in Religious Science and became a frequent contributor to *Creative Thought* magazine. Community Church of New Thought in Mesa, Arizona was founded by Lola and Rev. Cecil B. Mays, parents of longtime INTA President and CEO, Rev. Dr. Blaine Mays.

July 15, August 14, September 11

Elizabeth R. McClellan

Photo courtesy of Divine Science Federation Archives

1905-1991: Daughter of Alice R. Ritchie and raised in Divine Science teachings, Elizabeth contributed to *Aspire* magazine and wrote poetry in the New Thought tradition throughout her life.

February 28, September 14

Annie Rix Militz

1856-1924: Author and spiritual leader, reportedly taught by Emma Curtis Hopkins. Annie is best known as the founder in 1905 of Home of Truth Alameda, California. With her sister Harriet Hale Rix, Annie was a co-founder of the West Coast Metaphysical Bureau. She was named an Honorary President of INTA.

March 7, April 22, May 3, June 21, November 26, December 29

Marian G. Moon

Photo courtesy of Science of Mind Archives & Library Foundation

1924-2014: Marian served for many years as a teacher, practitioner and minister at Hollywood Church of Religious Science with Robert Bitzer. A self-published author, she later served at CSL Los Angeles, where she wrote numerous meditations and treatments for the "Newsletter." Marion was named Minister Emerita by her church in 2013.

January 3, April 8, May 31

Caroline Munz
Photo courtesy of Divine Science Federation Archives

1870-1955: Caroline "Carrie" Munz was ordained by Nona L. Brooks in 1923. Caroline was active in both the Denver church and college. She succeeded Nona Brooks in teaching Spiritual Psychology for the college and was a frequent contributor to *Divine Science Monthly*.
April 5, May 17, May 23, June 2

Elizabeth A. Nordman

1864-1942: Elizabeth was a longtime member of the First Divine Science Church of St. Louis where she also served as Registrar for the Missouri College of Divine Science. She was ordained by Rev. Herman Schroeder. Following his transition in 1925, Elizabeth became a senior minister of the "City Church." She was a frequent contributor to *Divine Science Monthly*.
July 10, December 19

Anna L. Palmer

1858-1944: Anna became a charter member of the First Divine Science Church of Denver in 1899. She taught at the Colorado College of Divine Science for many years, specializing in spiritual unfoldment. Anna was ordained by Nona L. Brooks in 1916 and at one time served as the President of the Colorado College of Divine Science. She was a frequent contributor to *Divine Science Monthly* and for some period served as its editor.

May 25, August 27

Clara A. Palmer

Photo courtesy of Unity Library & Archives

1884-1971: Clara worked in Silent Unity for many years. She wrote hundreds of articles for Unity including the anonymous column "Silent Unity's Message for You." Her book *You Can Be Healed* was published by Unity in 1937.

March 15, May 20, December 11

Vetura Papke
Photo courtesy of Science of Mind Archives & Library Foundation

1901-1997: Vetura was personal practitioner to Ernest S. Holmes and served as a practitioner for more than thirty-four years. She was a member of the faculty of the Institute of Religious Science for ten years and also was president of the League of Religious Science Practitioners. Vetura was ordained in 1989 at the age of 88.

June 20, July 24, October 27

Jane Paulson
Photo courtesy of Unity Library & Archives

1917-1996: With husband J. Sig Paulson, Jane was co-minister at Unity Village Chapel (1962-1978) and later at the Golden Pyramid (Unity of Houston) in Houston, Texas. She was a graduate of the Unity Training School. Jane and Sig conducted Unity seminars across the United States and around the world.

March 10, July 31

Dorothy Pierson
Photo courtesy of Unity Library & Archives

1916-2013: Dorothy was hired by Charles Fillmore in 1938 to work in Silent Unity. In the 1940s she began working in ministry and for sixty years served in numerous cities around the country. She also served as the president of the Association of Unity Churches (Unity Worldwide Ministries) and was the recipient of the Lifetime Achievement Award.

February 4, December 1

Peace Pilgrim

1908-1981: Born Mildred Lisette Norman, she was a non-denominational spiritual teacher, mystic, pacifist and peace activist. In 1953 she adopted the name "Peace Pilgrim" and walked and taught across America for twenty-eight years.

January 26, December 17

Ella Pomeroy

1868-1958: Ella was a close associate of H. Emilie Cady. She led her own vital Unity church in Brooklyn, New York for many years, well into the 1950s. Ella is best remembered for her book, *Powers of the Soul*, which is a companion to Charles Fillmore's *The Twelve Powers of Man*.

February 1, March 8, March 25, April 19, July 5, August 2

Nancy L. Purcell

1935-2015 After twenty-five years of teaching Nancy retired and entered the Unity School. Upon her graduation in 1990, she became the Senior Minister at Unity in the Seven Hills in Lynchburg, Virginia. She remained there until her retirement in 2012.

January 31, October 2

Rosemary Fillmore Rhea
Photo courtesy of Unity Library & Archives

1925-2012 Rosemary was the granddaughter of Unity co-founders Charles and Myrtle Fillmore. Ordained in 1980, Rosemary served for decades as Unity's world ambassador of goodwill. She is best known for her television broadcast, "The Daily Word" which ran for twelve years in the 1950s and 1960s.
February 29, July 17

Alice R. Ritchie
Photo courtesy of Divine Science Federation Archives

1876-1960: An early graduate of the Colorado College of Divine Science, Alice served as teacher, practitioner and minister and member of the College Board from 1911-1918. She earned her Doctorate of Divine Science in 1919; in 1921 she went to Chicago to take charge of the Divine Science church there.
January 14, April 12, October 5, December 28

Harriet Hale Rix
Photo courtesy of Science of Mind Archives and Library Foundation

1863-1931: Harriet was an early New Thought author and teacher. With her sister Annie Rix Militz she co-founded the West Coast Metaphysical Bureau and the Home of Truth in 1905. Reportedly she was a student of Emma Curtis Hopkins. She is remembered for her prayer ministry during World War I.

March 16, April 28, May 12, August 17, October 13, December 26

May Rowland
Photo courtesy of Unity Library & Archives

1890-1977: May was the director of Silent Unity for fifty-five years, from 1917 to 1972. She was a frequent contributor to *Daily Word* in addition to authoring several books. She also was Frank B. Whitney's wife until his transition in 1938. She later remarried.

February 14, March 20, May 24, November 1, November 14

Augusta E. Rundel
Photo courtesy of Science of Mind Archives & Library Foundation

1869-1960: Augusta "Gussie" Rundel was a Los Angeles socialite who personally financed several of Ernest Holmes' early endeavors. She became a practitioner, headed the Health Department for the Religious Science Institute for many years and frequently appeared in *Religious Science Monthly* and *Science of Mind*.

March 9, September 2

Agnes Sanford

1897-1982: Considered to be one of the principal founders of the Inner Healing movement, Agnes was the daughter of a Presbyterian missionary in China and the wife of the Episcopal priest Edgar L. Sanford. Her first book, *The Healing Light*, is considered a classic in the field of spiritual healing.

March 3, May 26, August 10, September 27

Helen Schucman

1909-1981: Helen was a professor of clinical psychology at Columbia University in New York City from 1958 until her retirement in 1976. She is best known for having "scribed" (with the help of colleague William Thetford) *A Course in Miracles*, the contents of which she claimed to have been given to her by an inner voice she identified as Jesus.

May 9, June 13, June 28, August 4, August 21, September 30

Clara H. Fiske Scott

1841-1897: Clara was a composer, hymn writer and publisher. She was the first woman to publish a volume of anthems, the *Royal Anthem Book*, in 1882. Clara was best known for her hymn, "Open My Eyes, That I May See," written in 1895 and inspired by Psalm 119:18.

June 6, August 18

Julia Seton Sears

1862-1950: Julia was a medical doctor and founder of the Church and School of the New Civilization. Julia was an important figure in the development of the New Thought movement from the esoteric-metaphysical point of view. Reportedly, she exercised considerable influence over Fenwicke Holmes and Ernest Holmes, founder of Religious Science. Julia also is remembered for *Destiny: A New Thought Novel*, published in 1917.

June 8, November 8

Imelda Octavia Shanklin

1865-1953: Imelda came to Unity in 1907, wrote for *Wee Wisdom*, becoming its editor in 1919 and chief editor for all Unity publications in the 1920s. Her articles appeared frequently among the "shoebox" pamphlets widely used by both Unity and Divine Science. Following her transition Imelda's book, *Selected Studies* (1926), was retitled *All Things Made New* by Unity.

January 10, June 4, July 3, September 15

Florence Scovel Shinn

1871-1940: Florence was an artist and book illustrator who became a spiritual teacher and metaphysical writer in her middle years. Shinn expressed her philosophy: "The invisible forces are ever working for man who is always 'pulling the strings' himself, though he does not know it. Owing to the vibratory power of words, whatever man voices, he begins to attract." She is best remembered for her book, *The Game of Life and How to Play It.*

January 5, February 6, February 24, August 16

Sue Sikking

Photo courtesy of Unity Library & Archives

1899-1992: Sue was the founder of Santa Monica's Unity by the Sea Church and senior minister for nearly forty years. In addition to working with her congregation of 5,000 she had a radio program called "A Letter to Adam." She also taught on television and lectured worldwide.

May 22, November 21

Alberta Smith

1873-1937: Alberta wrote the "Questions and Answers" column for *Religious Science Monthly* and *Science of Mind* for a number of years during the early Holmes era. Years later Religious Science published a book containing many of her columns, co-authored by Ernest Holmes.

February 17, May 10, September 9

Ruth B. Smith

1878-1933: For more than twenty years Ruth served as Secretary-Treasurer of the Colorado College of Divine Science. Through these years she also frequently wrote full months of "Daily Studies" for *Divine Science Monthly*.

April 9, June 17

Martha Smock
Photo courtesy of Unity Library & Archives

1913-1984: Martha worked in Silent Unity before becoming editor of Unity's *Daily Word* in the 1940s, a post she held for more than thirty years. She wrote many articles and several books during her Unity career.

November 3, November 7, December 7, December 12

Adela Rogers St. Johns
Photo courtesy of Science of Mind Archives & Library Foundation

1894-1988: Adela was a newspaper reporter who covered many big stories, including the abdication of King Edward VIII, earning her the title of "The World's Greatest Girl Reporter." She became a Religious Science minister and frequently wrote for *Science of Mind*. In 1970 President Nixon awarded Adela the Presidential Medal of Freedom.

April 11, September 24

Margaret M. Stevens
Photo courtesy of Divine Science Federation Archives

1920-2013: Margaret was ordained in Divine Science. In 1967 she became the minister-director of The Santa Anita Church (Independent) following the passing of founder, Ethel Barnhart. She served in that capacity for 22 years. Margaret served on the INTA Board and traveled internationally representing INTA. Following her retirement to Oregon she founded and led another small church for eight years.

February 15, September 25

Vida Reed Stone

1887-1965: Vida was a popular New Thought poet and writer. Based in Los Angeles, she established a strong New Thought following among the Hollywood elite of her era, reportedly including Frank Sinatra and Joan Crawford. Her work appeared frequently in *Divine Science Monthly* and *Aspire*.

February 20, March 12, April 18, July 12

Vera Dawson Tait
Photo courtesy of Unity Library and Archives

1907-1982: Vera was a Unity minister, teacher and author. She is best remembered as a teacher. Vera had the wonderful ability to quote directly from a Unity book. In addition, Vera could tell you page number and often if it was the second or third paragraph. This came from a time when she typed Unity books word for word to impress the teachings on her mind.
August 11, October 16

Sallye Taylor
Photo courtesy of Unity Library & Archives

1940-2015: Ordained in 1979, Sallye served in various capacities in Unity through 1990, when she founded Soul Food Unity Ministry. A Bible scholar, she co-presented with Mary A. Tumpkin "Unlocking the Book of Revelation" at the UFBL Bible Conference in 2007.
January 13, May 16

Elizabeth Towne

1865-1960: Elizabeth was the founder and publisher of *Nautilus Magazine*, an influential journal of the New Thought movement that ran from 1898 through 1953. For many years she was associated with INTA and she was named Honorary President during the time James Edgerton was President. Elizabeth served as INTA president in 1924-1925. She was a contributing author for *Mind Remakes Your World*, edited by Ernest Holmes in 1941.

January 15, February 8, August 9, October 3

Mary A. Tumpkin

Photo courtesy of Universal Foundation for Better Living

1949-2013: Mary was the president of the Universal Foundation for Better Living from 2007 to 2013, and founder of Universal Truth Center for Better Living in Miami Gardens, Florida in 1982. For more than thirty years Mary was a broadly acclaimed and beloved teacher, minister and Bible scholar.

June 7, July 14, November 12

Elizabeth Sand Turner
Photo courtesy of Unity Library & Archives

1897-1979: Elizabeth reportedly was a brilliant speaker, serving as the director of Unity Training School and author of three important books on the metaphysical interpretation of the Bible: *Let There Be Light*, *Your Hope of Glory* and *Be Ye Transformed*. She later built a successful Unity church in Florida.

January 21, February 16, March 14, March 28, March 29

F. Bernadette Turner
Photo courtesy of Divine Science Federation Archives

1903-1995: Bernadette was a Divine Science minister in the Chicago area and later Roanoke, Virginia (about 1969-1971). In December 1990 she was ordained an Episcopal priest, her lifelong calling, at age eighty-seven. Her writing appears in many New Thought publications.

February 9, April 21, June 12, October 22

Evelyn Underhill

1875-1941: Evelyn was an English Anglo-Catholic writer and pacifist known for her numerous works on religion and spiritual practice, in particular Christian mysticism. In the English-speaking world, she was one of the most widely read writers on mysticism during the first half of the twentieth century.

May 28, December 3

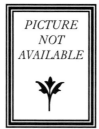

Helen Van Slyke

1888-1944: Helen was a poet, author and early teacher of Religious Science. She was first published (*Mountain Thoughts and Poems of Inspiration*) by the Institute of Religious Science in 1927. Helen served as Associate Editor for *Religious Science Monthly* from its inception. Her work appeared in the magazine for many years.

January 25, March 5, July 7, October 10, December 16

Judith G. Weekes
Photo courtesy of Universal Foundation for Better Living

1924-2006: Judith was the first UFBL minister in the Caribbean. She founded Christ Circle for Better Living (CCBL) in Diego Martin, Trinidad and Tobago, West Indies in 1976, making it the first UFBL church established outside the United States. She was a frequent contributor to *Daily Inspiration for Better Living*.

February 10, May 11, July 18, October 15

Eva Bell Werber
Photo courtesy of DeVorss & Company

1888-1962: Born in Indiana, Eva's love for art guided her to the Chicago Art Institute, where she later graduated. She then moved to California for health reasons and was able to establish a career in art and music, as well as in New Thought writing.

January 28, March 4, August 31, December 14

Georgiana Tree West

1882-1974: Leader of the Unity Center in New York City in the 1930s and 1940s, Georgiana also was president of the Unity Annual Conference during that same period. She is best remembered as the author of *Prosperity's Ten Commandments*.

April 26, August 22, September 29, October 21, December 4

Claudine Whitaker

Photo courtesy of Divine Science Federation Archives

1892-1970: Claudine was an Episcopal deaconess for an orphanage in Mexico prior to being ordained in Divine Science by Nona L. Brooks in 1919. Twenty-four years later she was ordained in Religious Science and served as the founding pastor of the Church of Religious Science in Chicago from 1943 to 1969. Through these years Claudine also continued to teach for the Divine Science Summer School each year in and around Denver.

April 4, June 14, October 20, November 19

Elena Goforth Whitehead
Photo courtesy of Center for Spiritual Living, Monterrey, California

1917-1987: Elena studied Divine Science in the late 1940s. Marrying fellow student Carleton Whitehead, she joined him in his Religious Science ministry in Monterrey, California before they moved to Chicago in 1969 following the retirement of Claudine Whitaker. Elena was a frequent contributor to *Creative Thought*.

April 14, July 23

Evelyn Whitell

1880-1963: The thirteenth child of a Quaker family in England, Evelyn became a teacher, newspaper editor and Truth student, moving to Kansas City and becoming a student of Myrtle Fillmore. She wrote articles for Unity from 1926 to 1948. Evelyn is best remembered for her book, *Lovingly in the Hands of the Father*, 1931.

April 17, July 9, September 26

Ella Wheeler Wilcox

1850-1919: An early New Thought devotee, Ella was an author and much beloved New Thought poet. She was often quoted by New Thought teachers including Malinda Elliott Cramer and Fannie Brooks James. For several years she wrote monthly spiritual poems for *The Nautilus*. In later life she became a close associate of Max Heindel of the American Rosicrucian Philosophy as she came to terms with the passing of her husband.

April 1, April 30, October 25, December 24

Helen Wilmans

1831-1907: Helen was a journalist, publisher and proponent of mental science. She was ordained by Emma Curtis Hopkins. Helen started her own newspaper, *The Woman's World,* and published a weekly magazine, *Freedom,* from Sea Breeze, Florida. She achieved a strong following. However, difficulty with Federal authorities over "distance healing" through the U.S. mail led to the end of her career and her own transition shortly thereafter.

May 2, May 19, October 12

Barbara L. Wolfe
Photo courtesy of Divine Science Federation Archives

1909-2003: Barbara was a long-time practitioner and New Thought writer from St. Louis' Divine Science "City Church." Her inspirational booklets were published by Divine Science Federation International. She also was a frequent contributor to *Aspire*.

January 17, February 22, May 13

Pearl C. Wood
Photo courtesy of Science of Mind Archives and Library Foundation

1892-1974: Pearl C. Wood was ordained in Kansas before moving to Los Angeles where she founded Triangular Church in 1932. For many years "Mother Pearl" published *Thinking With God: Daily Thoughts*. Pearl's church became a Religious Science church in 1956. Her grandson, Rev. Dr. Gregory Pitts, represents the third generation of her family to pastor the church that Pearl established when she was forty years old.

May 15, October 30

Clara M. Wright

1891-1979: Clara was a longtime practitioner at the Church of Religious Science in Los Angeles, California, and was a close friend of Ernest Holmes. She graduated from the College of Divine Metaphysics in 1955. Clara is best remembered for her books, *Ideas that Work* and *Prayer in Action.*

January 30, October 23

Jane W. Yarnall

1828-1914: Jane was ordained by Emma Curtis Hopkins. She and her husband William (also ordained by Emma) lectured widely from their Chicago home well into their later years. Jane passed to the next expression while visiting Detroit for a speaking engagement.

February 11, July 25, September 12, November 23

Helen Zagat
Photo courtesy of Divine Science Federation Archives

1893-1975: Helen was a Divine Science minister and Pastor of the Church of Divine Unity in New York City in the 1940s and 1950s. She was a frequent speaker at INTA Congresses during that period. Helen is best remembered for her book, *Faith and Works*.

July 6, July 29, September 16, October 11, October 28

REMEMBERED

The unpublished work of several noteworthy female ministers and practitioners is simply not available today or is accessible only on a very limited basis. Nonetheless these women deserve mention for the significant roles that they played in the New Thought movement. Alma Morse stands as the best-known member of this group. Her extant written materials are housed at Lakeside Temple in the care of Rev. Jennifer Lilburn.

Alma Morse

1900-1990: Alma Morse was ordained in Unity by Charles Fillmore in 1942. She taught during the summer at Unity Training School for more than twenty years. She is perhaps best known for editing M. Frederic Keeler's works after his transition in 1943, including *Christian Victory Instruction*. Alma was Minister Emeritus, Lakeside Temple of Practical Christianity in Oakland, California, which she founded in 1939 at Rev. Keeler's urging. She retired in 1966.

OTHER BOOKS BY
REV. DR. C. WILLIAM MERCER

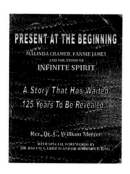

PRESENT AT THE BEGINNING
*Malinda Cramer, Fannie James and the
Study of Infinite Spirit*
Forewords by Dr. Rocco A. Errico and Dr. Barbara L. King
ISBN: 9780578151779
2014

THE CHRISTOLOGY CONNECTION
*Malinda Cramer, Oliver Sabin and the
Close of the Pioneering Era of New Thought*
Forewords by Dr. Ruth Miller and Dr. Helen Carry
ISBN: 9780578156484
2015

Dr. Will's books are available in hard-copy and eBook formats
and all books are available online through:
DivineScienceFederation.org
DeVorss.com
BN.com
Amazon.com (hard-copy and eBook)
Apple.com (eBook)
MalindaCramer.com

For more information about Dr. Will's books please visit
www.GreatNTWomen.com

ABOUT THE AUTHOR

Rev. Dr. C. William (Will) Mercer is Immediate Past President of Divine Science Federation International (DSFI) and co-ministers the United Divine Freedom Church of the Healing Christ with his wife, Rev. Sédare Coradin-Mercer in New York City's Harlem neighborhood. He is a life member of International New Thought Alliance (INTA) as well as Divine Science Federation International (DSFI).

Dr. Will's love for history is lifelong and plays a central role in his ministry. He recently completed two important books on the history of New Thought's oldest denomination, Divine Science, and the life and work of Malinda Elliott Cramer: *PRESENT AT THE BEGINNING* (2014) and *THE CHRISTOLOGY CONNECTION* (2015).

In this new book Dr. Will focuses his attention on the larger population of unique women that stood at the forefront of New Thought at its beginning -- as well as those who contributed to the growth and expansion of the movement's worldwide impact to the present day. All are now transitioned and yet the Timeless Truth of their lessons resonates with us today. All are recognized, acknowledged, thanked and loved for their fine stewardship of our shared teachings and for the love of God that we know through and with them.

COURAGE, CONVICTION AND CONSCIOUSNESS provides more than 365 glimpses into the spiritual core of more than 105 women who took a leap of faith into a fresh spiritual journey of joy and discovery in New Thought – and then sought to spread the Good Word in their own unique ways. What you'll therefore find within this loving volume are the voices of those who (along with their male counterparts) built and sustained the New Thought movement through its first 150 years. Many of them will be well known to you. Some will at first appear somewhat less familiar. All of them have lessons to share that were written especially for you.

Dr. Will can be reached directly at CWillMercer@gmail.com.